About the Auth

I, Segun Magbagbeola have studied Egyptology, black history and am a seeker of 'The Truth'. I practice the culture of Nuwaupu (The Science of Sound Right Reasoning) and have done so for 8 years, started by the one and only Master Teacher, H.E Dr. Malachi Z York, known by many other names. His profound teachings has exposed me to divine and sacred information and covered every topic under the sun. Through Nuwaupu I have discovered wisdom from other sources and have the blessing of taking a journey through life with confidence and true knowledge of self and kind. I come from the Yoruba tribe in Nigeria and I can trace my ancestry back to Egypt and Nubia. I have been a member of the Ancient Egiptian Order (AEO) since 2008 and given the name of 'Har-Aha Tepy Pet' (Fighting Hawk Chief of the Sky). I live in London working as a writer and director of Akasha Publishing Ltd, and also work as a personal trainer.

Black Egyptians

www.blackegyptians.co.uk

Black Egyptians

Segun Magbagbeola

Akasha Publishing

Akasha Publishing Ltd
145-157 St John Street
London
England
EC1V 4PW

A CIP record for this book is available from the British library.

ISBN-13: 978-0-9573695-0-4
E-book ISBN-13: 978-0-9573695-1-1

Printed and bound by Lightning Source

**Akasha
Publishing**
www.akashapublishing.co.uk
info@akashapublishing.co.uk

Acknowledgements

First and foremost I would like to dedicate this book to the first Pharaoh of Egypt Narmer/Menes. Your bravery and vision led to arguably one of the greatest civilizations in history.

To Dr. Malachi Z York, you are undeniably the Master Teacher. I thank you for opening my eyes to 'The Truth' and your countless devotion to us. To Tolu, for your constant support. To Tobi Kupoluyi, I hope you find peace within 'The All'. To 'Obicallys' the master is still the master!

Contents

Preface

A live audio recording from *'Who named God Part 1 and 2?'* (Audio CD) by
Dr Malachi Z York. Excerpt begins at 22m:30s.

<u>There's something about Egypt!</u>

So they'd have to accept, that there was something about that bible,
something about that Qur'an and something about that Torah which all
came from the Egyptian writings, you understand. Something about that
religion that they got from these Egyptians and their connection with the
stars and the talk about the soul and the spirit and the etheric you; the *ba*, the
ka, and the *kha* or the *ruwach* and the *ruwh* in the Torah or the Holy Ghost.
There's something about the fact that Horus was known to be a falcon and
Jesus was known to be a dove. There's something about the connection
between the birds and these so two so called divine children and Horus being
the Son of Osiris a god making him the Son of God and 'Ra Har Akhy', Ra the
God, so he was the son of God and God on earth in Egypt something like
10,000 YEARS! cutting it short before Jesus was born. Something about the
fact that that's written on the wall, carved in a stone, kept in a tablet, locked in
a vault and kept in a holy cave of those few fortunate beings that have access to
that information. Something about that you hear me, something about the
link between that information and **WHY THEY WANT US TO BE
EVERYTHING BUT EGYPTIAN!** They don't mind us being Christian,
they don't mind us being a Muslim, and they don't mind us being a Buddhist.
We can cut our hair off and get a little patch and a orange robe on and be a
hare Krishna, stand at the airport and stuff but **DON'T** link up and take
Egypt seriously. They fought against Dr Ben Jochanon for over 50 years as he
tried to reveal how powerful Egypt was you hear me. And the power the
Egyptians had once they start realising they're Egyptians. That's the first thing,
first realization is 'I'm not just studying Egyptology, **'I AM AN
EGYPTIAN!'** I know you're thinking walk like an Egyptian talk like an
Egyptian. They did that too, they put that in your mind and till it got turned
into a joke and away from reality in other words their present day scientists
have now got to face the reality that there is a spiritual world and that you are
directly linked to it..."

Authors Note

There is a concentrated effort to conceal and/or misrepresent the knowledge of African history from African people. In one of the greatest periods of our history that spanned over 3000 years, African's in Ancient Egypt had a highly advanced culture and led the world in all facets of civilization. Over time, as other nations heard of Egypt's greatness they sought to infiltrate, share in their power and even take over. During dynastic Egypt the Egyptians were conquered by foreign invaders on many occasions, but they managed to re-claim the throne each time until the end of the dynastic period by the Greeks. Most forms of western education and entertainment depict the Egyptians to be non-African, and great lengths were taken to wipe the presence of an African Egypt from the Egyptian landscape and from our hearts and our minds. There is no doubt that black people as a race are not in the best of situations, we have fallen from the gods we once were, but this is simply a small blip in our history, the future is there for the taking. In order for us to progress we must do so in unity, as one mind and one accord, and it is my hope that Egyptology/Nuwaupu will bring us together. The mind is the most powerful thing in the universe; we must receive the right education in order to feed our mind and our souls. We have received a warner to reveal our hidden past, changing present and our ruling future in Dr Malachi Z York. As we are now in the beginning of the new sun cycle, (a time when the forces of nature are geared towards our success) it is up to us to re-claim our history. In fact it is not history, *his-story*, it is *our story*, so it time for us to celebrate it and progress with a renewed sense of unity and future aspirations.

This book has been a long and exciting journey for me, filled with many obstacles, support, highs and lows. There were certain moments and conversations with people which sparked off the initial thought to write this book in the first place. *Maybe* they were supposed to happen, but I know that without my background and prior studies this would have been almost impossible. I had no definite idea of how I wanted the book to be written but like the saying in physics, if you can give an object an initial push after a while it will begin to generate its own force and direct it's self which is what happened with this book. Looking at the final product compared to an initial brainstorm at the start, I am proud of what I have accomplished. It was by no means *easy* to write and involved a lot of research, cross-referencing, having to make sense of it all and link it together. I needed to combine books from a wide plethora of schools including Egyptology, archaeology, astronomy the conventional and unconventional. I *doubt* I'll ever write a book as research intensive as this and it is funny how the hardest was my first. I have been in a position to learn the fascinating history of Ancient Egypt from multiple perspectives, so I simply want to share this with you, in the hope it empowers you as much as it has me. I hope you read this book with an open mind and pursue your own quest of research so the knowledge of Egypt is real to you. On that note I give you:

THE BLACK EGYPTIANS

Table A: Predynastic Chronology of Ancient Egypt (after Hassan 1985)

Date (BC)	Upper Egypt	Lower Egypt
3100	Protodynastic	Protodynastic
3300	Naqada III	Naqada III
3400	Late Gerzean (Naqada II)	Late Gerzean (Maadian)
3650	Early Gerzean (Naqada II)	Omari B (?)
3750	Amratian (Naqada I)	Omari A (?)
4400	Badarian	
4850		Merimden
5200		Fayum A

Table B: Outline chronology of Egypt. All dates are approximate. Chronology based on Murmane 1983.

Predynastic Period (4650 -3150) BC	
Early Dynastic Period: Dynasty 0-2 (3150-2686 BC)	
Dynasty 0	3150-3050 BC
First Dynasty	3050-2890 BC
Second Dynasty	2890-2686 BC
Old Kingdom: Dynasties 3-6 (2686-2181 BC)	
Third Dynasty	2686-2613 BC
Fourth Dynasty	2613-2498 BC
Fifth Dynasty	2498-2345 BC
Sixth Dynasty	2345-2181 BC
First Intermediate Period: Dynasties 7-11 (2181-2040 BC)	
Seventh-Tenth Dynasties	2181-2160 BC
Eleventh Dynasty	2160-2040 BC
Middle Kingdom: Dynasties 12 and early 13 (2040-1782 BC)	
Twelfth Dynasty	2040-1991 BC
Thirteenth Dynasty	1782-1650 BC
Second Intermediate Period: Dynasties 14-17 (1782-1570 BC)	
Fourteenth Dynasty	1650 BC
Fifteenth/Sixteenth Dynasty (Hyksos kings)	1663-1555 BC
Seventeenth Dynasty	1663-1570 BC
New Kingdom Dynasty: 18-20 (1570-1069 BC)	
Eighteenth Dynasty	1570-1293 BC
Nineteenth Dynasty	1293-1185 BC
Twentieth Dynasty	1185-1069 BC
Third Intermediate Period: Dynasty 21-25 (1069-656 BC)	
Twenty-first Dynasty	1069-945 BC

Twenty-second Dynasty	945-712 BC
Twenty-third/Twenty-fourth Dynasty (Libyan Kings)	818-725 BC
Twenty-fifth Dynasty (Kushite period)	772-656 BC
Late Dynastic Period: Dynasties 26-31 (712-332 BC)	
Twenty-sixth Dynasty (Saite Period)	656-525 BC
Twenty-seventh Dynasty (1st Persian domination)	525-404 BC
Twenty-eighth Dynasty	404-399 BC
Twenty-ninth Dynasty	399-380 BC
Thirtieth Dynasty	380-362 BC
Thirty first Dynasty (Second Persian domination)	342-332 BC
Macedonian Period (332-304) BC	
Ptolemaic Period (304-30 BC)	
Roman Period (30 BC-323AD)	
Byzantine Period (323 – 642 AD)	
Arab Conquest (642 AD)	

Chapter 1

The false representation of Egypt

All Egyptologist's would agree that Ancient Egypt was home to a highly advanced and civilized race. When the topic of 'race' is used to describe the Egyptians it is either conveniently left out, labelled insignificant or shown in the wrong image. When Ancient Egypt is shown in the media; such as movies, TV documentaries, and video games or in education; through books/articles and spoken about by everyday people and so-called scholars, the people are mostly depicted as Arab, Mediterranean or white. Just look at some examples of this in Picture 1.1. Now compare it with Picture 1.2, which shows evidence of a Black race in Ancient Egypt. There is a clear contrast in pictures; one of these has to be wrong!

What is said of the Egyptians in the academic world? The general view of the Ancient Egyptians being black by race is summed up by Basil Davidson in 'The History of Africa'. Ancient Egypt is left out of the history of Africa, due to the racist hierarchies of the nineteenth century who defended it by saying the Egyptians of the Pharaonic Age were not Negroes and therefore they were not Africans; and so their civilization, no matter how firmly and enduringly planted on the soil of Africa should be left outside the African context. He continues "Whatever their pigmentation or physical appearance the Egyptians of Pharaonic times were an intimate part of African history.[1] [Basil Davidson].

Keita S says, "The ancient Egyptians have been viewed as racial black-white hybrids, "Mediterranean whites," Negroid, or some combination of these. These terms all have problems."[2]

Dr. Zahi Hawass, the Secretary General of Egypt's Supreme Council of Antiquities says on the subject, "Tutankhamun was not black, and the portrayal of ancient Egyptian civilization as black has no element of truth to it. Egyptians are not Arabs and are not Africans despite the fact that Egypt is in Africa".[3]

This was said as a response to protestors in Philadelphia in September 2007 who cared enough to take to the street claiming that new images of King Tutankhamun were *altered* to show him with lighter skin. An earlier uproar took place June 2005 in LA when black activists demanded that a bust of the boy king be removed because the statue portrays him as white. Such actions

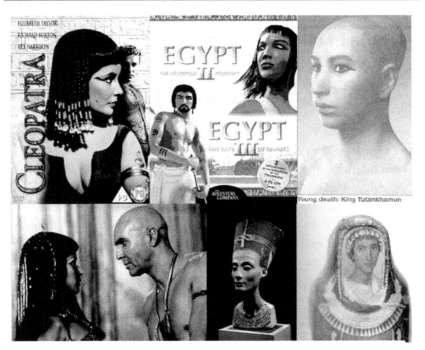

Picture 1.1 – Egyptians in the wrong image.

From left to right: Cleopatra movie 1963 starring Elizabeth Taylor, Egypt 2 & 3 by Jowood Games, Tutankhamun revealed after new CT scans in metro Newspaper London England, Pharaoh Ramses in the Mummy, the bust of Nefertiti, Greek Artemidorus shown in Egyptian funerary scenes.

show a shift in consciousness and gave me the willpower to continue this work. What Hawass is covertly saying in this quote is that Egyptians are white, due to the dismissal of African or Arab ethnicity. Of what particular family of whites is only a question he can answer? He lacked the strength to suggest openly they were white, and knew that by saying this would prove too controversial, so instead chose to leave the topic open, which attributes some sort of mystery to it when the subject can easily be concluded. This makes no sense, scientists are in no doubt that human life began in Africa and Africa is undisputedly the continent of the black race, just as Europe and Asia are the lands of the Caucasian and Asian people respectively. What's more, Mother Nature equipped the black race with biological attributes such as melanin to be able to cope with the fierce rays of the sun better than other races, so the idea of a non-black Egypt is dubious. This would make the true Egyptians, dynastic and pre-dynastic more likely to be black. Secondly, historians agree that Egypt only became a 'multicultural' society in the Greco-Roman Period.[4] (Dynasties

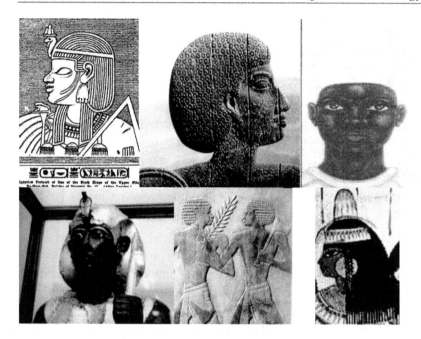

Picture 1.2 – The black features of Egyptians.

From left to right: 1) Ra-Maat-Neb in The crisis Newspaper by WEB Du Bois, 1911. 2) Afro of an Egyptian man. 3) The First Pharaoh Menes by Dr Malachi Z York, 4) Tutankhamun shown in dark skin. 5) Afros of the Egyptian army. 6) Dark skinned Egyptian woman wearing a wig.

26-31, 332BC-14AD), so before all the invasions, mixing, and trading, there must have been *one* original race of Egyptians!

David Icke, claims in The Biggest Secret says that "a white Martian race were the brains behind the Egyptian civilization," and "the Egyptians depicted their gods with blue eyes and white skin."[5]

The above quote doesn't mention the *human* race of the Egyptians, but the mention of white gods suggests indirectly that the Egyptians were also white if God made man in his image. The view that the civilization of Ancient Egypt was spearheaded by a group of non-blacks became known as the Dynastic Race Theory. William Matthew Flinders Petrie found evidence that Mesopotamia invaded pre-dynastic Egypt and imposed themselves on the rest of the country.[6] In the 1950's Egyptologists then assumed the population to be Asiatic from Mesopotamia. That Mesopotamians came into Egypt is factual as history confirms, but them dominating Egypt so much that the population was largely or wholly Mesopotamian is wrong, as the pictures and records say so. Even if they did rule or dominate Egypt, Egypt would still have been black because the Sumerians who ruled Mesopotamia at that present time (3300 BC) called themselves the black headed people.[7] Barry Kemp explains, the theory had always accepted that the original people of Ancient Egypt were Negroid, but the debate was really about whether or not the civilization was inspired by outsiders.[8]

If this was the case then the rest of the Egyptological world would follow suit which they obviously didn't or chose to ignore. The Egyptians actually trace their origin to Sudan, who are well known as dark skinned people but their earliest origins will be discussed in the following chapter. Cheikh Anta Diop disproves the Asiatic or Dynastic race theory in Chapter 5 of *The African Origin of Civilization*, for now we will just focus on the different views of a Black Egypt.

Count Volney states, "The Copts are the proper representatives of the Ancient Egyptians" due to their "jaundiced and fumed skin, which is neither Greek nor Arab, their full faces, their puffy eyes, their crushed noses, and their thick lips."[9] This description refers to a black race here, whilst he also uses Copt to describe a mixture of black Egyptian and foreigners, which leaves you unclear. Copt today is used to refer to the mixed version. Volney credits the African as being the inventor of arts, sciences and speech, which makes him trustworthy and proves he doesn't twist information, in this case he just failed to differentiate between the two versions of Copts.

Jean-Francois Champollion, in letters to his older brother Jacques Joseph Champollion-Figeac, states that "the Egyptians and Nubians are represented in the same manner in tomb paintings, reliefs," and that "The first tribes that inhabited Egypt, that is, the Nile Valley between the Syene cataract and the sea, came from Abyssinia to Sennar. In the Copts of Egypt, we do not find any of the characteristic features of the Ancient Egyptian population. The Copts are the result of crossbreeding with all the nations that successfully dominated Egypt. It is wrong to seek in them the principal features of the old race."[10]

Note that Abyssinia is present day Ethiopia and Eritrea; Sennar is a town on the Blue Nile in Sudan, both located in Africa. Eritrea is also said to be the land of Punt which the Egyptians claim is the land of the Gods.[11] They made several trade journeys there, although most authors trace the origin of the Egyptians to Sudan.

Another view is that black people were present in Ancient Egypt but as slaves or captives, led by pro-slavery supporters Samuel George Morton, George Gliddon and Josiah C Nott in the mid 1800s America. The fact that there were a few slaves in Egypt due to war captives can not be denied but to say blacks were *just* slaves in Egypt is not true. Slavery on a mass scale in Egypt cannot be proven. The one thing slavery is attributed to with the help of films such as 'Land of the Pharaohs, 1955' is the building of the pyramids. However recent reports in 2010 suggested the honourable manner of burial had to be that of paid labourers.[12] So there were practically no slaves let alone *black* slaves in Egypt. Furthermore, unless the Egyptians enslaved themselves, the only other place they would capture slaves would be in Nubia from which a handful of slaves were used. At the same time Nubian kings ruled Egypt in the Twenty-Fifth dynasty, in fact several pharaohs such as Amunemhet I (Middle kingdom: Dynasty 12) were said to come from the south i.e. Nubia.[13]

There is a collective of people and organizations who overtly claim a white, Arab or mixed race for the Egyptians, principalities as I call them. But as I said before they do most of their talking through pictures and movies or leave out the subject altogether in the academic world. The false images they leave behind are very powerful because they remain in our subconscious and shaking it off which many have tried to do is proving very difficult. Most pictures of Egyptians generally follow the examples listed above. In the academic world what they fail to do is *intentionally* attribute the Egyptian civilization to a black race and this is evident from their encyclopaedias, Egyptology, archaeology and anthropology books. You just read about the greatness of the Egyptians, their pharaohs and major accomplishments but are not told what race they belonged to. It seems that the advocators of this non black theory are incapable of admitting the truth that Egypt; the cradle of civilization served as the benchmark for all other civilizations because then they would have to give credit and respect to us as members of the black race. You see it's all really about power and empowerment. There is a very sinister project called the 'Spell of Leviathan' that has been cast on black people to keep us from knowing who we are, this is fully documented in Nuwaupian doctrine. There are several other books exposing the lie of a non black Egypt such as 'The African Origin of civilization: Myth or Reality' by Cheikh Anta Diop, 'Black Athena' by Martin Bernal, 'Egypt Child of Africa' by Ivan Van Sertima and 'Black Genesis' by Bauval and Brophy. Bauval/Brophy are both white 'unconventional' Egyptologists and deserve special praise for actually writing a book that promotes black people as the true founders of the Ancient Egyptian civilization. They explain that Black Genesis is not only a scientific thesis but also a testament of respect and admiration to black people. We still have to tell *our own* story, it means *much more* coming from a Nubian, that is why I'm here. This marks an unprecedented time in Egyptology history when both sides (Afrocentric and Eurocentric) reveal a common theme, representing a shift in consciousness as a benchmark for the rest of the world to follow in this pivotal year of 2012. Many black people around the world are still unaware of their link to Egypt, or simply don't care. This is evident by a standard conversation and observation of their actions. And if you tried to get into a serious discussion about it they would call you an idol worshipper, and say you're part of a cult. Of course there are some with an Afrocentric mind who associate themselves with Egypt and promote the greatness of kingdoms such as Timbuktu, but this in my view needs to grow exponentially! It is one thing to come across Egyptology from a black perspective and another to practice and truly identify yourself as an Egyptian; with clothes, pictures, books, customs and a general way of life. However most Africans/Caribbean's would rather follow western religions which I think is rooted in fear and a lack of understanding. The Bible rightly says *'My people are destroyed for lack of knowledge'*. Hosea 4:6.

We as black people do in fact have our own way of life, a culture, not religion called Nuwaupu which has been brought back to us by Dr Malachi Z York. "Nuwaupu means to convey a message that results in sound right reasoning" mentioned in The Holy Tablets 1:1:15.15[14] (Further references to The Holy Tablets will be HT). This is done by right knowledge, right wisdom and right overstanding. This was the same culture practiced by the Ancient Egyptians millennia ago. Nuwaupu is the true universal and spiritual science of the black race,[15] and this is what we must return to, in order to be unified again. Make no mistake Nuwaupu is very deep, this cannot be made clearer than Dr Malachi York's sentencing of 135 years. But that is another story!

Despite the obvious deception and cover up of the Egyptians being a black race there is evidence to show that they were African, black in origin. Some of which are mentioned below:

"It is certain that the natives of the country are black with heat." [Herodotus][16]

"The Egyptians said that they believed the Colchians to be descended from the army of Sesostris. My own conjectures were founded first, on the fact that they are black-skinned and have woolly hair." [Herodotus] [17]
"Ancient Egypt was a Negro civilization. The History of Black Africa will remain suspended in air and cannot be written correctly until African historians dare to connect it with the history of Egypt... The Ancient Egyptians were Negroes. The moral fruit of their civilization is to be counted among the assets of the Black world". [Cheikh Anta Diop] [18]

"It appears from the remark of Herodotus [i.e. an ancient Greek historian] that woolly hair like that of the Negroes prevailed among the

Egyptians, and by comparing this fact with the other characteristics mentioned by Lucian [i.e. another ancient Greek writer], we are led to infer that this nation had the distinguishing marks of an African race. This conclusion is confirmed by the travellers, who have described some of the most ancient Egyptian monuments [i.e. Norden, De Volney, Sonnini and Denon] and particularly the Sphinx which stands amidst the pyramids, and is probably coeval with those venerable fabricks [sic]. These figures have exactly the characteristic features of the Negro". [James Cowles Prichard.] [19]

"Egyptian skeletons, statues and countless pictures of Egyptians in their temples and monuments show the same racial characteristics as the Nubians and Nilotic tribes, the brown-skinned hunters of the steppes and the savannah husbandmen of the Sudan... of African origin were such great personalities in world history as Rameses the Great, the Sun King Akhnaton [sic], the many Pharaohs who bear the names of Amenophis [i.e. Amenhotep], Thutmosis [i.e. Thutmose] and the Set[h]os [i.e. Seti]. Of African inspiration are the pyramids, the golden-burial chambers, the statues, platic arts, temple friezes and other great Egyptian works of art. The Sphinx is an African monument, the hieroglyphs are an African script, and Ammon [i.e. Amen], Isis and Osiris are African gods." [Herbert Wendt] [20]

"According to the almost unanimous testimony of the ancient historians, they [i.e. the Ancient Egyptians] belonged to an African race which, first established in Ethiopia on the Middle Nile, gradually came down toward the Mediterranean Sea, following the course of the river." [Gaston Maspero].[21]

"Egypt is in Africa, Egyptians are Africans and there is now overwhelming evidence that ancient Egyptians have a black African origin".[22] [Bauval and Brophy]

"The Egyptians were a great civilization with many Nubian scientists, spiritual healers, mystics, astronomers and mathematicians like Zoser..." [HT 13:3:24]... "Egypt was the land inhabited by the Nubuns, Nubians." [Dr Malachi K York, The Holy Tablets, 13:11:9]

"There is now absolutely no doubt that the Ancient Egyptian Civilization was overwhelmingly African." [Ivan Van Sertima]. [23] Whenever a black person attributes the civilization of Ancient Egypt to a black race they are labelled Afrocentric and never taken seriously. An article 'Building Bridges to Afrocentrism' by Ann Macy Roth, Professor of Egyptology at Howard University states "In America, however, Afrocentric Egyptology is less a scholarly field than a political and educational movement, aimed at increasing the self- esteem and confidence of African-Americans by stressing the achievements of African civilizations, principally ancient Egypt."

Afrocentric Egyptology has four main points: (1) Ancient Egyptians were black, (2) ancient Egypt was superior to other ancient civilizations, (3) Egyptian culture had tremendous influence on the later cultures of Africa and Europe, and (4) there has been a vast racist conspiracy to prevent the dissemination of the evidence for these assertions.[24] Considering the past and present condition of the Black race throughout the world, self esteem and confidence boosts are sometimes necessary, but with evidence of a Black Egypt it is *more* than just a means of self esteem it is factual history that needs to be taken seriously and in my view adopted as part of our culture *globally*. Books are excellent source of knowledge; but as they say, a picture tells a thousand words. This and the many movies and documentaries on Ancient Egypt tips the scales in this debate which all show them to be white/Arab looking. And of all the hundreds of productions it's funny that not one shows the Egyptians in their true light. Now ask yourself why, there must be a particular reason? It's either they are all unknowingly wrong; but with the logic, remains and scientific study, this is highly unlikely. The only other assumption is; that the knowledge of our great past has been hidden from us because this is the key to unlocking our mental and physical bondage and returning to the kings/queens we once were. This same tactic has been used since slavery where our names, religions and cultures were stripped from us and we had nothing but what our slave masters gave us. This even happened straight after pharaonic Egypt where the Egyptian religion was made illegal under the guise of paganism and the priests and practitioners were in some cases executed. The fact remains, that there was a period of time before any invasions/battles/trading/immigration that the Egyptians all belonged to the same race. I have given myself the job of proving what race and colour they belonged to.

Introduction to Egypt

Egypt is considered the cradle of civilization. The ancient Egyptian kingdom spanned over three millennia and left a lasting legacy still recognized to this day. They produced such feats as the pyramids of Giza, the Sphinx, and were great mathematicians, astrologists, and healers. Egypt was the nucleus of a global diffusion of ideas spreading out to the rest of the ancient world. Egypt now called the 'Arab Republic of Egypt' is a country located in the North East of Africa. The capital is Cairo. It covers an area of (385,210 sq mi). From the North going clockwise it borders with the Mediterranean Sea. Israel and Gaza to the North East, the Red Sea to the East, Sudan to the South and Libya to the East. Its current population is estimated at 83,082,862 million.

Picture 1.3 Flag of the Arab Republic of Egypt.

Picture 1.4 Anwar Sadat. President of Egypt from 1970 – 1981.

The current president is Mohammed Mursi of the Islamist Muslim Brotherhood which founded the Freedom and Justice Party. Two presidents' before him was Anwar Sadat the last black president of Egypt. (Picture 1.4) Now why would there be a black president of an Arab country if black people were not long rooted in its history? Its climate is desert; hot, dry summers with moderate winters. Egypt is associated with the Nile, although it runs through 9 other countries. The Nile is the longest river in the world at 4,132 miles, is made up of three main streams, The Blue Nile, the Atbara and the White Nile. Egypt owes its existence to the Nile River which provides its main source of water. In the middle kingdom, circa 2000BC, Egypt was called *to-meri* 'the cultivated land' or Tama-Re by Nuwaupians. It was also called Kemet, the black land, and Mizraim in the bible, land of two straits. Egypt was invaded by the Arabs in 642 AD and it has remained an Arab country to this day, most of the people living in Egypt today are of Arab descent, the main religion is Islam and the national language is Egyptian Arabic. So the question is, "What race were the original, indigenous, native people in the area of land that we now call Egypt, what did they look like and what language did they speak?" Because there is an obvious difference the between that of Ancient Egypt and modern Egypt. To do this we will have to do a *thorough* dissection of Ancient Egypt, and look closely at Ancient Egyptian culture and lifestyle including language, art, religion, and major wars and invasions which changed the scene. We can start by looking at Egypt's chronology. (See Fig 1.1)

According to historians early Egypt was not land but sea when the universe was being formed. Afterwards as the Nile during the times of its inundation carried down the mud from Ethiopia (south) and land was gradually built up from the deposit. This could be the possible reason the Egyptians told Greek historians i.e. Diodorus that they were colonists (immigrants) sent out by the Ethiopians (with reference to inner Africa, south of Egypt).[25] The Sahara desert dried out over a period of several thousand years, which reached its final desiccation at the end of the 3rd millennium BC. During which time people must have migrated from there to the Nile Valley.[26] Pre-dynastic Egyptians established settlements in both Upper and Lower Egypt. They made high quality pottery, slate palettes for grinding cosmetics, and rock drawings of motifs including boats. Around the 5th and 4th millennia BC there seems to have been a rapid transition from a Palaeolithic hunter gatherer way of life to a Neolithic food producing way of life.

Although the start of the Egyptian dynasty is approximately 3100BC, "In some methods of dating, dynasty 1 falls around 5500BC, off by almost 2400 years." Even the acclaimed unifier of Egypt 'Narmer or Menes' has been brought into question by ivory labels from tombs in cemetery U at Abydos that attest to kings of a unified Egypt who predate him.[27] However Menes a Thinite from an area called 'Thinis' in Upper Egypt is shown on the Narmer palette unifying the two lands, which we assume to be the case because the reverse side shows him wearing the white crown of upper (southern) Egypt, and the front side wearing a red crown of lower (northern) Egypt.

Furthermore, this is the first name given by the Egyptian priest Manetho, who as an Egyptian we have good reason to believe. What is very important and denotive of human nature, is the Narmer palette shows him defeating an Asiatic enemy from the North, so this unification couldn't have taken place without an act of war. Some disagree and say the picture is symbolic of the king's power and doesn't record specific events of his reign but the extremely graphic beheaded bodies and slain men prove otherwise. The Egyptians were known to draw and record all aspects of their life and culture.

Picture 1.5 – The Narmer Palette

Picture 1.6 – The first pharaoh Narmer/Menes.

Figure 1.1 A chronology of key events in Egypt (with a particular focus on rulers, kings and wars): BBC Egypt website

circa 7,000 BC – Settlement of Nile Valley begins.

Circa 3,000 BC – Kingdoms of Upper and Lower Egypt unite. Successive dynasties witness flourishing trade, prosperity and the development of great cultural traditions. Writing, including hieroglyphics, is used as an instrument of state. Construction of the pyramids – around 2,500 BC – is a formidable engineering achievement.

669 BC – Assyrians from Mesopotamia conquer and rule Egypt.

525 BC – Persian conquest.

332 BC – Alexander the Great, of ancient Macedonia, conquers Egypt, founds Alexandria. A Macedonian dynasty rules until 31 BC.

31 BC – Egypt comes under Roman rule; Queen Cleopatra commits suicide after Octavian's army defeats her forces.

642 AD – Arab conquest of Egypt.

969 – Cairo established as capital.

1250-1517 – Mameluke (slave soldier) rule, characterised by great prosperity and well-ordered civic institutions.

1517 – Egypt absorbed into the Turkish Ottoman empire.

1798 – Napoleon Bonaparte's forces invade but are repelled by the British and the Turks in 1801. Egypt once more becomes part of the Ottoman empire.

1859-69 – Suez Canal built.

1882 – British troops take control of Egypt.

1914 – Egypt becomes a British protectorate.

1922 – Fu'ad I becomes King of Egypt and Egypt gains its independence.

1936 – April – Faruq succeeds his father as King of Egypt.

1952 – King Faruq abdicates in favour of his son Fu'ad II.

1952 – Gamal Abdul Nasser leads a coup by the Free Officers' Movement, now known as the July 23 Revolution, which results in Muhammad Najib becoming President and Prime Minister of Egypt.

1953 - June – Egypt is declared a Republic by Najib.

1981-6 October - Anwar al-Sadat is assassinated by Jihad members.

It is clear from looking at this chronology, and timeline that Egypt has been invaded on numerous occasions and foreign rulers have been in power. The Hyksos 'rulers of a foreign land' were the first foreigners to rule Egypt in Dynasties 15/16 of the Second Intermediate period. Since then Egypt has been ruled and taken over by Assyrians, Persians, Greeks, Romans, Arabs, Turks,

French and British consecutively. The question we are faced with now is, "If dynastic Egypt was an African population where did they all go?" My hypothesis is that due to foreign invasion and religious persecution the Egyptians spread out into other parts of Africa, and a cultural diffusion took place between these tribes. (See Chapter 4&5). Apart from immigration, EB solves some of the puzzle by saying, 'most of Egypt's population, comprising of the Nile Valley and the Delta are a mixture of an indigenous African population with Arabs. The towns especially the northern Delta consist of the foreign invader, Persian, Roman, Greek, Crusader, and Turk',[28] who can be safely regarded as the Copts spoken of by Jacques Joseph Champollion-Figeac earlier. 'Egypt: Lonely Planet' also mention two Nubian villages Siou and Koti on Elephantine Island in Aswan, home to the Nubia Museum, and Nubian houses and restaurants and others in West Aswan and Seheyl.[29] Some of the Eastern desert is inhabited by an African tribe of blacks called the Beja while people of the Western Desert, outside the oases, are of mixed Arab and Berber descent who have subsequently mixed with Egyptians from the Nile Valley, Arabs, Sudanese and Turks.[30] This can be summed up in 'Lets Set The Record Straight' by Dr Malachi Z York (2004). On p.359 he quotes "The Modern Egyptians today are descended from the successive Arab settlements that followed the Muslim conquest in the 7th C, mixed with the indigenous pre Islamic population. 60% of the population are Fulani or Peasant. 5% are Egyptian Copts, a Christian minority. Nubians live south of Aswan".[31] The only indication of black people in this quote is the *Nubians* who live south of Aswan which means the majority of the country is non-black African. The Nubians are mentioned last, meaning they are a minority. This proves they know the Egyptian civilization belonged to black Africans. If this is the case and the earlier quote from EB is a trusted source, why then is the image of Egypt still propagated as non-black?

Egypt and religion

Egypt features very heavily in the bible, it is mentioned 546 times. In fact the modern monotheistic religions are based on Egypt. Hosea 13:4 reads, *"Yet I am the Lord thy God from the Land of Egypt, and thou shalt know no god but me..."* is a testament to this. **This is the show-stopper!** In fact Egyptian Gods are mentioned in the Bible (Jeremiah 46:25) such as Amun (Revelation 3:14) who was the father of the gods in Egypt. The God of the bible is also referred to as the sun in Psalm 84:11" For the Lord God is a sun and shield" which is identical to Re, the sun-god in Egypt. And it also happens that Amun merged with Re to form Amun-Re. Nun is mentioned in Judges 2:8, who is one of the Ogdoads in Egypt and represents the primordial waters. Egyptian civilization predates the bible by several thousand years and these cannot be mere coincidences. The Egyptian religious stories although they appear mythological are symbolic of real events. The main characters in the bible all visited Egypt at one point. Abraham to escape a famine in Genesis 12:9, Jesus to hide from Herod in Matthew 2:13, Moses to free his people from Egypt in Exodus, Joseph after being sold into slavery by his brothers was made ruler of Egypt in Genesis 45:8, given an Egyptian name 'Zaphenath Paaneah' and married Asenath an Egyptian woman in Genesis 41:45. 'On' is also another Egyptian God and is called Annu in Sumerian Doctrine. Jesus' skin colour is likened to burnt brass in Revelation 1:14 which is obviously a black colour, and hair like wool describing the texture to that of an afro or nappy hair. Now if the Egyptians were white, God wouldn't have been able to send Jesus there to hide because he would have stuck out like a sore thumb, he would have only been able to hide with people of the same skin colour. What's more if Jesus is black and from the lineage of David as the bible says in Matthew 1:1 then all the other Israelite prophets descended from Adam, must have also been black. This would make the Israelites and Egyptians related, hence why God also claims in Exodus 34:23 that he is the God of Israel and Jesus discriminates in Matthew 15:24 saying he is only sent to the Israelites. There is reference to the Opening of the mouth ceremony in Exodus 29:21, a major ceremony in Egypt to allow a pharaoh to become a god and seek eternal life. The Golden Calf worshipped in Exodus 32:4 relates to the goddess Hathor, who was associated with a cow; even chapter 2 of the Qur'an, Surah al-Baqarah is called the chapter of the cow. More clues will be discussed later on in the chapter, but this is backed up by Egyptologists such as Joyce Tyledsley who states in Ancient Egypt and the Modern World that "Some of these myths passed from Egypt to Rome, and have had a direct effect on the development of modern religious belief".[32] It is thought that Rameses II (son of Seti and Tuya) was the Pharaoh spearheading Israelite captivity in the biblical story of Exodus. As already mentioned before, slavery was rare in Egypt, and more importantly the dates do not coincide. Dr Malachi K York explains in 'Jesus found in Egypt' that according to the Bible, Abraham was in Egypt before Moses, which if true would have had to be at the time of Narmer, recorded to exist between 3100 to 2890 BC. There are 9 generations from Abraham to Moses, and 247 pharaohs from Narmer to Rameses II in Dynasty 19, so the time of Moses would have been gone when Rameses came to the throne.[33] Dr Ben Yosef Jochannan an African Egyptologist also agrees that there are no records of Moses existing anywhere in Egyptian history. [34] However if we look through Egyptian history we see the names Thut*mose*, Ah*mose* and Ka*mose* showing that the biblical Moses was grafted from these names.

It is shocking what lengths have been taken to erase the African presence from Egypt. Some of you might already be aware of the alteration of Egyptian statues. It was the Arabs who were responsible for destroying and distorting the statues and monuments of Egypt to hide the African features. This took place since the Arab invasion (642 AD) at various times until the 19th century. An Arab historian Mak Rizi records that in 1378, an Arab named Mohammed Sa'im al-Dahr shot off the nose of the Sphinx, (picture 1.5) and in retribution for the damage was lynched by local inhabitants. [35] Nubians have a distinctive wide nose so it is evident why they would want to conceal this evidence especially if they planned on taking over the country. The sphinx is a subject of controversy, not just because it's mysterious in nature but also due to the debates of its race and its time of construction. A trustworthy Count Volney said the Sphinx's head was typically Negro in all its features. [36] A magazine from 1833 comments on the Sphinx, "The features are Nubian, or what, from ancient representations, may be called Ancient Egyptian, which is quite different from the Negro features." [37] This is a fallacy, because Nubian and Negro both refer to the black race. Jacques Joseph Champollion-Figeac in an attempt to discredit Volney even claims that the physical qualities of black skin and woolly hair do not suffice to characterize the Negro race. This is probably one of the biggest contradictions told on the subject of racial origin and for this he deserves a medal for deception and bravery; but later says "woolly hair is the true characteristic of the Negro race"[38] which ironically is 100% true so he is obviously confused and has his own agenda.

Picture 1.7 – The Sphinx   Picture 1.8 – Shabti of Pharaoh Ahmose

Egypt in the Media

Cleopatra (1963). Played by English actress Elizabeth Taylor. EB claim that "Cleopatra was of Macedonian descent and had no Egyptian blood"[39] however other sources disagree. Rapper Nas in Track 15 of God's son says "Caesar and Cleopatra, we need another actress to play her cause Liz Taylor's hot, but the Egyptian queen on the movie screen needs to be portrayed in a proper flava".[40] York M writes "Cleopatra was neither Roman nor Greek like Caucasoid history pretends; she was a Phoenician, a Mitsrayim which would be an Egiptian from the pure Negroid seed of Noah who was perfect in his generations 'genealogy' Genesis 10:6". The Romans, Jews and Greeks who controlled Egipt allowed the Phoenicians to rule Egypt until Cleophas was rejected as King much like they control parrot rulers and puppet establishments today. He gives a short history of the Phoenicians: the original Phoenicians are black skinned from Accad, son of Nimrod, in Genesis 10:10 which means 'the heads of black faces'. The Phoenicians descend from Hamath 'meaning black' in Genesis 10:18 and his Nubian wife Salha. The Hamathites lived on the East Bank of the Orontes (river in between Lebanon and Syria), and later moved into Phoenicia between Lebanon and the Mediterranean sea, so became known as the Phoenicians by the Greeks. They then moved to Tunis in North East Africa also called Carthage and finally into parts of Europe and were known as Black Canaanites.[41]

Stargate (1994). Cast includes:
Anubis – Carlos Lauchu. Born in Panama.
Horus - Djimon Hounsou. Born in Benin. An Egyptian.
Ra – Jaye Davidson. Son of a Ghanaian father an English mother. However the God Ra is unlikely to be mixed race.

The Prince of Egypt (1998). Although a cartoon, the image is not Nubian.

The Mummy (1999). Cast includes:
Pharaoh Seti I - Ahahron Ipale. Born in Morocco.
Imhotep: High Priest of Osiris - Arnold Vosloo. Born in Pretoria, South Africa but not a native like the Zulu or Xhosa tribe.
Anck Su Namun - Patricia Valesquez. Born in Guajira, Venezuela.

Egypt: Rediscovering a lost world. (2005).

Cast includes:
Tutankhamun - Arkin Chandaril.
Ay – Neji Nejah
Ankhesamun - Nicola Liberos
Rameses II – Fuman Dar
Kher-Heb – Aiman Zahabi

CHECK OUT THE PICTURES OF THESE FILMS ONLINE. ARE THEY ACCURATE DEPICTIONS OF PHARAOHS, MUMMIES AND THE GENERAL EGYPTIAN POPULATION OF ANCIENT TIMES?

We shall now proceed to end this chapter by showing exactly how the Egyptians saw and drew themselves. We shall start with (Picture 1.8) a scene from the Book of Gates in the tomb of Seti I. The painting shows the souls of different races known to the Egyptians entering the next world through gates, associated with different goddesses. Jean Francois Champollion writes a letter to his brother about this picture, which I will outline briefly. Starting from right to left, first is the Egyptian also called Rot-En-Ne-Rome, which means 'the race of men par excellence'. They are described as having a dark red colour and long braided hair. Next is the Asiatic or Namou, their skin colour borders on yellow or tan, strongly aquiline nose, thick black pointed beard. There can be no uncertainty about the racial identity of the man who comes next: he belongs to the black race Nubian or Nahisi. Last is the Libyan or Tamhou, who are described as having flesh coloured skin, a white skin of the most delicate shade, a straight nose, blue eyes, blond or reddish beard, clad in a hairy ox skin, a veritable savage tattooed on parts of his body. [42] The Egyptian has more or less the same hairstyle, (according to the picture) as the African and Libyan, resembling braids, plaits or twists. This hairstyle is possible by any race if done properly, however an African has thick, curly hair (See Chapter 10). This would account for the Libyan having the same hairstyle as the Egyptian and Nubian, the Asiatic has his hair unstyled.

Picture 1.9 - Book of Gates Tomb of Seti I Dynasty 19 1820. From right to left to right, Egyptian, Asiatic Nubian, Libyan.

Rameses III of Dynasty 20, the eighth king in succession after Seti I had a very similar scene in his tomb. However this time both the Egyptians and Africans (Nubians) are identical. This shows the Egyptians did not always portray themselves as light skinned as some would say.

Picture 1.10 - The table of Nations scene in the tomb of Rameses III. From left to right Egyptian, Libyan, other African, Asiatic. Simplified reproduction by Kurt Sethe and Richard Lepsius.

The Egyptians always represented the white invaders: Hyksos, Assyrians, Persians, Greeks, as races apart and were never influenced by them for the simple reason that their civilization was less advanced than their own.[43] There are several pictures in Egypt of blue, green, yellow and red skinned people. In an article from New England, 1833 when referring to wall paintings it was said that, "It may be observed that the complexion of the men is invariably red, that of the women yellow; but neither of them can be said to have anything in their physiognomy at all resembling the Negro countenance."[44] Picture 1.12 shows red and yellow skin tones below.

Picture 1.11 - Painting from the tomb of Sebekhotep at Aswan.

This contrast in colour is due to lifestyle habits, the men are shown to have darker skin because they spend more time working in the sun, and the women are shown as lighter because they spend more time indoors.[45] However Robin Walker (2008) states that the colours were "clearly symbolic. No groups of indigenous males and females ever had this colour contrast." He also added in reference to picture 1.11 of a turquoise coloured woman that "we cannot always interpret the colours used in Ancient Egyptian art too literally. Turquoise people do not exist."[46] well maybe on Pandora!

Picture 1.12 - Temple of Rameses II at Abydos 1394 – 1328 BC. Taken from Walker R, fig 30, p.41.

Only a thorough study of Ancient Egypt would reveal what race/colour they were. Such clues are present, for example The British Museum Book of Ancient Egypt, admits that "The dark skinned people of Nubia, while speaking a different language to the Egyptians, shared with their neighbours a common ethnic background and similarities of material cultures".[47] This clearly shows the Egyptians belonged to the same race as the Nubians, black Africans.

So any reference to them being light was either symbolic or a close shade of the black race, e.g. South Africans or the Igbo tribe are known to have light or fair skin but still black. They didn't have to paint themselves 'jet black' in every single picture just to show their colour. The Egyptians, black people in general actually have a brown/dark brown complexion and is not actually black, this is just a term used in modern day to describe us. However some black people have really dark skin such as the Sudanese/Nubians and is evident in their drawings. The term black is thrown around carelessly these days; anyone can be called black according to the rule 'one drop of black blood makes you black.' Kola Boof despite her somewhat weird life, is in her words 'against the racist American notion that Black people should think so little of themselves that just anybody can BE them." She continues that "it is seen as "racist" to proclaim one's blackness, to cherish it and to separate it from the ownership of those who are not black. But still, if my people are to survive...and to survive as themselves, it's a position that must be taken. And taken without apology or hesitation..... We are not so worthless...that just anybody can be us."[48] I for one agree with her. "Africans are the indigenous people of Africa and their descendants in the Diaspora" [49] [African code] and we have to take back our identity!

Summary

• There is a concentrated effort to hide the greatness of the Ancient Egyptian civilization from their descendants, black African people. Pictures are deceptive, statues were vandalised and some academics say they were anything but black. Others choose to give race in Egypt the silent treatment.

• Many academics including Herodotus, Cheikh Anta Diop, James Cowles Prichard, Herbert Wendt, Bauval/Brophy, Dr Malachi York and Ivan Van Sertima all agree that Egypt was a black civilization.

• Egypt was invaded many times in its history so by the end of the dynastic period the civilization was mixed.

• There are two important Ancient Egyptian drawings which show their skin tone. In The Book of gates they are dark brown and in The table of Nations they are identical to the Nubians who are dark skinned.

• The history and mythology of Egypt and Sumeria have been plagiarised to form the monotheistic religions.

Notes and References

1. Davidson B, (2001) *Africa in History*. P.25/26. Weidenfeld & Nicolson; New edition.

2. Keita S (1993) *Studies and Comments on Ancient Egyptian Biological relationships*. History in Africa. Vol. 20, published by African Studies Association.

3. *Tutankhamun was not black: Egypt Antiquities Chief*. Accessed 6/9/10, written Sept 25, 2007 AFP. [September 25 2007, MENA News Agency. Agence France Press website. http://afp.google.com/article/ALeqM5iB6u3XEMp9IrJfl-kH6FHNgZCg_A

4. Brewer D, Teeter E, (2007) *Egypt and the Egyptians*. Cambridge University Press; 2nd edition. P.58.

5. Icke, D (1999) *The Biggest Secret: The Book that will change the world*. Bridge of Love. 2nd edition. p.13,14.

6. Lefkowitz M, Rogers G (1996) *Black Athena revisted*. The University of North Carolina Press. p.16 & 67.

7. Walker R (2005) *When we ruled*. Every Generation media. p.597

8. Kemp B (2005) *Ancient Egypt: anatomy of a civilization.* Routledge, 2nd Edition. p.47

9. Volney, Constantin-François. *Principles Physiques de la Morale, Déduits de l'Organisation de l'Homme et de l'Univers.* P.131

10. Champollion-Figeac. (1839) *Egypte Ancienne. Paris: Collection de'l Univers,* 1839, p.27.

11. Chami (2006) cited in Acholonu, 2009, p.107

12. *Egypt: New find shows slaves didn't build pyramids.* Available from: http://www.sfexaminer.com/world/egypt-displays-new-archaeological-discovery-tombs-of-workers-who-built-the-great-pyramids-81126157.html#ixzz0zQ5HkLKh [Accessed 5/8/2010]

13. Ibid (4) p.43

14. York-El, Dr Malachi Z. *The Holy Tablets.* Scroll #172. ISBN 1-59517-116-9. Egipt Publishers. Athens, Georgia. 1:1:15 Or read online at: http://holytablets.nuwaubianfacts.com/

15. York-El, Dr Malachi Z. Book. Scroll #43 *Breaking The Spell.* (Revised) ISBN # 1-595-17-001-4. Egipt Publishers. Athens, Georgia P.14

16. *The History of Herodotus,* translated by George Rawlinson. New York: Tudor 1928, p.88. cited by Diop C 1974. p.1

17. Ibid p.115

18. Diop C (1974) *The African Origin of Civilization: Myth or Reality.* A Capella Books. p.xiv

19. Walker R (2008) *Before the slave trade.* African World History in Pictures. Black History Studies Publications. p.115

20. Ibid p.44.

21. Ibid (18) p.71.

22. Bauval R, T Brophy (2011) *Black genesis: The Prehistoric origins of Ancient Egypt.* Bear and Company. p.178

23. Van Sertima, Ivan. *They Came Before Columbus.* Live Documentary.

24. Roth A (1995) *Building Bridges to Afrocentrism: A letter to my Egyptological colleagues.* Available from: http://www.africa.upenn.edu/Articles_Gen/afrocent_roth.html [Accessed 26/1/10]

25. Ibid (1) p27

26. "Ancient Egypt." Encyclopaedia Britannica. 2010. Encyclopædia Britannica 2006 Ultimate Reference Suite DVD

27. Ibid (4) p,30 & 37

28. Ibid (26)

29. Virginia Maxwell, V. Fitzpatrick, M. Jenkins, S. Sattin, A (2006) *Egypt (Lonely Planet Country Guide)* Lonely Planet Publications. 8th Revised edition. p.128

30. "Egypt."Encyclopædia Britannica. 2010. Encyclopædia Britannica 2006 Ultimate Reference Suite DVD 17 Sept 2010 .

31. York-El, Dr Malachi Z. (1996) Scroll #360 *Let's Set the Record Straight.* (Revised). Egipt Publishers, Athens, Georgia. p.359.

32. Tyldesley J (2009) *Ancient Egypt and the Modern World.* Available from: http://www.bbc.co.uk/history/ancient/egyptians/egypt_importance_01.shtm l [Accessed 24/11/2010]

33. York-El, Dr Malachi Z. (1996) Book #203 *Jesus Found in Egipt.* Egipt Publishers, Athens, Georgia. p.366.

34. By Yosef A.A. Ben-Jochannan B (1986) *We, The Sons And Daughters Of "AFRICA's" Great Sperms And Ovum, Let Us This Day Of 6086 N.Y. / 1986 C.E. Speak As One Voice Academically.* http://www.africawithin.com/jochannan/drben_ascac_address_prelude.htm

35. Ibid (4) p.5

36. Ibid (18) p.27

37. *Original papers, Ancient Egyptians.* (1833) The New England Magazine, October, volume 0005 issue 4. p.276 Available from: http://digital.library.cornell.edu/cgi/t/text/pagevieweridx?c=nwen;cc=nwen;i dno=nwen00054;node=nwen00054%3A1;size=l;frm=frameset;seq=283;vie w=image;page=root [Accessed 13/10/2010]

38. Ibid (18) p.52

39. *Cleopatra VII Thea Philopator.* "Encyclopædia Britannica. 2010. Encyclopædia Britannica 2006 Ultimate Reference Suite DVD 17 Sept.2010.

40. CD. Nas. Gods Son. (2002) Track 15/Bonus Track 1: *Thugz Mirror Freestyle.* Columbia Records.

41. York-El, Dr Malachi Z. (1996) Book #15 *666 Leviathan The Beast as The Anti-Christ. Part 1 of 4.* ISBN# 1-59517-143-6. Egipt Publishers, Athens, Georgia. p.117 & 212

42. Ibid (18) p.46

43. Ibid (18) p.239

44. Ibid (37)

45. Spencer A, (2007) *The British Museum book of Ancient Egypt.* British Museum Press. p.194

46. Walker R (2008) *Before the slave trade. African World History in Pictures.* Black History Studies Publications. p.40 and p.41

47. Ibid (45) p.262

48. Boof K, *An Essay through photos.*

49. *Motherland.* Documentary DVD. (2010) by Owen Alek Shahadah. Quote by Dr Kimani Nehusi, scholar author university of East London.

Chapter 2

Extraterrestrial Origins

A fter the introduction in Chapter 1 I now want to tell the story of the Egyptians from the earliest possible source. Hold on to your seatbelts you're in for one hell of a ride! This will take you to unknown territory but will be critical to identifying their race and understanding their culture. Ancient Egypt is filled with mystery, wander and controversy concerning their wealth of knowledge in the sciences and arts, construction of architecture, religious texts and lifestyle. The greatest mystery of Egypt is the last remaining monument of the 7 wonders of the Ancient world, The Giza pyramids. Several of the world's best Egyptologists, architects and engineers have tried to explain the methods used to build them using basic and simple techniques but when weighed up against the facts it is clear they simply don't know. On the other hand 'free thinkers' offer more logical and practical solutions which are labelled 'conspiracy theories', simply an idea or theory used to explain a particular event. Conspiracy theories are not taken seriously by academics and governing bodies as they are seen to lack sufficient evidence, claimed to be false and passed off as ridiculous. However *any* evidence behind a theory makes it more probable and when examined under logic deserves more credibility than a mere co-incidence. It seems the principalities hide the truth because they are afraid of the impact this would have on society.

It is said the Great Pyramids of Giza were built by aliens or Extra-Terrestrials which literally means beings from outside of the Earths atmosphere. For example, an Egypt holiday guide says of the pyramids "Their extraordinary shape, geometry and age render them somehow alien constructions... It's easy to laugh at such seemingly out-there ideas, but visit the Giza plateau and you'll immediately see why so many people believe such awesome structures could only have unearthly origins." [1] The Egyptians are said to have acquired almost overnight, the arts of writing, calendar calculation, and stone building from a foreign influx of people, [2] which some say is Mesopotamia. The Egyptians and Sumerians were very close in development, most notably in the age of their writing systems, however Egyptian writing has proved to be the oldest of the two. [3] The foreign influx theory seems very likely, given this sudden increase in knowledge but instead of

Mesopotamia, would it be more suitable to look further afield when searching for evidence? As further afield as another planet? Since the 1970's evidence of an Egyptian city on Mars surfaced but was passed off as a conspiracy theory. The basis of Nuwaupu is to accept and follow facts that can be proven, based on experience, evidence and reason. The experience test is not always possible but right evidence and reason can be credible. If an explanation cannot substantially satisfy these three tests, then it cannot be proven so is wrong or doesn't exist. This chapter will explore the earliest origin of the Ancient Egyptians and answer some of the so called conspiracy theories of paranormal association with Egypt. This chapter should be read with an open mind and heart in order to get a clear and complete overstanding of Egypt's unexplained mysteries. You are being exposed to divine and sacred information that is not to be misused and wasted. So, where did it all begin?

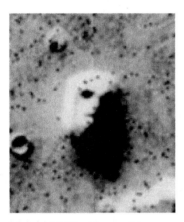

Picture 2.1 The Face on Mars

In July 1976 a satellite, Viking Space Orbiter, sent back images of the plains of Mars. In an area called 'Cydonia', two particular images 035A72 and 07013A captured something very interesting, dubbed 'the face of mars'. It was given the name because it resembles a human face. This face is similar to the face of the Sphinx at Giza. [4] This is also agreed at NASA. An article from the science at NASA website entitled 'Unmasking the face of mars' admits the face looks 'like an Egyptian pharaoh.' [5] The deep Egyptian Sahara is even described by Bauval/Brophy as the location on Earth most like the Martian landscape. For people new to Egyptology the Sphinx is an interesting figure which comprises the head of a human and the body of a lion. In the same area, there are several pyramids nearby. Both the face and Martian pyramids are similar to the Sphinx and Giza pyramids in Egypt today and all of them are artificial, meaning not natural, implying it was built by someone. Kate Tuckett asks, whether it was a superior civilization on Earth that went there to build them or an ancient civilization from Mars came to build them here?[6] She goes on to say that if the structures are related, "there must be a totally radical rethinking of our whole civilization." This would cause major problems for the powers that be so are labelled conspiracy theories, to keep people in darkness so they can remain in power. Could this really be true? Are the structures and findings on Egypt and Mars really related? And if so who was responsible for building them? In order to answer these questions we will need to take a closer look at Mars to see if it really can or could support life. We will begin by comparing it to Earth which we already know can support life.

Mars Examined

Table 2.1 - Statistical facts on Earth and Mars

	Earth	Mars
Distance from the Sun (miles)	93 million	142 million
Planet from the sun	3	4
Diameter (miles)	7,926	2,110
Mass (kg)	$5.9736*1024$ kg	$6.418*1023$
Time to orbit sun (days)	365	680
Angle tilted on axis (°)	23.45	25.2
Average temperature (°C)	14	-46C
No of moons	1	2
Weather	Habitable, extremes of desert, polar caps and moderate temperature.	Unpredictable, mostly freezing.
Atmosphere	Nitrogen, 77% Oxygen, 21% Argon 0.93% Carbon Dioxide 0.04 Water vapour 0.4% Variable	Carbon Dioxide 95.32% Nitrogen 2.7 Argon 1.6 Oxygen 0.13 Carbon Monoxide 0.07

The Sun

The first factor to consider when examining the probability of life on a planet is the distance from the sun. The Sun is the ultimate source of life. It gives heat, light, and allows organisms to perform their proper biological processes. There exists in astronomy something called the goldilocks zone or habitable zone, when a planet is a certain distance from the sun that it's not too hot or too cold but 'just right' to grow and sustain life. The estimated 'H Zone' extends to the semi major axis of Mars[7] The Earth is closer to the sun than Mars, so logically one can assume it is warmer, and has a better chance of supporting life than Mars, which is 49 million miles further away. But is the current position of Earth and Mars the same as it was at the time of Martian civilization? I ask this question because objects in space are constantly moving and run the risk of collision which alters their orbit. David Icke in *The Biggest*

Secret explains the findings from a scientist involved with aerospace research, Brian Desborough. His account goes like this. Jupiter crashed with a planet. Part of Jupiter broke away to become Venus. Venus was projected into space destroying the atmosphere and life on Mars. Venus made several orbits of Earth before it took its current place in the solar system. Physicists and Brian believed before this time Mars orbited where the Earth is now and Earth was closer to the sun. He further explains that there are vibratory fields orbiting the Sun or fixed paths of energy waves which planets are caught in to orbit the sun. The planets also create the same kind of wave circles around themselves, which then attract lighter bodies to orbit them, e.g. the moon orbiting the Earth. If a planet is disrupted from its course it will eventually lock into another orbit. Desborough believes, the vibrational pressures of Venus passed close to Mars and Earth, it hurled them into different orbits. [8]

Water

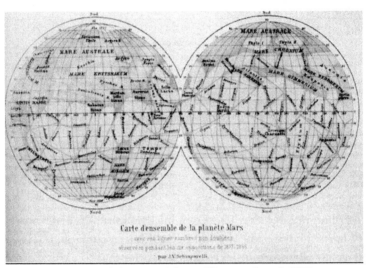

Picture 2.2 - Giovanni Schiparelli's map of canali 1877

Picture 2.3 – Martian channel

Water is essential to life. The first inkling of water on Mars first came about by an Italian astronomer, Giovanni Schiaparelli. He studied the surface of Mars in September 1877 and found 40 faint linear features which he called 'canali' meaning channels. He later produced a detailed map showing these adjoining channels. This was done at the Brera observatory in Milan and was known as the Great Opposition. Most astronomers didn't agree. However a strong supporter of this theory, Percival Lowell an American businessman and astronomer, began studying Mars in the 1890's and carried on trying to prove the channels did exist and life had existed on Mars. He stated 'the canali really were canals and the geometric and planet wide construction implied the work of rare intelligence'.[9] The entire surface of Mars was photographed, but the canali phenomenon was ignored by the scientific community who said the channels were optical illusions and he imagined them. But what's interesting, is they acknowledge the existence of channels, just not the ones by Schiaparelli and Lowell. An article on Mars speaks of outflow channels which state "These are true channels in that they were once completely filled with flowing water, as opposed to most river valleys, which have never been close to full but contain a much smaller river channel.[10] NASA commissioned many studies on the surface of Mars. In 1976, NASA sent two Orbiters around Mars which brought back pictures of the entire planet from pole to pole. They showed pictures of a network of eroded channels, floodplains and river valleys.[11] Notice the word erode. Erode means to wear away or destroy gradually, confirming the existence of water. In 2007, Mars Express found ice 3.7 km (2.3 miles) below the surface of Mars in the South Pole region. The ice is said to cover an area bigger than Texas and contain enough frozen water to cover the whole planet in a liquid layer approximately 11 meters (36 feet) deep. This was done using (MARSIS) a radar instrument.[12] In 2008, the Mars Phoenix Lander confirmed the existence of water ice in a soil sample.[13] The Mars Global Surveyor produced images of gullies in the southern highlands which were formed from liquid water, such as the Nanedi and Nergal Vallis.[14] These findings are all strong evidence that water once existed on Mars. Now when Mars would have reached its demise the water would have sunk into the soil and accumulated in the Polar Regions as mentioned above or escaped in the air in the form of vapour.

Temperature

The next important factor to consider is temperature. The average temperature of Mars is currently -46°C, and temperatures range from -87°C in winter to 20°C in summer. The planet is also 1.52 times as far from the sun as Earth, resulting in just 43 percent of the amount of sunlight.[15] However a planet closer to the sun might not necessarily be warmer as in the case of Venus. Venus has high atmospheric pressure which increases the greenhouse effect and results in a higher surface temperature than Mercury.[16] The conditions of Mars a long time ago wouldn't necessarily be the same now. Mars currently has a low and thin atmosphere, which make it impossible for liquid water to exist over large regions for a long time, and prevent it storing solar heat. The high amount of carbon dioxide is due to Mars' lack of plate tectonics that prevent it recycling the CO_2 back into the atmosphere and sustaining a significant greenhouse effect to keep the planet warm.[17] There is no carbon cycle in Mars; CO_2 is prevalent in the atmosphere at 95% and isn't used by any organisms. Algae and plants account for most of the CO_2 absorption in Earth's atmosphere by diffusion used in photosynthesis. Oceans also absorb a small amount of CO_2. Carbon compounds from plant or animal waste exist as fossil fuels but would be unlikely to decay due to lack of bacteria. So because no plate tectonics exist to recycle CO_2 and no organisms exist on Mars this would explain the high amount of CO_2. Martian temperatures are simply too cold to presently support life.

Martian Tilt

William Herschel a German Astronomer proved that Mars has seasons due to its axial tilt of 24.9°, which (Picture 3) explains below.

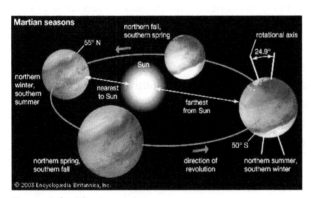

Picture 2.4 – Martian seasons.

The seasons of Mars, a result of the planet's inclination of 24.9° to its orbital plane. At present, southern summer occurs when Mars's elongated orbit brings it nearest the Sun. As the seasons change, the polar caps alternately grow and shrink. At its maximum size the southern cap extends about 5° more equatorward than the northern cap.

Moons

Mars has two moons. We know the moon helps, by 1) reflecting sunlight (light gives heat) and 2) by forming tides which help to cool the planet. This would help establish a balanced climate much like we have on Earth between night and day. To conclude there is very strong evidence that at some point in Martian history it had a very similar life supporting climate to Earth. They say liquid water is the only thing stopping them from believing however ice is just frozen water. Now let's examine these hills.

Martian discoveries

Now back to 'The face'. They say the goal of Viking 1 was to acquire images of the Cydonia region of Mars as part of the search for potential landing sites for Viking 2. Now any one who sees the hill captured in 035A72 and 070A13 would come to the conclusion that it is a human face. It clearly has all the attributes of a face, two eyes, a nose, a mouth, and the shape of the hair is very well defined. It has been described by some as the Martian sphinx, which also has a human face, but the fact remains it still looks very much like a human face. The dimensions of the face measure roughly 2.5 km (1.6 miles) long, 2 km (1.2 miles) wide and up to 940 m (2,600 ft. high), and seem very much to be artificially constructed, meaning not natural, or man made. So why have most of the astronomical world dismissed it? It's funny, that everything has been said to debunk the face from being connected to an ancient Martian civilization such as:

- a trick of light and shadow[18]
- "We've over-learned human faces so we see them where they aren't." [19]
- it's just an ordinary looking hill. With no shadows there are no facial features at all. [20]
- The human brain is programmed to recognize patterns and shapes that are familiar from everyday experience especially faces. [21]
- Pareidolia' The term for neurological or psychological phenomena where vague images are interpreted by the brain as specific images. [22]

Surely this is a work of intelligent design or do the face disbelievers know something we don't. Do they need to buy special sunglasses like in the movie 'They Live' or should we all get our eyes tested? On April 5 1998 the Mars Global Surveyor released new pictures of the face with their newer high resolution camera. On April 8 2001 the Mars Reconnaissance Orbiter released another picture using a HiRise picture of the face. (Refer to Picture 2.5)

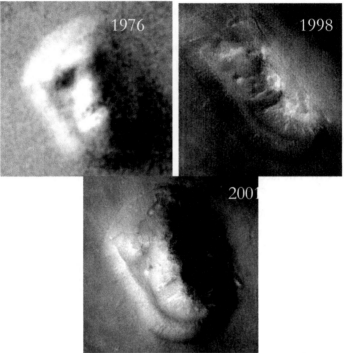

Picture 2.5 - Faces on Mars

All three pictures are completely different and more or less photographed from the same angle. The latter two taken with a higher resolution camera should show a clearer image not a *different* one. The conclusion? Something was done to the original face and then photographed again or the new face was graphically reconstructed. The 1998 picture is flat and according to the dimensions given above, cannot be taken seriously. The 2001 picture is slightly better given that it shows a fuller figure but is still miles apart from the original photo captured in 1976. The 1998 and 2001 pictures must have been changed either by computer software or the actual face distorted by NASA spacecrafts. It seems we are being lied to! Even if the 1976 picture was discredited, there shouldn't be that much of a difference between 1998 and 2001. An article by Van Flandern from Meta Research says that "JPL-MIPL personnel processed the image through two filters having the effect of flattening and suppressing image details."..."This step is documented at a JPL web site." [23] We are constantly bombarded with excuses such as the original photo was captured at a certain angle, with a certain amount of sunlight and resolution which makes it look like a face. These are just excuses. The end result is, if it looks like a face, then it most probably is a face, but the questions that would emerge if this was verified and accepted; like Kate Tuckett says 'would force us rethink our civilization.' The Mars observer vanished in August 1993. This didn't go well with sceptics who thought NASA was purposely withholding images from the public. One would think that NASA would be itching to get to the bottom of this theory and prove once and for all whether it was or wasn't a face with the MGS. However they had no real intentions of taking new photos and are even cited saying they will try and acquire new images, and there is no certainty the

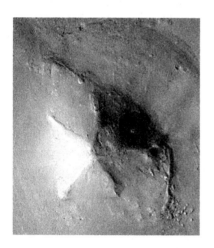

Picture 2.7 – Cydonia region of Mars.

Picture 2.6 – D&M pyramid

images will include the features of interest. I urge readers to read the full article, this is documented on the Malin Space Science Systems website. [24] The Cydonia region has more than just a face it also contains a number of pyramids and has been called the city. The most famous of this is the D & M pyramid which is five-sided, about 800m high and 3 km long, located 16 km from the face. Six other pyramids are reported nearby. There are also buttes (fortress hill) and mesas (table mountains) [25] Since Mars and Egypt both have pyramids and versions of the sphinx this drastically increases the chance of a connection. It's worth mentioning a Martian meteorite ALH84001 which showed 10-12 segments of what some thought to be a fossil. This was found by Dr Everett Gibson a NASA planetary scientist, however this was also discredited. The most recent project was The NASA Curiosity Rover which landed on Mars on the 6th August 2012. Its assignment according to the Mission fact sheet is to 'Investigate whether conditions have been favourable for microbial life and for preserving clues in the rocks about possible past life.'[26] but 1976 is all the proof they would need.

So if the Ancient Egyptians built cities and monuments on Mars, and Mars is currently desolate what caused life to end? For the small minority who actually admit to sentient life on Mars they would take this question more seriously than those who don't even believe or rather acknowledge. Finding the truth about an event which took place on another planet such a long time ago is not an easy task. The first clue is that the surface of Mars is covered with craters. This suggests that Mars suffered an onslaught of meteorites which probably led to a cataclysmic calamity. The biggest crater is called Hellas Planita, located in the Southern Hemisphere. The impact basin measures 7,000 km (4,400 miles) across, including the ring, and 8 km (5 miles) deep. A similar theory is said to have wiped out the dinosaurs on Earth. A huge meteorite hit the Earth causing an 'impact winter'; a dust cloud which enveloped the Earth blocking the suns heat and light for months/years, eventually causing all life to die.[27] Some scientists say one meteorite hit the Earth, and the dinosaurs already experienced terrible climatic conditions and a second meteorite would have been the decider.[28] The high incidents of craters on the surface cannot be overlooked. Some researchers have shed light on Mars' destruction. Percival Lowell, claimed the 'canali' really were canals and that "getting the water round was the major task of a civilization on a dying planet."[29] This view is also shared by Dr York, who writes 'mars died because its oxygen and water were slowly evaporating into space.'[30] There has been a stream of movies about Mars in Hollywood such as Total Recall (1990) Mission to Mars (2000), Red Planet (2000) Mars Attacks (1997), The Box (2009) and the most recent John Carter (2012). In the movie 'The Box', the co-star played by James Marsden works in the optics lab at NASA and helped to design the camera for the Viking Lander. The movie is set in 1976 (no co-incidence there) at Langley Air Force Base, Virginia. Near the start of the film he enters the 'Viking Results Press Conference'. A reporter asks the speaker "Why is the National Security Agency involved?" As you can imagine everyone turned to look at the troublemaker and there was an uneasy silence. The speaker tried to play dumb by asking "The NSA?" The reporter replied "Yes, the Deputy Director of the NSA is here in Langley". This prompted a series of questions by the audience such as "Why is the NSA here in Langley? Tell us about tests being conducted on the labs? Is there an ancient Martian civilization that left something behind?" The speaker replied, "I'm sorry I have no comment on that but I thank you for the information, any other questions." Arthur Lewis tells the reporter 'If we find water beneath the surface and the Orbiter photos of utopia Phoenicia indicate that there were once rivers on the surface of the planet, it's quite possible we will eventually find evidence of life". Funnily enough nothing was mentioned about the face or Cydonia region, which the film was based on and it followed it's own plot. Either way those questions need answers.

Enough has been said about the Martian and Egyptian monuments, but we still don't know 1) who made it? and 2) why?

MARS EXPLAINED!

> "The face on Mars is the face of Homo erectus. It is the face of Zakar or who you know as Adam. The **Annunaqi** set up bases on the planet Mars 450,000 years ago before coming to the planet Earth. **Homo Erectus** were being abducted from the planet Earth and then taken to a **laboratory** on the planet Mars, where they were being made into homo sapiens. What you are seeing are remnants of **cities**, bases and monuments of an Ancient Egyptian type civilization."[31] Dr Malachi Z York

If you find the above paragraph hard to digest. Let's take it step by step.

1) Annunaqi – means 'those who came down in 50's.' These are the real Gods of the bible who made man in Genesis 1:26. They appear in Hebrew in the Key Word Study Bible #430 as the title 'elohiym' in plural form, meaning gods. 29 The 'us' and 'our' prove this, because one God would not say that. So many Christians battle an idea of more than one God to the bitter end, and then say, 'The Father, the Son and the Holy spirit', when the father and son are actually two different beings (Read Scroll #196 Is Jesus God?). An overstanding and acceptance of this will set you in the right direction and shatter the basis of the monotheistic (one god) religions: Christianity, Judaism and Islam. (THINK ABOUT IT!) The Annunaqi are mentioned in ancient texts of Mesopotamia, where the Sumerians lived. E.g. Enuma Elish, Atra Hasis, Gilgamesh Epics in Cuneiform script. And the religious people who only deal with the bible would have to explain the presence of Nergal an Annunaqi in 2 Kings 17:30, or Tammuz, Ezekiel 8:14 (The Holy Bible).

Picture 2.8 – Anunnaqi

2) Most are familiar with the term 'Homo Sapien', meaning 'wise man' or 'knowing man'. Homo erectus is simply an earlier type of humanoid which existed in the Pleistocene age 1,600,000 to 250,000 years ago. The 450,000 years event is clearly within this given time period.

3) Laboratory. Today couples with fertility problems have procedures to help them, such as In-Vitro Fertilisation (IVF), Intrauterine Insemination (IUI), egg and sperm donation. If you mentioned the term 'test tube babies' say 100 years ago, you would have been called crazy. The treatments carried out by doctors today were the same being carried out 49'000 years ago, by the Annunaqi. We just thought this was the first time it was done.

4) Cities. One isolated face on Mars could be considered an anomaly. However the high concentration of pyramids, a tholus and a mound indicate that this must have been a city.

The face on Mars is only part of the story of creation. The Nuwaupian story of Extraterrestrials and creation goes a little something like this. It is said that we are in the 18th galaxy 'The Milky Way' because the density of the stars give it a white or milky appearance. There is a 19th galaxy called Illuwyn 'Abode above', which is home to three suns, 19 planets, and 38 moons. (Picture 2.8) One of the planet's is called Rizq, from Razaqa meaning 'to provide'. Rizq is located between the suns Utu and Shamash. (Read Man from Planet Rizq. Scroll # 80) There are three continents on the Planet Rizq; Darnuriyya, Kusmusta and Zarantu. The galaxy Illuwyn is mentioned in the Quran 83:18

"No. Indeed the record of the righteous is in Illiyyun. And what can make you know what is Illiyyun?" Psalm 83:18 mentions the Most High; the corresponding Hebrew word is 5945 'elyown', taken from 5927 'alah' a verb meaning to go up, to ascend, to take away to lift, to offer. Here we can see the common notion of a heavenly abode up there.

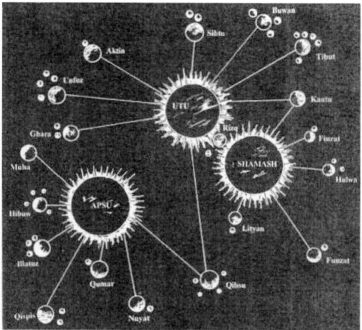

Picture 2.9 – Illuwyn the 19th galaxy. Tri Solar system.

The leader of Rizq was Murdoq, the grandson of Anu the Most High God. Another being who went by the name of Humbaba, Tarnush, Shakhar wanted to rule instead of Murdok. When he couldn't have it he shot a plutonium bomb at the atmosphere of Rizq. This severely depleted its atmosphere and led to a war in heaven (Revelation 12:7). Murdok battled against Humbaba by using the Tillu missile similar to the Thel missile (Tactical High Energy Laser), an air defence weapon used by the marines. Murdoq was given this red light beam ray gun made from the sardius stone by his grandfather Anu 'The Heavenly One' which he used to defeat Humbaba. However the planet Rizq which already had a high level of radiation from being in between two suns, now had extra radiation from the bomb which depleted its ozone layer. The Rizqiains, led by Murdoq, set out on a mission to search the galaxies for gold and other minerals. They needed to create a dome of gold dust particles suspended in the atmosphere that would protect it from the UV rays of the suns. As they passed through the Milky Way they discovered gold particles in the asteroid belt signalling the presence of gold on the planet Earth. That's why the Bible says in Genesis 2:12 'And the gold of that land is good: there is bdellium and the onyx stone'. Rizq became uninhabitable so many Rizqiyians fled to Orion and Pleiades. When they found Earth they started mining the gold themselves but soon it became tiring for them. So they decided to create a slave or a 'lulu amelu' *primitive worker* to do the work for them. The beings on Earth 'Homo Erectus' were still evolving so they sped up their evolution by mixing in their genes to mine gold for them, hence began the process of ET intervention. Once the gold was mined it was taken to Mars and the dark side of the moon then transported onto the Motherplane Nibiru.

Among the many images of Mars, are images of dolphins.[32] Dolphins are one of the most intelligent animals/sea creatures and one of the only animals to voluntarily associate with humans. The Black Book, mentions 'The Dolphin project'. The Neteru (Egyptian gods) used the dolphin for the process of artificial insemination and to transport the seed of humans between Earth and Mars. [33] Scientists have admitted that dolphins are closer to humans than monkey's are,[34] which would make the transportation easier and increase the possibility of this even happening. The English word for womb comes from the word dolphin, because, womb is *delphinus* in latin and delphis in greek, and modern English is a combination of different languages including Latin and Greek. The subject of dolphins is not to be taken lightly. A documentary *Tales of the Unexplained – UFO Chronicles, Series 1: Episode 1* mentions the same event.

People claim that dolphins and whales are here for a purpose and these sea mammals possess the answer and questions about mankind and the universe. Trisha Lamb Fauerstein who made it her life long mission to explore the existence of dolphins claims "There's a lot of channelled information that indicates that dolphins and whales came here from Sirius. Some say that they were god like beings on Sirius and that they came to this planet to colonize and take care of it. Whales and dolphins were sent here to store the history of this planet, of humans, of dolphins and whales and all other beings." The video also mentions how they can heal people with emotional problems such as disabled and autistic children. "With their sonar abilities they can actually see into your body and detect problems, imbalances in your energy field and then they beam back that helps to bring you back into balance. Another function they have is interdimensional or intergalactic travel. Supposedly dolphins and whales can take on their light body and travel anywhere in the galaxy or to any dimension they want to." With the capability of interdimensional travel it's said that dolphins transport humans from this realm into the afterlife.[35] It is sad to see dolphins and whales are being massacred by the Japanese who have no care or idea of their divine purpose.

Picture 2.10 – Adam, a successor on Earth was fashioned after the likeness of the Elohyeem, Gods, Judges, Angels, Genesis 1:27 49,000 years ago.

This Is Adam Notice The Gradual Transition Of The Face.
Notice How The Face Matches Perfectly With The Face On Mars.

Picture 2.11 - 'Transition of Adam to Face on Mars' Shamballah

Out of all the speculation none are as clear as Dr Malachi York. Nuwaupian doctrine teaches that Gods called Annunaqi or Neteru created and bred a new type of being, Adamites, or what is called Adam in the Bible 49,000 years ago. These Gods were scientists and mixed their DNA with the 'homo erectus' and several types of monkey. The whole breeding process took up to 600 years. 100 years to gather species or abduct homo erectus from the earth. 400 years for breeding. 100 years to educate and civilize the new being.[36] The Holy Tablets also records this incident.

> 1:2:23 Adamites, of the 14 generations, before the completion of the Adama project in the laboratory in Cydonia called Shimti. The Lahmu (Mars Project", or the Sphinx project.) This genetic breeding and splicing, chromosome tampering is that, which gave birth to Kadmon, called Zakar and even Adam.

> 1:4:54-57 Here, you will find prototypes of Homo Sapiens. Thus, the word parthenogenetic, which explains that this site, where there are pyramids, and ruins of temples of the Anunnagi, were used for the cloning of Homo Erectus to Homo Sapiens, called the Adama Project. This is where the face of Kadmon can be found. Today, the site is called Siddoneeah, or Cydonia from Sidon, the first son of Canaan.

[The Holy Tablets, Dr Malachi Z York]

Dr York (Amun Nub Re Akh-Ptah) isn't the only one to state this. 'The Lost Book of Enki' by Zachariah Sitchin also records this incident.

> Some 445,000 years ago, astronauts from another planet came to Earth in search of gold. Splashing down in one of Earth's seas, they waded ashore and established Eridu, "Home in the Faraway." In time the initial settlement expanded to a full-fledged Mission Earth with a Mission Control Center, a spaceport, mining operations, and even a way station on Mars. [37]

Catherine Acholonu-Olumba an African historian, wrote a book entitled, 'The Gram Code of African Adam – Stone Books and Cave Libraries, Reconstructing 450,000 Years of Africa's lost Civilizations'. So one can see that there is a common theme of 450,000 years, regarding the supposed time of Earth colonisation by the Martians who set up their new home in Egypt. Richard Hoagland, a former NASA scientist also confirms that Cydonia has the ruins of an entire Martian city because of the large number of monuments all located within the same area.[38] An article entitled, 'The Face on Mars: Once and for all' makes an excellent comparison between the Face on Mars and the sphinx. He says the FOM is looking straight up into the sky and the sphinx is built for admirers on ground level. Then it points out that it would be meaningful to the Martians if they built it purposely to be seen from space.[39]

Dr York writes, "The face on Mars was used as beacons to warn aliens of the Adama project taking place on Mars."[40] The logic is there for all to witness. The article worked this out on pure common sense, with no knowledge of Nuwaupu or The Black Book. "Due to successful disinformation campaigns, science and the media still treat the Face on Mars as fantasy." In the movie 'The 4th kind' sceptics saw believers in UFO's as entertainers of wild theories. They used weather balloons, atmospheric effects, optical illusions and hypnotic hallucinations as explanations for UFO's.

One might ask, 'If these Egyptian Gods or aliens did come to Earth, then are there any traces of their journey or evidence of them being here? Well the answer to that question can probably be answered in two words. Nazca lines! The Nazca lines are lines and figures of animals located in southern Peru similar to crop circles in England. According to Dr York the Nazca lines were left by the Neteru when they came to earth. [41] Erich Von Daniken says the lines are runways of an ancient airfield that were used by extraterrestrials. It should not be discredited just because Peru is far from Egypt for they could have landed anywhere then gone to settle another continent. [42] This is not about believing because someone says so, this is about critically evaluating evidence using ancient knowledge and common sense. Research the pictures for yourself and if you still disbelieve I would love to hear a better explanation!

The scientists and media know that Mars was once home to an ancient civilization and are seriously planning how to make Mars hospitable. An article 'Mars in Earth's image' discusses different techniques they can use to simulate life there. [43] They wouldn't be willing to go this far if they knew there was no chance of transferring human life there.

> 1:4:57 This is why today astronomers are interested in the planet Mars, because they have discovered that life existed there before, and that there is a possibility that they might be able to bring human life to that planet again with its Martian atmosphere. [The Holy Tablets, Dr Malachi Z York]

Now on to the pyramids in Egypt. The pyramids of Giza are the only remaining of the Seven Wonders of the World, the term wonder implies there is still speculation attached to it, an unsolved mystery. The main areas of debate are how the stone blocks were prepared, how the stones were transported and placed meticulously in position, and how they were perfectly aligned with the Orion star constellation. Thought to be built around 4,500 years ago [44], Egyptologists, and archaeologists don't know how, why, or who built them. Somebody built them because they are in no way natural formations by the Earth, just like the face on Mars though they do replicate natural formations such as mountains and volcanoes. However the image of 'non African' men building the pyramids is still circulated even by academics. (See picture 10)

Picture 2.12 – Non African image of Pyramid builders

Quick facts about Khufu pyramid.

• Height: 480 ft. (146m)
• Length: 756 ft. (230m)
• Blocks: Approx. 2,300,000 blocks of stone, each averaging 2 1/2 to 15 tonnes in weight.
• Mass: 5.9 million tonnes
• No side is more than 8 inches different in length than another
• The nearest quarry is 500 miles away in Aswan.
• The whole structure is perfectly oriented to the points of the compass.
• If you cut and placed 10 of these stones a day it would take 664 years to make 1 pyramid.
• Built in 20-30 years.
• Was the tallest building in the world until Lincoln Cathedral in 1300 AD.[45]

The pyramids are said to have been built by using basic techniques, for example "a system of ramps must have been used to *drag* the millions of blocks into their positions in the various pyramids" and "it is usually assumed that wooden and bronze levers were used to manoeuvre the blocks into position".[46] Could it have been that simple and still satisfied these basic engineering principles? 1) They had no steel, in fact used copper tools so how did they cut them? 2) How did they transport all the 2.3m stones 500 miles, especially with no machines or trucks? 3) There is no evidence of the straight or spiral ramps to move the stones up the pyramid, which to reach the top would have to be over half a mile long. 4) To be strong enough to support the weight, the ramps would need to contain as much material as the pyramid itself.[47] 5) How did they drag all these stones around the ramps when they were so heavy? 6) With no telescopes or modern astrological materials, how did they align the three pyramids with the 3 stars of Orion?

I'm not saying that manual labour was not used *at all* in constructing the pyramids, but given the scenario I argue that they must have used some advanced techniques to build them. Even with our high skyscrapers in modern cities the pyramids are still something to be revered and some might argue even more advanced than anything we can produce today. More people are now catching on to the idea that 'the ancients' had superior knowledge. Despite several weak explanations, some professors admit 'there is still a great deal that remains mysterious about the basic structure of pyramids.'[48] My argument now goes beyond trying to prove that black people were the main contingent during Ancient Egypt, but that black Gods or ET beings interfered with our evolutionary development on Earth and were responsible for the advanced knowledge of the Egyptian civilization! An Egyptian by the name of Malachi Z York explained some of the mysteries behind the pyramids.

> 3:5:11 The ancient Egyptians had an advanced knowledge of astronomy, and they knew about Sirius B, which is why the 3 Great **Pyramids** of Giza are lined up perfectly with the **Orion** star constellation. (12) They made their map face south towards Sirius. (13) The 3 pyramids of Giza were originally built by **Adafa,** with the help of **extraterrestrial beings**. Adafa was in tune with the celestial beings that originally erected the pyramids... The Giza pyramids today were reconstructed by the pharaoh Khufu, also known as Cheops, and his son Khafre and Menkure. [The Holy Tablets, Dr Malachi Z York]

1) Pyramids – The three pyramids of the Giza complex were reconstructed by Khufu (Cheops) Khafre (Chephren) and Menkure (Mycerinos). Khufu was the pharaoh of Egypt in the 4th dynasty and ruled for 23 years. Khafre was the son of Khufu and Menkure was the son of Khafre. HT 3:5:14.
2) Orion – is a star constellation, depicted as a hunter holding a lion in one hand and a club in the other. Orion's belt, a belt worn by the hunter contains 3 stars Alnitak, Alnilam and Mintaka which appear in a straight line. They line up with Khufu, Khafre and Menkure's pyramid's respectively. Orion is mentioned in the bible 3 times.

Picture 2.13 – The pyramids of Giza in relation to Orion's belt.

Heaven appears in the bibles NT as the Greek word 'Ouranos'. Ouranos is listed as #3772 in the Hebrew-Greek key word study bible and is described as sky or heaven, the abode of God.[49] Mark 13:25 'And the stars of heaven' show a strong link with astrology.

3) Adafa – known as *Enoch* in the bible, was a direct descendant of Adam. Genesis 5:24 And Enoch walked with God: and he was not; for God took him. The Holy Tablets say he was in tune with the celestial beings that originally erected the pyramids. This quote shows Enoch was extremely important! Who can claim to have walked with God? And the fact God 'took' him... need I say more.

4) Extraterrestrial beings – Almost all cultures speak of the Gods coming down to mix or teach them. As I mentioned the Annunaqi, Nazderu, Orisha, Eloheem, Thunderbirds, Allahuma, Nommos, Kachina. Genesis 6:2 also mentions, sons of God.

York also adds that the step pyramid of Saqqara was built by Imhotep for Zoser, and Imhotep also acquired the science from the Eloheem Annunaqi.[50] Although sceptics of alien life might disagree, the facts speak for themselves. Here is a brilliant quote by Robert Temple. "A number of people cannot bring themselves to think seriously about Extra terrestrials because their minds do not run that way, I suppose". [51] Most sources say the pyramids were built by Khufu but its clear there is more to the story. If they were originally built by Adafa (Enoch) and ET's this would make them older than the accepted date of 2,500 BC so how old? Our clue may come from the finding that water erosion has eroded the paws and wings on the Sphinx; this wouldn't have been possible since before 5000BC because Egypt has had a desert climate. Even accepted Egyptology textbooks such as 'The British Museum book of Ancient Egypt' admit that Egypt experienced strong floods between 15-10,000 BC, p.14, however they still fail to put two and two together. So just how old are the Sphinx and Giza pyramids? A psychic called Edgar Cayce was able to access the mental reservoir while in a self-induced hypnotic state and answered questions on various topics called 'readings'. When asked about Egypt he revealed this place was built in the year 10,500 BC and that this date would be supported somewhere around 1998 AD. Robert Bauval confirms "10,500 BC is when the sphinx is gazing directly at its own image the constellation of Leo, and if we are to turn 90 ° and face due south we could see the three stars of Orion's belt in a pattern that mimics exactly the pattern of the pyramids on the ground, so we have here a perfect conjunction taking place in and only in 10,500 BC."[52] In Black Genesis he explains, "there is a possibility that the pyramids of Giza were indeed built during the fourth dynasty but were built on top of a location where there was some pre-existing, symbolic much older architecture. [53] York also confirms in Science of the Pyramids that some of the pyramids had to have a hard core such as a hill or a rock, from which a pyramid could be built upon. While we are on the subject of location did you know the pyramids of Giza sit directly on one of the many major points or vortices of the Earth's energy grid and were built geometrically 23 ° from the centre of the Earth. I guess that is just another co-incidence. Our planet is on a 23 ° axis so the pyramids must be used to maintain balance. It's specific location is 31.72 N, 31.20 E. (We will see the reason why later) These

Egyptians whatever colour they were went through hell and back to build the pyramids and the reasons behind their construction must be monumental! An important factor that is overlooked when trying to date the pyramids is that the Ancient Egyptians recorded literally everything on papyrus, walls, and stone. There are pictures and records of scantily clad women at a banquet, fishermen on the Nile, taxes, women throwing up after drinking too much beer, religious ceremonies, trade missions and wars. Why wouldn't they draw pictures of themselves building the pyramids, one of their greatest achievements? They had 20-30 years to do it? Is there 1 picture showing this, because I haven't seen any? This is just another reason why the dating should be revised.

Cayce also predicted that the records of Atlantis could be found in three locations, Guatemala, the Bahamas (see atlantis.com) and you guessed it; Egypt, in a hidden chamber under the left paw of the sphinx. It just so happens that in May of 1993 a seismologist Dr Robert Schoch, Professor of Geology at Boston University may have found it. This is his account:

> "We were able to model what was underneath the Great Sphinx. We found under and in front of the left paw of the sphinx what I believe is a major chamber maybe up to 25m below the surface. Based on its regularity it looks like it was human carved and not only is it definitely there, but it seems to have something in it. The way it resonated, the way it ringed seems to indicate that there was something in the chamber."[54]

According to the documentary the Egyptian government hold the rights to determine if and when the secrets of Atlantis will be revealed to the world, so these predictions can not be fully tested. The date given by Cayce was dismissed by the various authorities and even though so called rogue Egyptologists like John Anthony West, Graham Hancock and Robert Bauval were able to prove these findings they are still dismissed. This is evident by the omission of this information in Egyptology and history books.

Cayce was probably the first to date the pyramids to that time and Dr Malachi York supports that dating for the Giza complex including the Sphinx. York adds the pyramids were built after the fall of Atlantis,[55] which happened circa 11,500 years ago. This link with Atlantis is probably the principal reason for their construction.

What Most People Don't Overstand Is That Pyramids Are
Electromagnetic Antennas, That Create Standing Columnar

Waves, To Prevent The Wobbling Of The Earth. After The Destruction Of Atlantis The Earth Needed To Be Balanced. The Pyramids At Giza Were Built To Balance The Magnetic Fields And Land Masses Of The Earth After The Axis Shift, Of 23 Degrees, Which Takes Place Every 50,000 Years Called An Epoch. The Axis Needle Completes A Cycle Every 24,000 Years, Called An Equinox, And Every 50,000 Years, The Crust Of The Earth Shifts, Like The Skin Of A Grape. (York-El, Science of the Pyramids p.8)

The pyramids served other purposes:

- Temples and tombs
York says it was the mastaba that was used as a tomb not the pyramids as we have been taught. However some of the Nubian pharaohs used their pyramids as tombs.
- Refocus light into 3 different electromagnetic charges of tachyon pairs.
The word pyramid means light or fire measures. There is a light emitted from the top of the pyramid. This is actual energy called Standard Columnar Wave or SCW. This double helix is generated by the sides of the pyramid bending light and creating a vortex. This is the glue or energy that runs the Universe. It is the bond between the spiritual and physical realms of reality. If humans are to advance into the spiritual world, then we must learn to overstand Tachyon Energy. According to the American Heritage dictionary, Tachyon means 'a hypothetical subatomic particle that travels faster than the speed of light'.
- Landing sites for our ancestors
The pyramids were built as beacons, so that they would know where to land their ships, and once there, it could recharge.
- Storehouses of universal knowledge
In the underground chambers of the pyramid are libraries of all the books of the prophets. These books make up what is known as the Archaic records which can be now found in The Holy Tablets. When the pyramid is sealed you can only go in mentally so no one should ever try to enter or damage them because Egyptian curses are real!
- Initiation into higher levels of consciousness.
We all have an aura or electromagnetic field around our body. However it is negative and the pyramids can be used as sort of tuning device to turn it into a more positive electrical charge.
- Connection with angelic beings

After the Planet Rizq was destroyed the Annunaqi escaped to Orion. The Egyptians were imitating the civilization that was found in heaven or Orion, (Ouranos in Greek) by aligning the pyramids to the 3 stars of Orion.

• Entrance into inner caverns of the Earth called Shamballah and Aghaarta. In the centre of the planet there is another world. There are several subterranean pathways to different chambers leading to these underground cities. And the pyramids are just one of many entrances there. Bauval/Brophy also speak of subterranean passages at Khufu's pyramid and beneath Sneferu's bent pyramid at Dashur. Movies such as 'Journey to the Centre of the Earth' are not a joke.

This is described in more detail in 'Science of the Pyramids' Scroll #191. The Holy Tablets relates how they were built:

> 13:3:44 Arts, this is where hieroglyphics a device used for cutting stone originated 45 Architecture he initiated the use of levitation 46 The process which the elders used to move some of the stones in the construction of the pyramids. 47 He also initiated the use of the laser, a device for cutting stone. 48 Imhotep, under the guidance of Zoser, acquired the knowledge needed to calculate the precise dimensions for the construction of the first pyramid, the step pyramid. [The Holy Tablets, Dr Malachi York]

The pyramids of Giza were built with the help of ET beings who had knowledge of levitation and the laser. They used levitation to change the polarity of the stones thereby making it weigh next to nothing and used lasers to cut the stone. (Read Daniel 2:34) The name laser was achieved by using the initial letter of the five words which describe it. Thus a laser Is "Light that is amplified by stimulated emission radiation."

In order to truly understand the origin of Ancient Egypt it is imperative that their relationship with astronomy is addressed. HT 1:9:120/227 say that '9 ether' or woolly hair is a symbol of an Extraterrestrial being. This might be hard to swallow but research into any of these things will confirm it, and the evidence cannot be denied.

The Sirius Star Constellation

Any research on Ancient Egypt will reveal their advanced knowledge of astronomy and mathematical genius. The Egyptians are known to have tracked celestial events such as the heliacal rising of the star Sirius. This is when Sirius rises just before or with our sun, 93 million miles away. The star Sirius is also known as Alpha Canis Majoris and is visible in February under the Southern Hemisphere and March in the Northern Hemisphere. Scagell states "Canis Major also known as Laelaps, was the fastest dog and was owned by Diana The Goddess of hunting. Canis Major contains the brightest stars in the sky called Sirius also known as the Dogstar."[56] The Koran 53:49 says "And he is the Lord of Sirius", and 6:97 shows the influence of astronomy on major religions today. Rising floodwaters, and the rising of the dog star Sirius indicated a new year which was carefully monitored approximately July 19 in the Julian calendar. New Year's Day was called 'emergence of Sepdet' Sepdet being the personification of Sirius as a goddess. So who is exactly is Sepdet?

> Sothis[Greek] Astral goddess. Egyptian. She heralds the Nile inundation as the personification of the star Sirius which rises coincidentally in the dawn sky in July. She is depicted as a nude figure wearing the conical white crown of lower Egypt surmounted by a star. Late in Egyptian history she becomes largely syncretized with Isis. Also Sopdet (Egyptian).[57]

Make note the word personify, which means to take human form, showing the Egyptian gods were human as in the numerous pictures of other gods, not mythical or invisible.

In fact the tomb of Osiris was rediscovered over a century ago on January 1st 1898 by a French archaeologist and Egyptologist named Emile Amilineau.[58] This was discredited and said to be Tomb O of Djer, however a body was not found there. A skull was found on chamber 'D' of the east side of the site which Emile believed was Osiris himself. The skull was examined and said to be that of a woman but it didn't alter his conclusions.[59] In short Emile's conclusions were met with academic scepticism. Now jump roughly a hundred years to 2000, Osiris' tomb was announced to the world located in the lowest of three underground levels in Abydos. It could be that Emile Amilineau was well ahead of his time and saw what everybody else failed to see, but this is another example of how things are dismissed or covered up to hide the truth. An article even claims that Egyptologist's never seriously questioned the possibility that the Egyptian gods might actually be real, contrary to the story of his body being dismembered by his brother Set. Now this God, who was a real human, with a real body not a formless entity, has been found and proven to exist. Therefore his wife Aset (Isis), his son Haru (Horus), his brother

Sutukh (Set), Nebthet, Amun and all the other Gods of Egypt must have also been real. In fact, Egypt and the Egyptians also mention a 'time of the Gods' where the land was ruled by deities.

> According To Manetho, In The Beginning, Seven Deities
> Ruled Egypt For 12,300 Years: Ptah For 9,000, Ra For 1,000,
> Shu For 700, Geb For 500, Osiris For 450, Seth For 350 And
> Horus For 300 Years. The Second Dynasty Of Deities Included
> Thoth, Maat And Ten Others, Who Ruled For 1,570 Years.
> The Third Dynasty Consisted Of Thirty Demi-Deities Who
> Reigned For 3,650 Years. The Fourth Period Lasting 350 Years
> Was A Period Of Chaos, When Egypt Was Disunited And
> Had No Ruler, It Ended With A Reunification Under Menes.
> You Were Never Taught This, This Is The Kind Of
> Information That Is Kept From The Public.
> [York-El, Science of the Pyramids p.48]

Sources say that during the excavation of Osiris' tomb led by Dr Zahi Hawass, US and Egyptian military units were present. To date, outside entities including archaeologists and historians have not been allowed to inspect the tomb which shows there is something 'special' about this tomb that the Egyptian government want to keep secret.[60] It's also a co-incidence and a fantastic conspiracy theory, but if you go into the Temple of Osiris in Abydos you will find pictures of crafts including a helicopter, submarine, flying saucer, and a jet plane which are obvious pictures of the real thing. York says the Elders had built aircrafts, and ships for travelling to their different stations across the globe.[61] This could be the source of those crafts in Abydos, but he didn't link the two.

Picture 2.14– Sirius Star constellation.

Now back to Sirius, The Holy Tablets, Tablet 3, Chapter 5 'The Dogon and the Sirius mystery' explains Sirius in great detail. As Sirius is linked with Isis, the proper Egyptian name Aset, Orion is linked with Asaru (Osiris). (HT 3:5:93). Sirius A is known as Aset, Sirius B is known as Nepthys (Aset's sister) and Sirius C is known as Anubu (HT 3:5:104). Sirius was the most important star in the sky to the ancient Egyptians. (HT 3:5:96). They built temples which aligned with Sirius, (HT 3:5:100) and the Opening of the mouth ceremony was centred on it. (HT 3:5:5). A book was written about Sirius, called The Sirius mystery, by Robert Temple, with the purpose of solving the question, "Has the Earth in the past been visited by intelligent beings from the region of the star Sirius?" It explores the findings by French anthropologists Marcel Griaule and Germaine Dieterlan (G & D) who visited the Dogon in 1931 and lived with them. Their findings are presented in a journal 'Sudanese Sirius System'. By speaking to their elders, Manda D'orosongo, Ongnonlou, Innekouzou and Yebene they revealed their vast knowledge of Sirius to them. Sirius B was also the most important star to the Dogon. (HT 3:5:180) They named it Bo Tolo meaning 'cereal star', or fonio, from a grain found in West Africa. Its scientific name was Digitaria exilis. The fact the Dogon even knew of the existence of Sirius B, which is invisible to the naked eye, when they obviously had no telescopes is amazing. This knowledge must have been passed down from generation to generation, and originally come from celestial beings or aliens. They also knew Sirius B had an elliptical (egg shaped) orbit, rotated around Sirius A, rotated on its axis and completed its orbit every 60 years, which they celebrated with a Bado rite or Sigui ceremony. They even knew of the existence of Sirius C which wasn't discovered till 1995.[62] If both the Egyptians and Dogon both had such extraordinary knowledge of astronomy, does this make them related? This and the fact they are both African, the logic points to yes. The Holy Tablets confirm that the Dogon are descendants of Egyptians (HT 3:5:114) and moved from Kemet in Cush into Mali (HT 3:5:3). The same way the Egyptians were in tune with celestial beings such as the Neteru the Dogon must have also had their celestial counterpart. This was the Nommos meaning, 'the masters of the water', also called 'instructor' or 'the monitors.' The Nommos were reptilian creatures from Sirius B, in the Canis Major constellation. They came here when their planet was destroyed and interbred with a tribe in Mali and named them Dogon after their great deity Dagon. Dagon is described as a sea god with the tail of a fish, mentioned in the bible in Judges 16:23. The Nommos lived in water and during the shadow hours they returned to the waters and came on land to teach and mix with the Dogon. The maps that these Dogons have are so accurate that they match modern maps of today. (HT 3:5:157) Humans have webbed fingers and toes, a constant need to bathe, produce semen or sea-men which fuse with an egg in conception, a foetus can survive in water during pregnancy. These are all reptilian traits that humans share with reptiles, or humanoid reptilians. So in fact these reptilians that visited the Dogon could be in fact their ancestors and Nuwaupian doctrine confirms this.

The temple of Hathor at Denderah, although it is in Egypt is classed as foreign because it was built by the Greeks during the Ptolemaic period (54 BC) based on their knowledge of Babylonian-Chaldean star lore. However an older temple existed in the same site under Tutmosis III around 1450 BCE. The ceiling shows all 12 signs of the zodiac, and is referred to as solar biology. Within the temple is a picture of a light bulb which some say they used to perform brain surgeries and blood transfusions, again suggesting they were taught by supreme beings.[63] This temple is dated to the Ptolemaic period, just before or during the reign of Cleopatra, around 50BC, well after dynastic Egypt.[64] Most authors acknowledge the zodiac to have come from Babylon, previously called Sumer linked to 3000-2000BC, and historians such as Wallis Budge speak of a similarity between their Gods. An Egyptian board game called 'senet' is said to originate from Sumer. Chapter 1 showed that both groups came in contact with each other, highly probable given the same time

period. Robert Temple writes, "The Sumerians seem to have called Egypt 'Magan' and seem to have been in contact with it." The zodiac from Babylon in Sumer is what we use today. The Egyptians had the same calendar. This was split up into 3 seasons of 4 months, each month had three weeks of 10 days, and 5 days were added after the last season, which makes 365 days exactly.
1) akhet – time of inundation. July to October.
2) peret – time of growing. November to February.
3) shemu – time of harvest. March to June.

Chapter 1 mentioned the Sumerians referred to themselves as 'Sag Gigga' black headed people. Unless this is in reference to their hats, this means the Sumerians were also black, hence why they shared so many similarities with Egypt. Wallis Budge was convinced that Sumer and Egypt both derived their cultures from a common source which was exceedingly ancient. This common source could very well be the mysterious land of Atlantis. However, few people, except those in tune with ascended beings/masters or psychics who can tap into the mental reservoir have any knowledge of Atlantis. Apart from Edgar Cayce another is Richard Kieninger or his pen name Eklal Kueshana, his work is published in 'The Ultimate Frontier.' According to the 'brothers' who taught Richard, Atlantis flourished for 14,000 years and was submerged 10,500 years ago. One group abandoned Poseid (one of the islands in Atlantis) several centuries before it submerged, and went to North Africa (Egypt) under their ruler Osiris who was a high adept. Cayce referred to it as 'Poseidia' so we see an identical name being used here. These pre-dynastic Egyptians managed to salvage some of their culture after the fall of Atlantis, while the rest of the world was reduced to a brutal struggle for survival. Egypt was the world's third ranking civilization after Atlantis second and Lemuria first.[65] The evidence of Osiris ruling this Egyptian empire and evidence of his body being found would make him older than 8500BC. So is there any indication of the race of Osiris or his followers? Nothing is said on the Atlantean's race by Kueshana. Edgar Cayce does say "Later we find there was the entering into the black or the mixed peoples, in what later became the Egyptian dynasty."[66] Whether Egypt is a subculture of Atlantis is another topic entirely, John Gordon wrote a book on this, and the Pyramid Texts also contain Atlantean records. Did Atlantis and Mu ever exist? The evidence points to yes. That Osiris (a God) started the Egyptian civilization by leaving Atlantis before the deluge is one way to explain the Egyptians advanced society, together with Enoch's involvement with ET's stated in the Holy Tablets. According to Robert Temple, "Atlantis can no longer be ignored by anyone seriously interested in the truth". The facts here are documented and widely available, it is now almost certain that Egyptian culture was influenced by Extraterrestrials.

Picture 2.15 – Mazzaroth, Temple of Hathor at Denderah

Giorgio Tsoukalos another alien enthusiast and editor of the Legendary Times Magazine calls it the 'ancient astronaut theory'. He says "the only way the ancient astronaut theory can be disproven is when the Extra terrestrials show up and say we were never here in the past." As mentioned before, the Egyptian Gods took human form, as personifications of stars and elements, hence were able to make their descendants in their image and likeness whether through sex or genetic manipulation so the real Egyptians must have been black skinned. The pictures on walls and DNA evidence all confirm this. Even alternative writers such as David Icke are right to say that Martian Gods started the Egyptian civilization however his melanin content seems to be a little undercooked. If these Egyptian Gods were 'white, blond hair and blue eyed' this would make their descendants in dynastic Egypt the same thing and I would like to see some pictures. This is erroneous, pictures in ancient Egypt clearly depict the Egyptians and their gods in dark brown skin. Picture 2.8 of the Annunaqi clearly shows their race and complexion, the descriptions given in the 1996 Nuwaubian calendar are "Dark-Greenish Brown skinned Olive toned beings with supreme 9 ether hair texture or what you'd call "Kinky" or "Kingly" hair. They look like humans with a few exceptions, such as their eyes." The Rizqiyians are also human in appearance. They have dark reddish brown skin, dark pupils, hair is silver, white to black and wavy, they are 5-7 feet tall, some with facial hair and some without. They claim "We are the parents of

Nubians on the planet Earth, and father of the ancient Sumerians, Egyptians, and various other cultures of south America,"[67] the opposite of David Icke's description. The Annunaqi and Neteru are separate beings from Sumeria and Egypt and are not to be mistaken as the same or equivalent Gods since several equivalents have been made in the past e.g. Enki to Bes and Enlil to Ptah. According to Dr. York in recent updates *the Annunaqi are not for us and are disagreeable in nature*. Earth has been visited many times by different groups of ET's and both groups refer to separate incidents. Many cultures across the world have accounts of being visited by ET's. Some people have a genuine, deep rooted interest in ET life and will investigate with an open mind to find the truth. Others lack the temperament to even conceive this as a possibility and insist on 'I have to see it to believe it.' Either case is fine but we are nearing the time when we will witness these beings for ourselves!

Picture 2.16 – Nibiru (The planet that crosses the skies)

1:1:8 You should know that eventually the time will come when these supreme beings, Annunagi, would have to descend upon this planet Earth, in order to guide the inhabitants back towards their home, in and beyond the stars. [Dr Malachi Z York, The Holy Tablets]

Summary

• Ancient Egyptian history is incomplete without the knowledge of Extraterrestrials.

- There was an Egyptian civilization on Mars before they came to Earth. The face on Mars dubbed 'The Martian sphinx' and pyramids in Cydonia are remnants of an ancient Martian civilization.
- There is evidence that Osiris and his group escaped Atlantis before it's destruction to start an Egyptian civilization in North Africa which explains why there were so technically advanced.
- ET's helped the Egyptians to build the Pyramids and Sphinx 12,000 years ago whilst Khufu helped to re-construct it.
- Egyptians had great knowledge of astronomy and were linked to the star constellations Sirius and Orion.
- The Egyptian Gods, Neteru/Rizqiyians are coming back to Earth to claim their children and will take them back to the skies.

Notes and References

1. Virginia Maxwell, V. Fitzpatrick, M. Jenkins, S. Sattin, A (2006) *Egypt* (Lonely Planet Country Guide) Lonely Planet Publications. 8th Revised edition. p.128

2. Davidson B, (2001) *Africa in History*. Weidenfeld & Nicolson; New edition. P.26

3. Dreyer G (1998) The New York Times. *Inscriptions Suggest Egyptians Could Have Been First to Write.*
http://www.nytimes.com/1998/12/16/world/inscriptions-suggest-egyptians-could-have-been-first-to
write.html?n=Top%2FReference%2FTimes%20Topics%2FSubjects%2FR%2
FReading%20and%20Writing%20Skills [Accessed 6th September 2010]

4. Tuckett, K. (2004) *Conspiracy theories*. Sussex. Summersdale. P.54 Sphinx

5. *Unmasking the Face on mars,* NASA Science. Available from:
http://science.nasa.gov/science-news/science-at-nasa/2001/ast24may_1/ [Accessed 12th February 2010]

6. Ibid (4).

7. Nowack, Robert L. *"Estimated Habitable Zone for the Solar System".* Department of Earth and Atmospheric Sciences at Purdue University.

8. Icke, D (1999) *The Biggest Secret: The Book that will change the world.* Bridge of Love. 2nd edition. p.13, 14.

9. Horizon. Percival Lowell – *Canals on Mars.* Clip from BBC website, taken from Horizon. Available from:

http://www.bbc.co.uk/solarsystem/sun_and_planets/mars#p0063x9z [Accessed 13/02/2010]

10. "Mars."Encyclopædia Britannica. 2010. Encyclopædia Britannica 2006 Ultimate Reference Suite DVD 13 May 2010.

11. The Planets Revisited. Clip from BBC. *River Channels on Mars.* Available from: http://www.bbc.co.uk/programmes/p0063x5rs [Accessed 18/2/2010]

12. JPL-Nasa. *Mars' South Pole Ice deep and wide.* Available from: http://jpl.nasa.gov/news/news.cfm?release=2007-030 [Accessed 13/5/10]

13. NASA (2008) *NASA Spacecraft Confirms Martian Water, Mission Extended.* Available from: http://www.nasa.gov/mission_pages/phoenix/news/phoenix-20080731.html [Accessed 13/5/10]

14. "Mars."Encyclopædia Britannica. 2010. Encyclopædia Britannica 2006 Ultimate Reference Suite DVD 13 May 2010.

15. Kluger J. Discover (1992) *Mars in Earths Image.* Available from: http://discovermagazine.com/1992/sep/marsinearthsimag105 [Accessed 11/3/2009]

16. *The Nine Planets.* Available from: http://www.nineplanets.org/venus.html [Accessed 03/04/2010]

17. *The Nine Planets.* Available from: http://nineplanets.org/mars.html [Accessed 03/04/2010]

18. http://paranormal.about.com/library/weekly/aa052900a.htm http://www.think-aboutit.com/Mars/TheVikingPhotos.htm

19. Schirber M (2005) *Face on Mars: Why people see what's not there.* Available from: http://www.livescience.com/health/050613_mars_face.html [Accessed 11/3/2010]

20. *Internet Encyclopaedia of Science.* Face on Mars. Available from: http://www.daviddarling.info/encyclopedia/F/face.html [Accessed 5/2/2010.]

21. About.com- Paranormal Phenomena. *The Face on mars: Once and for all.* Available from: http://paranormal.about.com/library/weekly/aa052900b.htm Accessed 13th March 2010. [Accessed 23/3/2010]

22. CNN. Britt R. (2005) *Scientist attacks Alien claim on Mars.* Available from: http://edition.cnn.com/2004/TECH/space/03/17/alien.debunk/index.html [Accessed 14/3/2010]

23. MetaResearch. Flandern T (2000) *Proof that the Cydonia Face on mars is Artificial.* Available from:

http://www.metaresearch.org/solar%20system/cydonia/proof_files/proof.asp
[Accessed 14/4/2010]

24. Michael Bach. (2004) *Face on Mars.* Available from:
http://www.michaelbach.de/ot/fcs_face_on_mars/index.html [Accessed
15/4/2010]

25. "mesa." Encyclopædia Britannica. 2010. Encyclopædia Britannica Online.
09 March 2010. http://www.britannica.com/EBchecked/topic/376530/mesa
[Accessed 12th March 2010]

26. *Mars Science Laboratory: Overview. Mission Fact Sheet.* Available from:
http://mars.jpl.nasa.gov/msl/mission/overview/ [Accessed 8/8/2012]

27. BBC Science and nature: *Horizon. What really killed the dinosaurs?*
http://www.bbc.co.uk/sn/tvradio/programmes/horizon/dino_prog_summar
y.shtml [Accessed 14th June 2010]

28. Ibid

29. Ibid 9

30. York-El, Dr Malachi Z. (1995) Scroll #131. *Shamballah and Aghaarta,
Cities Within the Earth.* ISBN# 1-59517-081-2, Egipt Publishers, Athens
Georgia. p.23

31. Ibid p.30

32. Matthews K. *Bad Archaeology. Other Martian sites.* Available from:
http://www.badarchaeology.net/extraterrestrial/others.php [Accessed 4th
May 2010] http://www.ufos-aliens.co.uk/cosmicmarsanoms.htm

33. Discovery Channel Online. Texas Alumni. (1998) *Human genes closer to
dolphins than any land animal.* Cited in P.315 Black book.
http://www.aquacranial.com/Home.html

34. York-El, Dr Malachi Z. *The Black Book.* Egipt Publishers. Athens,
Georgia, p.315, 410

35. *Tales of the Unexplained – UFO Chronicles,* Series 1: Episode 1
http://video.uk.msn.com/watch/video/ufo-chronicles/1geckb0qm [Accessed
03/04/2011]

36. York-El, Dr Malachi Z. (1995) Scroll #80 *Man From Planet Rizq.* ISBN
#1-59517-075-8, Egipt Publishers, Athens, Georgia p.109

37. Sitchin Z (2004) *The Lost Book of Enki.* Inner Traditions International.
p.1

38. Hoagland R (2002) *Monuments on Mars A city on the edge of forever.* USA.
North Atlantic Books. 5th edition.

39. About. *The Face on mars Once and for all.* Available from: http://paranormal.about.com/library/weekly/aa052900a.htm Ibid [Accessed 20th May 2010]

39. York-El, Dr Malachi Z. *The Black Book.* Egipt Publishers, Athens, Georgia P.2

40. Think about it. *The Viking Photos: Photographic Evidence of Humans on Mars.* Available from: http://www.think-aboutit.com/Mars/TheVikingPhotos.htm [Accessed 1/5/2010]

41. York-El, Dr Malachi Z. Scroll #91 *The mystery clouds ~ Are there UFOs.* ISBN#? Egipt Publishers, Athens, Georgia p.89

42. Von Daniken, E (1998) *Arrival of the Gods: Revealing the Alien Landing Sites of Nazca.* Element Books; First British Edition.

43. Ibid 39

44. *Pyramids of Giza: Facts, Legends and Mysteries.* (2007) Thames & Hudson. P.

45. *Sacred Destinations. Giza pyramids.* Available from: http://www.sacred-destinations.com/egypt/giza-pyramids [Accessed 5/9/2010]

46. Shaw I (2009) *Building the Great pyramid.* Available from: http://www.bbc.co.uk/history/ancient/egyptians/great_pyramid_01.shtml [Accessed 5/9/2010]

47. Khufu's great pyramid. Available from: http://www.unmuseum.org/kpyramid.htm [Accessed 21/4/2010]

48. Ibid 46

49. Ibid 29. #3772 Ouranos. New Testament Dictionary.

50. York-El, Dr Malachi Z. *The Dog.* Scroll # 143 ISBN #? Egipt Publishers. Athens, Georgia p.33.

51. Temple R, (1998) *The Sirius mystery.* Century. 2nd Edition. p.13.

52. *Sightings, Secret of the Sphinx.* Aired on Sci-Fi Channel. Director Kathryn Douglas.

53. Bauval R, Brophy T, (2011) *Black genesis: The Prehistoric origins of Ancient Egypt.* Bear and Company. p.287

54. *Decoding the Past – The Sleeping Prophet.* Aired on History Channel. Available from: http://www.history.com/videos/the-sleeping-psychic#the-sleeping-psychic [Accessed 25th November 2010]

55. York-El M, *Who and What are You.* Live audio CD.

56. Scagell R (2004) *Night Sky Atlas.* Dorling Kindersley Publishers Ltd.

57. Jordan M (2000) *Encyclopaedia of Gods: Over 2500 Deities of the World.* Great Britain: Kyle Cathie. p.240

58. York-El, Dr Malachi Z. Scroll # *Jesus Found in Egipt.* ISBN#1-59517-044-8. Egipt Publishers. Athens, Georgia p.196

59. R Peter, *The Tomb of Djer and Later, The Tomb of Osiris at Abydos.* Available from: http://www.touregypt.net/featurestories/djertomb.htm [Accessed 23/10/10]

60. The Tomb of Osiris http://praylu.blogspot.com/2007_03_01_archive.html [Accessed 23/10/10]

61. York-El, Malachi Z York. Scroll #? *Mission Earth and the Extraterrestrial Involveent.* ISBN#1-59517-077-4. Egipt Publishers, Athens, Georgia,

62. Ibid (51)

63. York-El, Dr. Malachi Z. Book No #1. *Are there Black Devils?* (Revised) ISBN#?, Egipt Publishers, Athens, Georgia, 2000 AD. p.49

64. Linda Hall Library. *Napoleon and the scientific expedition to Egypt. The Zodiac of Denderah.* Available from: http://www.lhl.lib.mo.us/events_exhib/exhibit/exhibits/napoleon/zodiac_dendera.shtml [Accessed 27/8/2010.]

65. Eklal Kueshana (2000) *The Ultimate Frontier.* The Adelphi Organization. USA. 10th edition. p.88

66. Cayce E (2000) *Edgar Cayce On Atlantis.* Little, Brown and Company. P.61 Reading 364-4.

67. Dr Malachi K York (1996) *Nuwaubu Nubian Calendar 1996.* The Holy Tabernacle ministries, USA.

(*Books written by Dr Malachi K York are mostly available from Nuwaupian bookstores. Certain books have gone out of print)

Chapter 3

A gap in time

The Neteru came to Earth 49,000 years ago during the time of the Lemurian /Atlantean civilization for the Adama project. A series of nuclear wars destroyed Atlantis and sunk the entire continent. The God Osiris fled with his followers to Egypt and continued their civilization there as a replica of Mars. The following chapters will attempt to trace the movement of peoples from Egypt into other areas of Africa and find links between Egypt and other African countries. To identify yourself with Egypt you need to know whether or not you are a descendant, otherwise why bother? And saying the Egyptians were black just because Tutankhamun had a round nose is not good enough in this day and time, we need the whole story and the facts to prove it. Now that we know the first Egyptian civilization was on Mars we now need some knowledge of the origins of humanity and the inception of the black race. What happened since the beginning of time and 5000 years ago at the start of the first dynasty? We now need to ask ourselves a few questions;

• Are all black people descended from the same source, if so any Negroid can say they are Egyptian?
• Were the Egyptians a particular type of Negroid amongst other types in Africa meaning that only their descendants can claim Egyptian ancestry?
• During and after dynastic Egypt, did the Egyptians migrate to other areas and mix in with the local inhabitants? Because if so there are likely to be remnants of a cultural exchange still present today?

It is said that Africa contains a large range of human types, more so than any other continent.[1] According to Picture 3.1, by 8000 BC anthropologists had divided Africans into 6 categories, Egyptians and Cushites north of the Sahara; sub Sahara: Negroes, Nilo-Saharans, Pygmies and San.[2] The Holy tablets say there are 7 types of Negroid however don't mention each type.

> Therefore, the Melanin-ites and their evolutionary descendants are the personification of the original creative forces, HU, 7 in all. As the 7 species of RIZQIYIANS, you

have 7 species of Melanin-ites or NUWAUBIANS, called
Negroids. And you have 3 species of Mongoloids, and 2
species of Caucasoid, all growing out of the original
Nuwaubians.) [The Holy Tablets 1:1:20]

So we see a general consensus of 6 or 7 Negroid types. Africa also possesses an
extremely large number of tribes, languages and cultures which has stopped
our unity. We see this in the Bible when the Gods wanted to confound their
language because they were unstoppable (Genesis 11:6/7). Though there are
certainly differences between Africans let's not forget the most important
thing. According to the Nazderu they are the parents of all Nubians or
Melanin-ite children on the Planet Earth. The cause of physical and cultural

Picture 3.1 - Language families of Africa, c. 2000.

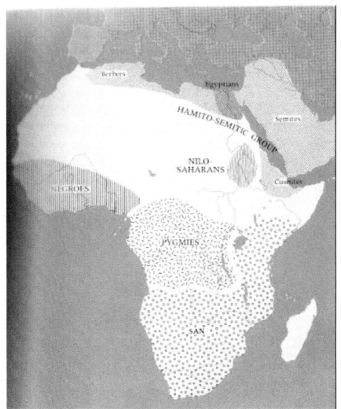

Picture 3.2 – 6 African types

differences between us might deserve a whole book in itself, but Nuwaupu gives clear reasons for this in the strategies the Gods used to make man i.e. (the Black Book). From the arrival of the Nazderu to this planet, the subsequent making of modern man (homo sapiens (49,000 years ago) to the start of the Egyptian dynasty (3100 BC) is a very big gap. 'Questions to Dr. Malachi York El About The Beginning' Scroll #203, and the Black Book deal with this in more depth. The Nuwaupian perspective on creation is that man had evolved out of the waters of the ocean from a living cell into homo-erectus.[3] (Read Holy Tablets 3:4:17) At this point the Nazderu came to Earth and sped up the evolutionary process by mixing in their DNA. Archaeology has identified the remains of what may be our oldest humanoid ancestors to Ardi 4.4 million years ago and Lucy 3.2 million years ago in the region of Ethiopia. (See Picture 1 & 2) Chapter 2 has introduced the possible event that Osiris led a group of Egyptians from Atlantis into Egypt before its destruction. Dr York says the Garden of Eden or 'Gan - the prepared enclosed garden of delight' where this event took place was known as Mu or Lemuria,

Picture 3.3 – The Afar Rift Valley where the bones of Ardi and Lucy were found.

Picture 3.4 – Possible apperance of Ardi

present day Saudi Arabia, Mecca.[4] Lemuria according to Eklal Kueshana existed between 76,000 BC and 24,000 BC. This is within the timescale of Adam according to Nuwaupian doctrine, and we are also told that the human animal evolved in Mu, which makes this even more credible.[5]

Picture 3.5 – Africa 8 million years ago

For those who may say that this contradicts the theory that life started out in Africa, geology confirms that before 8 million years ago, Africa and Arabia were joined and a crack broke Arabia away from the rest of Africa.[6] Dr York says this was due to the Neteru who caused a great explosion which made Asia split from Africa creating the red sea. [7] Whether this was due to natural or artificial means, geological data confirms there was a time when the two were joined. 'The Beginning' mentions 5 cataclysmic calamities which destroyed the life on this planet[8], the last point of reconstruction would be what we know as the birth of Adam/Eve which took place 49,000 years ago. David Icke says there has been 6.[9] This gives us a great starting point to begin our history of the Egyptians. Let's use religion to add to the equation (taken with a pinch of salt). The Bible tells us that after the creation of Adam, God destroyed the world in 40 days and 40 nights and Noah was the only one who survived (Genesis 6:17). You don't *have to* believe in or use Noah because a similar story of a flood is present in the Gilgamesh Epics, a Sumerian tablet dated to the 3rd millennium BC well before Genesis was written in 1512 BCE. Noah's equivalent in this tablet would be Utnaphishtim. The Holy Tablets gives a useful insight into what could have happened next. 13:11:4 speaks of 3 migrations however one wasn't registered.

> HT 13:11:5 The first migration is when Seth moved into what is called Egypt today, originally called Tama-Ra, meaning "Land Of Ra."

> HT 13:11:7 The old migration was when Utnafishtim's sons moved over out of Asia as being Asiatic into what is called Africa today. 8 So they moved in there and settled in the land.

HT 13:11:9-12 then explains how each of the sons inhabited a part of Africa i.e. Mizraim went to Egypt and was inhabited by the Nubuns, Nubians. Cush to Ethiopia, Ham to Sudan and Phut to Libya. This is also present in Genesis 10:6 "And the sons of Ham; Cush, and Mizraim, and Phut, and Canaan."

Notes and References

1. McEvedy, C (1995) *The Penguin Atlas of African history.* Penguin. 2nd Revised edition. p.20

2. Ibid (p.20)

3. York-El, Dr Malachi Z. Scroll #70 *Lets Talk about the end.* ISBN 1-59517-069-3. Egipt Publishers. Athens, Georgia,P.43

4. York-El, Dr Malachi Z. Scroll #28 *The right knowledge.* ISBN 1-59517-116-9. Egipt Publishers. Athens, Georgia, P.85

5. Eklal Kueshana (2000) *The Ultimate Frontier.* The Adelphi Organization. USA. 10th edition. p.80&81

6. Ibid (1) p.85

7. York-El, Dr Malachi Z. Scroll # *The Beginning.* ISBN 1-59517-116-9. Egipt Publishers. Athens, Georgia, P.107

8. Ibid (7)

9. Icke, D (1999) *The Biggest Secret: The Book that will change the world.* Bridge of Love. 2nd edition. p.13,

Chapter 4

Ancient Egypt and African countries – Sudan

Chapter 1 has indicated that the Egyptians shared strong links with Nubia. This prompts an in depth study of Nubia, in present day Sudan. Sudan used to be known as 'The Republic of Sudan' and since July 2011 the country has been divided into North and South Sudan. The Southerners

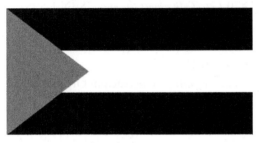

Picture 4.1 – Flag of Sudan

voted in a referendum after a long period of conflict and neglect. The name Sudan derives from the Arabic expression bilād as-Sūdān ("land of the blacks"). It should be rightly called by its ancient name Nubia from the word 'Nuwb' the original term for Africa,[1] or the Egyptian word 'nbw' meaning gold. Nubia is the area between the first cataract at Elephantine to the sixth cataract near Khartoum. Egyptians called the southern region of Nubia, Cush since the 18th dynasty. The Ancient Greeks called it Ethiopia. Sudan is located in North East Africa directly below Egypt. Its population in 2010 was 45 million, and the capital is Khartoum, at the junction of the two Niles. It had an area of 966,757 sq miles making it the largest in Africa. The colours of the flag are 1) Red; represents Sudan's struggle for independence and the sacrifices of the country's martyrs. 2) White; represents peace, light and optimism. It also represents the White flag league which was a nationalist group that rose up against colonial rule in 1924. 3) Black; represents the black original people of Sudan and the Mahdiya revolution, who fought colonial rule during the Kimokino Revolution, 1881. Green; represents Islam, agriculture and the prosperity of the land. The River Nile runs through Sudan and splits the country from east to west. The Nile runs for 4,132 miles, 6,650 km starting from the top Egypt, Sudan, Ethiopia, Eritrea, Kenya, Uganda, Rwanda, Burundi and Tanzania. Early civilizations would logically build their settlements along the Nile, providing water to drink, bathe, farm, fish, trade goods and transport. This gives the origin of the Egyptians a wider scope as the country we know today may not have been

confined to the present day limitations and may have extended further into any one of these 10 countries. It is accepted that the Nubians/ Sudanese were of African origin, all of it's names implies 'blackness'. The Sudanese shared a variety of different skin tones as shown in Picture 4.2. I quoted in chapter 1 that "The dark skinned people of Nubia, while speaking a different language to the Egyptians, shared with their neighbours a common ethnic background and similarities of material cultures. This is backed up in an Egyptian tourist guide book, 'Egypt: Lonely Planet'. "Although the two were ethnically linked, the darker skinned Nubians had more African features than the Egyptians."[2] The word ethnic was used in both quotes so it's important we get a proper understanding of that word. ethnic adj 1a (of a social group) having a common national or cultural tradition. b (of music, clothing, etc.) inspired by or resembling those of an exotic people. 2 denoting origin by birth or descent rather than nationality. [The Oxford Dictionary of Current English]
So as we can see that they shared the same origin and were both Negroid, what we now need to establish are the finer details.

Picture 4.2 - Part of a wall-painting from the tomb-chapel of Sobekhotep showing Nubians presenting the produce of the southlands to the Egyptian king. The items shown include gold rings, jasper, ebony logs, giraffe tails, a leopard skin and live baboons. 18th Dynasty, c.1400BC; from Thebes. H. 80 cm. Taken from picture 161, p.270 spencer.

Picture 4.3 - The Nubian prince Maiherpi, here shown on his funerary papyrus, was raised at the Egyptian court, but died aged about 20. Taken from p.58 Morkot.

Reference 25 in Chapter 1 by Basil Davidson says the Egyptians told Greek historians from 500 BC, that they were colonists i.e. immigrants sent out by the Nubians. The reason for this was that early Egypt was not land but sea, when the universe was being formed, afterwards as the Nile during the times of its inundation (July – October) carried down the mud from Nubia (south), land was gradually built up from the deposit. These were direct word of mouth accounts by Egyptians themselves when the Greeks started visiting Egypt. Now until the building of the Aswan dam in 1970 the floods were a sight to behold, this certainly makes it even more believable. Reference 22 of Chapter 1 by Gaston Maspero "According to the almost unanimous testimony of the ancient historians, they [i.e. the Ancient Egyptians] belonged to an African race which, first established in Ethiopia on the Middle Nile, gradually came down toward the Mediterranean sea, following the course of the river." This alludes to the fact that the Egyptians came from Sudan and settled in Egypt so we now have good reason to take Nubia seriously. The relationship between Nubia and Egypt has been intertwined from the very beginning. As Picture 4.2 indicates they were partners in trade, and also enemies or allies at war at different points in time. Nubia is referred to in Egyptian records as Ta-Seti, meaning 'the land of the bow' because the Nubians were skilled archers. Since the First Dynasty the Egyptians viewed the Nubians as their rivals and maintained an aggressive foreign policy towards the Nubians. They often referred to it as 'miserable Nubia'.[3] They sought to control Nubia's economic resources such as gold, and other items and also the trade routes along the Nile. The Egyptians clearly regarded them as inferior and many paintings revealed they used some as slaves. Egypt also valued Nubia for its dancing girls and famous wrestlers.

Earliest Origins of Nubians

Dr. Kryzstof Grzymski directed an expedition for The Royal Ontario Museum, Toronto in the 1990's and about 70 miles south of Dongola, found several sites containing Palaeolithic axes. They are given a date of up to 70,000 years old[4] making it one of the oldest pieces of evidence of life and tools in Ancient Sudan. The lost kingdoms of Africa documentary reveals rock gongs dating to 50,000 BC. These are huge fine slabs of rock that when tapped with stones make a bell sound. These could have been used to make music and communicate across the country. The axe findings are a good 40,000 years earlier than what EB say are the earliest inhabitants of Sudan. They give this honour to Negroid hunters and gatherers living in Khartoum during the Mesolithic (Middle Stone Age) times

Picture 4.4 - The Nilotic Sudan in ancient and medieval times.

(30,000–20,000 BC). EB also add they were 'clearly' in contact with predynastic Egyptians (before 2925 BC) to the north of Egypt but the desert separating Egypt from Nubia discouraged settlement.[5] This *contact* will be uncovered later on in the chapter.

In Wadi Halfa, Sudan a Khormusan culture is identified to have established a settled community from around 25,000 to 8000 years ago close to the (Upper Palaeolithic).[6] They built mud-brick villages and subsisted on hunting, fishing, grain foraging and raising cattle.

In 1974 an American Anthropologist, Fred Wendorf found artefacts and monde structures in a site which they dated 11,000-9,300 years ago.[7] A further investigation showed that the site area had enough water supplies to support the Nabta community prior to dessification in that region. Egypt: Lonely planet also recognize this settlement, which they say is 100km West of Abu Simbel and date it to 10,000 years ago.[8] Nabta is famous for the Nabta Playa, a circular formation of stone slabs very similar to Stonehenge. (More on this later) The timeline in Fig 1.1 (Chapter 1) also confirm that around 7000 BC was when settlement of the Nile Valley began.

The completion of the dessification of the Sahara brought about migrations to the Nile Valley, the area located in Upper Egypt. Dessification shows the changing of one environment to another and like the Valley of the Kings; recent research has shown that 7000 years ago the Sahara was in fact green. There are visible outlines of dry valleys or wadi's. They were once big rivers which flowed into the Nile.[9] Perhaps this is credible due to the rock art of cattle drawings dating from 6000-5000 BC. Camels are the only animals designed for deserts and they weren't introduced till much later.

5000BC is a significant part of Egypt and Nubia's pre-history. Spencer says this was the time that a rapid cultural transformation occurred. About 5000BC, farming peoples of the lower Nile and delta evolved out of their obscurity and across a few brief centuries, built an urban civilization which had all the characteristics and acquirements of Egypt's later glory.[10] In fact 5200 BC is the first date assigned to a Predynastic Egyptian civilization, in the region of Fayum A, Lower Egypt. This was the transformation from a Palaeolithic (hunter gatherer) to Neolithic (food planter and domesticated animals) way of life. If the Egyptian oral tradition is true that they were sent there by the Nubians, it would probably have occurred during various stages from 7000 to 5200BC.

In 1907, an archaeologist George A. Reisner discovered the remains of a settlement belonging to an indigenous population. He called them the A Group, as it was the earliest culture to be found in Lower Nubia. The remains here were more or less ignored and thought to be insignificant until Keith C. Seele from the Oriental Institute of Chicago discovered Cemetery L, at Qustul in 1964. The site contained tombs of 12 A-Group kings buried with belongings such as gold jewellery, pottery, and stone vessels that rivalled the wealth of the Egyptian kings. In cemetery L-24 two incense burners were found which would throw the date and place of pharaonic kingship in Egypt into disarray. The incense burners were made no later than 3300 BC, a good 200 years before pharaonic kingship in Egypt. The question was now 'Were the artefacts an Egyptian import or Nubian product? '

Picture 4.5 – Incense burner found in a Qustul cemetery. [Taken from Figure 23, p.32 Walker]

An article by the New York Times revealed that Nubian monarchy was the oldest in the world and came before Egypt.

> We are assured that "Evidence of the oldest recognizable monarchy in human history, preceding the rise of the earliest Egyptian Kings by several generations, has been discovered in artefacts [sic] from ancient Nubia." Nubian kings buried at Qustul, pioneered political and religious symbols, that were later adopted with Egyptian pharaohs. Artefacts such as pottery, jewellery, stone vessels and ceremonial objects such as an incense burner were buried with these early Nubian pharaohs.[11]

Picture 5 shows a multitude of links with Egyptian royalty. In the centre of the picture a seated figure wears a tall crown. The crown indicates kingship and is the white crown of Upper Egypt. He carries a flail in his hand also denoting kingship, and a beard or khebes similar to the dynastic pharaohs of Egypt. Above the king is an abstract bird which could be a falcon. Horus was associated with a falcon or hawk, and in some cases was seen as the first ruler of all Egypt.[12] This is probably indicative of the fact that every pharaoh had a 'Horus name', which was the chief name as one of their five names.[13] The bird is perched on a serekh, a rectangular frame containing the hieroglyphs of a pharaoh's name. In front of the bird is what appears to be a star, but is actually a rosette; a symbol of royalty before the First Dynasty. There is also a similarity with the figure's penis and many Egyptian drawings such as 'The Image of Atum at the moment of creation' (Figure 23 from Existence How and Why Actual Fact #36.) and figures of Min (God of fertility) holding his penis. This was done in Egypt to show sexual potency because a major theme of their religion was fertility and procreation.[14] References by Brewer and Spencer will now be quoted in the text as they have collectively a large range of Egyptian history between them. There is evidence of kingship in Upper and Lower Egypt before the first dynasty but none with such a clear symbolism of royalty as the incense burners found in Qustul, Sudan. The incense burners were found to be made from local stone found in Nubia. Even if it was found to have an Egyptian origin, it would seem highly unlikely that the Egyptians would have quarried Nubian stone, transported it back to Egypt, carved it into a distinctly Nubian style of incense burner, then export it back to Nubia! [15] This indicates that kingship existed in Nubia before it got to Ancient Egypt and the Nubians actually set the trend for royalty and symbolism in Ancient Egypt. This also verifies that the oral accounts given to Diodorus by the Egyptians were in fact true. In light of this important discovery we should now examine other archaeological evidence that reveals a link between the two.

Archaeological similarities between Nubia and Egypt

Though Egypt is famous for its pyramids and Sphinx, Nubia also has its own wonders. One of which is Nabta Playa, a circular formation of stone slabs first mentioned on page 5. It was found in 1998 by an anthropologist Fred Wendorf. It's location is 100km west of Abu Simbel and was built between 6500 – 6000 BC. Nabta playa has been confirmed by most sources as a calendar. We have already seen in chapter 2 that the Egyptians had an excellent working knowledge of astronomy in which they used to construct some of their monuments. In fact, there was an official ceremony *pedj shes* ('stretching the cord'), which relied on the sightings of the Great Bear and Orion constellations to align their monuments to each point of a compass. The *pedj shes* is first attested on a granite block of the reign of the Second-Dynasty king Khasekhemwy (c.2650 BC).[16] Thomas Brophy was perhaps the first to correctly identify the symbolism of the stones in relation to the stars from his work in 2005.[17] Dr York writes, as well as a calendar, it was also a star viewing diagram. 3 of the 6 centre stones were markings of Saahu 'Orions belt' as it would appear at the summer solstice in 6400 BC. "So in fact the stone diagram depicts the time, location, and tilting behaviour of the constellation of Saahu (Orion), through its celestial cycle."[18] The advanced knowledge of astronomy needed to align the stone slabs to Orion 'nearly 9000 years ago!' gives the Nubians a direct link to Egypt, in that they could also have had a direct link to extra galactic aliens just as the Egyptians with the construction of the pyramids. In fact, Bauval and Brophy call these Saharan Nubians 'star people' the true founders of ancient Egyptian civilization.[19]

Picture 4.6 – Graphical representation of Nabta Playa

Picture 4.7 – Photograph of Nabta Playa

The Nubian desert is littered with remains of pyramids temples and palaces almost identical to the ones found in Egypt. After the Nubians ruled Egypt in the 25th dynasty they picked up Egyptian habits and began to build their own pyramids. The oldest Sudanese pyramids date back to 8th century BC,[20] which coincides with the start of the 25th dynasty. Their pyramids had their own style being much steeper than the Egyptians and generally between 20 and 30 metres high. Since then more pyramids were built to serve as tombs for dead kings.

Picture 4.8 – Empire of Kush (Sudan). Pyramids at Gebel Barkal. c.100 BC. There are at least 223 pyramids in Sudan as a whole. Sudan has more pyramids than any other country on earth – even more than Egypt. Photo: Louis Buckley, Black Nine Films). Walker[32]

Walker says there are approximately 90 pyramids in Egypt, much less than the 223 in Sudan. In Napata is a mountain dedicated to the Egyptian God Amun called Gebel Barkal 'the pure mountain'. On the outside of this giant mountain is a cobra carved in the rock, symbolic of 'Wadjet' a cobra goddess of Lower Egypt which is on the headpiece of pharaohs to symbolise royalty. A relief sculpture on a wall (200BC) shows the Nubians had their own traditions. A Nubian ruler is being presented with a snake (i.e. granted rulership) by the lion headed war God Apedemak (local to Nubia) to the far right. Horus is last on the left and Amun is one place in front of him. This shows the Nubians in this scene saw Apedemak as more important. However, Amun was just as important to the Nubians as the Egyptians were. There is an avenue of ram statues leading up to the temple paying homage to the God Amun. Inside the base of the pinnacle lies a temple to the Goddess Mut, wife of Amun. There are lots of drawings of Hapi, the Nile River god on the inner courtyard of the Temple. He was associated with bringing the fertility of the Nile to his people. Kings and Queens were officially crowned first at Jebel Barkal and Nubians make an annual pilgrimage there to this day. (Nubia: The forgotten kingdom)

Taharqa a Nubian pharaoh of the 25th Dynasty is shown on pictures in this temple, celebrating his joint Nubian and Egyptian kingdom by painting

Nubian gods on one side and Egyptian deities on the other. He is shown giving an offering to Amun.

The pictures below show both Egyptian and Nubian kings striking the same pose, their right hand outstretched in the air and their left hand grabbing their enemy by the head.

Picture 4.9 Temple in the Nubian desert

Picture 4.10 King Den smiting an Asiatic enemy
2950BC Abydos.

Picture 4.11 was the largest complex in the whole of Ancient Sudan, according to Robin Walker. The style of pillars is very similar to ones in Egypt such as the Temple of Isis in Philae although this was built by Greeks.

Picture 4.11 - Empire of Kush (Sudan). Central Temple within the Great Enclosure at Musawarat. C.220 BC. Photo: Derek Welsby.

Picture 4.12 - Temple of Isis at Philae

Now that we have seen similar archaeological remains and gods worshipped by both groups let's examine the view of scholars to see what they have to say about the relationship between Nubia and Egypt.

Scholarly accounts of the relationship between Nubia and Ancient Egypt

Diodorus Siculus an ancient Greek historian discusses the origin of Ancient Egyptians. They originated in Ethiopia, which in this context means the region of modern Sudan, and then migrated north to occupy the land of Egypt.

The Egyptians were originally Sudanese and thus preserved Sudanese culture in the belief that their kings were gods, and also the pomp associated with their royal burials. He continues the shapes of their statues and the forms of their letters are Ethiopian." [John G Jackson in Man, God, and Civilization, p.213. cited in Walker, 2008, p.35.]

"when comparing the anthropometric features of the ancient Egyptians to the Beja, Bishari and Barabra, there is at first sight nothing against them being closely related. And we need not relinquish a relationship merely because the pharaohs fought against them... Why is it that the various writers who have examined them have not dared, despite the findings of multiple resemblances, to relate them [i.e. the Nubians] to the ancient Egyptians." [Race and history: An ethnological Introduction to History p.432 Eugene Pittard. cited in Walker, 2008, p.44.]

"Diodorus of Sicily reports that each year the statue of Amon, King of Thebes, was transported in the direction of Nubia for several days and then brought back as if to indicate that the god was returning from Nubia. Diodorus also claims that Egyptian civilization came from Nubia, the centre of which was Meroe."[21] [Diop, 2004, p.150]

Dr Derek Welsby of the British Museum and Charles Daniels commented on a recovered Sudanese artefact. They noticed similarities between the Negroid representation of the face and Egyptian representations throughout the Pharaonic period such as, cows ear's said to be the goddess Hathor, thick braids of hair, a large nose with widely flaring nostrils and thick lips. (Walker, 2008, p.73.)

"Egyptian skeletons, statues and countless pictures of Egyptians in their temples and monuments show the same racial characteristics as the Nubians and Nilotic tribes, the brown-skinned hunters of the steppes and the savannah husbandmen of the Sudan. Herbert Wendt. (Quote 20 – Chapter 1)

We have already seen in 'The table of Nations' scene from the tomb of Rameses III that the Nubians and Egyptians are identical, which Jean-Francois Champollion confirms in quote 10, chapter 1.

Early Sudanese kingdoms

During its history 'The Kingdom of Nubia' was centred on major sites such as Kerma, Napata and Meroe. Dr Charles Bonnet from the University of Geneva led an expedition in 1986 and discovered what was termed the Pre-Kerma settlement from 3500 – 2700 BC who were famous for their round houses. There are traces of older towns dating to 4800 BC and 3500 BC respectively which suggest Pre-Kerma was the latest of a major town. Around 2700 BC the

Nile channel shifted to the West and the Pre-Kerma site was abandoned for the newer site of Kerma. During the Old Kingdom (2575-2134 BC), Egyptian texts speak of a land in Upper Nubia called "Yam." Troops from Yam were enlisted into the Egyptian army and they did trade with the Egyptians, including a Pygmy. By the end of the Old Kingdom and the beginning of the New Kingdom (2134-2040) political changes in Egypt and Nubia led to the disuse of Yam in Egyptian texts. Yam was replaced by Kush, the Egyptians modified it to mean vile or contemptible[22] into what I think may be Kassite.

Kerma, located ten miles south of the third cataract is known as the first Nubian city, the first capital of the Kingdom of Kush. It is dated from 2500 - 1500 BC and further split into three chronological periods Early Kerma (circa 2450-2050 B.C.), Middle Kerma (circa 2050-1750 B.C.) and Classic Kerma (circa 1750-1480 B.C.).[23] Kerma was noticeably powerful by 2000 BC, however they never developed writing. A newly found inscription of Sobeknakht in the 17th Dynasty about (1575-1550 BC) shows evidence that Kushites raided Egypt for precious objects; had their objective been occupation or control they could have fully taken over.[24] This event is said to have been embarrassing for the Egyptians therefore it was wiped out of history. Kerma houses a monumental mud brick building; the Western deffufa and a smaller eastern deffufa, which served as temples for religious purposes. The Western deffufa is 60 metres high and is dated to between 1700- 1500 BC. Kerma incorporated a central city, surrounded by a series of defensive walls and moats built by the Egyptians to control trade and prevent invasion by the Nubians, most of which were built in the 12th dynasty. Lost Kingdoms of Africa suggests they were the descendants of the same people who drew rock art between 6-5000 BC, because 15,000 cattle skulls were found at a mound. The kingdom's collapse was brought on by a number of factors, such as the overexploitation of soils and increased desertification which led the Kushites to move further south into Meroe. Another factor was Nubia's vast amounts of wealth, desired by the Egyptians. One letter stated; "gold is like dust in the land of my brother......there are more horses than straw in the land of my Kassite brother." (Spencer, 2007, p.51) Egypt invaded Nubia many times in the 18th dynasty, perhaps as payback for the invasion written by Sobeknakht. 1480 BC is the date given for the end of the Kerman settlement, with evidence that it was burnt down and overthrown.

The next cultural phase of Nubia was Napata located just below the 4th cataract. Thutmose I invaded a part of Nubia and the Nubians put up strong resistance until Thutmose III managed to fully conquer the whole of Nubia. He built a fort in Napata and is therefore credited as being the founder.

Egypt continued to dominate the whole of Nubia and had established a system where the children of the defeated Nubian chiefs were sent to Egypt in order to be educated in the Pharaoh's court and then brought back to Nubia as district governors to teach the rest of their people. Official dates of a major Napatan city are 747–275 BC (Wysinger)[25] or 661-300 BC[26] (Nubianet) which corresponds with the reign of Nubian pharaohs of the 25th dynasty. Napata is famous for the Amun temple complex also called the Pure Mountain called in Arabic, Gebel or Jebel Barkal, it was one of the holiest places in Nubia because the great God Amun was thought to reside there. Both the Nubians and Kushites (Egyptians) identified Gebel Barkal as the source of kingship because it was thought to be the place where Amun first brought the crown to Earth, thus each pharaoh would receive the royal crown by Amun at their coronation.

For Egypt's survival the accumulation and occupancy of other lands was paramount so the Pharaohs such as Amunhotep III and Rameses II,[27] began trying to encourage Egyptians to settle in Nubia. They did this by building Egyptian style statues and temples in Nubia so it would feel like home. Egyptians would eventually settle in Nubia and choose Nubian spouses, the Nubians would learn the Egyptian ways such as language and writing and hence a process of cultural and religious assimilation would begin. When Egypt was taken over by the Assyrians the Nubian kings were forced to return to their spiritual homes in Napata. In 590 BC an Egyptian army sacked Napata forcing the Cushites to retreat further south, further threats were felt by the Greeks until eventually they re-located to the area of Meroe. Meroe is located on the east bank of the Nile between the 5th and 6th cataract. It was a populated town as early as the 8th C BC, most historians recognize it as the official capital of Nubia in 300 BC. It was a good location which offered important strategic and economic benefits because rain was more frequent and is situated within a network of trade routes.

The Nubians used Egyptian hieroglyphs but by 200 BC had adapted it to form their own 23 sign cursive script as well as a language spoken later by the regions people.[28] This script has been translated but the language is a mystery. Egyptologists are searching for a 'Rosetta stone' of the Meroitic script and until it is deciphered scholars can only use Greek and Roman reports to learn about the Kingdom, they don't have the Nubians point of view on life. The Meroitic kingdom was famous for smelting iron which they used to make useful tools for famers and advanced weaponry for the army. It is called by many the Birmingham of Africa, as Birmingham had a thriving metalworking industry from its large supplies of iron ore deposits. The Meroites showed

Egyptian gods Anubis and Nephthys as deities, another indication of religious similarity between the two groups. Meroe eventually was ravaged by King Ezana, King of Aksum (Central Ethiopia) in 350 AD, although the area shows signs of emigration from 320 AD. Meroe has 84 pyramids; most of them were built within the Meroitic phase of Nubia.

Peoples of Sudan

We have seen evidence of some of the earliest people and cultures to have occupied Nubia, such as the Rock gong people of 50,000 BC, the Khormusan culture of 25-8000 BC, the Nabta playa builders or 'star people', and the newly transformed Neolithic people of 5000 BC. In more recent times, close to the pre-dynastic period of Egypt there were mainly two groups of people inhabiting Nubia at the time. These were the A & C Group. The A-Group were a prehistoric people that dominated lower Nubia, between the Fist and Second Cataracts from about 3800 to 3100 B.C. By about 2600 BC the Egyptians referred to the Nubians by the name *Nehesy*, this was another name used by Champollion-Figeac to describe the Nubian in the Book of Gates. These were the same people who produced the incense burners which are noted by EB to be similar to those in neighbouring Egypt from the Naqada II-III period. Many of these luxury objects were of Egyptian origin, indicating that the A-Group carried out extensive trade with Egypt, especially since the area of Lower Nubia lacked natural resources.

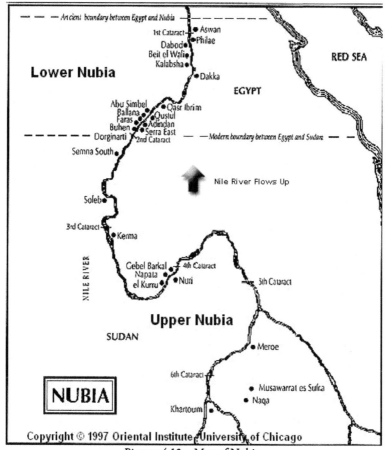

Picture 4.13 – Map of Nubia.

The dead were arranged flexed, facing west, which is exactly the same position of the pyramid builders in Cairo, described in the article 'Great Pyramid tombs unearth 'proof' workers were not slaves'.[29] The A- group culture is said to have come to an end, with the rise of the 1st dynasty in Egypt. The Egyptians invaded Nubia on many occasions, this could have stopped production of archaeological remains belonging to the A-Group, since for the next 500 years none were found. A text from Fourth dynasty King Sneferu, says that 7,000 Nubian captives were taken to Egypt, which could suggest that over a period of time a large Nubian population was assimilated into Egypt or were driven away from Nubia further into desert grasslands.[30] EB also dates the end of the A group between late pre-dynastic times and the 4th dynasty.[31] Any further attempts to investigate the A-Group were made impossible with the construction of the Aswan Dam.

The old Aswan dam was completed in 1902 at the 1st cataract, and its height was raised again in 1912 and 1934 to increase the area of cultivable land and provide the country with most of its hydro-electric power. The area containing many Nubian villages and monuments was flooded which foddered archaeological surveys. In 1968 the Aswan High Dam was completed, and Lower Nubia was completely covered by the artificially created Lake Nasser which would destroy all archaeological evidence forever. Headed by UNESCO a Nubian rescue campaign went into operation to save as much as possible, however much of the antiquities were still lost. This has made it impossible to uncover any secrets that were waiting to be discovered from the A-Group and others, however there is still a wealth of material that has been excavated.

The C group were centred in Upper Nubia (Wawat) between the third and fourth cataracts around 2300-1550 BC. Much of their material culture appeared to stem from the A Group. (Spencer p.264) The autobiography of Weni (Dynasty 6) records that troops of many tens of thousands of Nubians and Libyans were drafted to the army through conscription. (Brewer p.40). Within this period are Egyptian references to Wawat, Irtjet, and Setju (from north to south), chiefdoms or small kingdoms in Lower Nubia occupied by the C-Group. From the Second Intermediate period the majority of the Egyptian army were Nubians from a tribe of people called Medjay that dwelled in the Eastern desert around the 2nd cataract region. This name is still preserved today by the eastern Sudanese camel herding nomads, called the Beja. By the end of the Old Kingdom these Medjay or Nubian mercenaries settled in Egypt, married Egyptian women, and became assimilated into the Egyptian population. (Nubianet) They would represent much of the Egyptian army for a very long period of time.

Picture 4.14 – The Medjay. Nubian warriors in the Egyptian army.

Picture 4.15 – Nubian bowmen also known as Medjay on a temple relief.

The start of the Middle Kingdom was not a good time for Nubia. Amunemhet I was the first pharaoh in Dynasty 12. The 'Prophecy of Neferty' states a character Ameny, attributed to Amunemhet came from the south and was the son of a woman from 'Ta-Sety' Nubia. Kush was annexed into the Egyptian empire under his rule. (Brewer p.51) The new province was ruled by an official named Kings son of Kush. During the reigns of Senwosert I - Senwosert III

Egypt led military campaigns against Nubia which the C-Group Nubians rebelled against but eventually succumbed. The local C-Group population seem to have co-existed amicably with the occupying Egyptians. Five dynasties later the Nubians had acquired some power. The Kamose stela (Dynasty 17) mentions foreign rulers, one in Avaris who would be the Hyksos, and one in Nubia, with each man having his own slice of Egypt. The Hyksos occupied Egypt during that time so the Nubians used that situation to their advantage and made an alliance with them to control part of Egypt. After Ahmose, every pharaoh in the New Kingdom continued military campaigns. This resulted in the gradual Egyptianisation of the C-group until their culture disappeared. In the 19th/20th dynasties desiccation caused a partial depopulation of Wawat. (EB) Spencer also dates the end of the C-Group to the 18th dynasty. This was Egypt's Golden age and was especially bitter for the Egyptians since Tutankhamun's mother Queen Tiye was a Nubian. By this time Nubians were incorporated into society and married the Egyptians.

Another group of people in Nubia, Lower Nubia are the X-Group, identified with the Ballana culture (250-550 AD). A tomb was found at Ballana and excavated before the raising of the old Aswan Dam in 1934, now the area is covered by water. The Ballana are identified with the Nobatae people, a group of Nubian nomads from the west of the Nile (Spencer p.278) who inhabited the Meroitic area, southern lower Nubia. Another group was called the Blemmyes who were from the eastern desert, they took over northern, upper Nubia. Both groups utilised the fast camel in warfare. Although the X-Group still worshipped Egyptian Gods, there are signs of a general decline in Meroitic culture and strong trading with Rome.

Nubian pharaohs of the 25th dynasty

Picture 4.16 – Stone figures of Nubian pharaohs in the 25th dynasty found at Kerma by Swiss archaeologist Charles Bonnet in 2003.

In Dynasties 23 and 24 the Egyptian administration was usurped by Libyan Kings, Egypt had fought fierce battles with the Sea peoples in Dynasty 20 and was likely to have not yet fully recovered. Separate kings ruled Upper and Lower Egypt so Egypt wasn't in its strongest position. From 2000 BC Nubia had been growing steadily under their independent royal family headquarters at Napata. This allowed King Kashta from Nubia to conquer Upper Egypt from Osorkon III and rule Thebes. His successor Piankhy or Piye managed to subdue the Delta and bring all of Egypt under Nubian rule to start the 25th dynasty of Nubian pharaohs. He was the first Napatan ruler to use the full titulary of and iconography of a pharaoh, followed by Shabaqa, Shebatata and Taharqa. The Nubian pharaohs ruled Upper Egypt for a 100 years rounded off (747 – 656 BC) and the whole of Egypt for approximately 61 years (728 - 667 BC). Wysinger (dates are approximate). Taharqa is mentioned in the Bible (2 Kings 19:9 & Isaiah 37:9) as the King of Ethiopia, though the name ethiops means 'burnt face' so was a broad term used to describe dark peoples.
2 Kings 19:9 And when he heard say of Tirhakah king of Ethiopia, Behold, he is come out to fight against thee: he sent messengers again unto Hezekiah, saying...

Anthony Arkell says "it is most improbable that Taharqa was a Nubian though he may have had some Negroid blood in his veins".[32] (Arkell 1955, cited in Sertima p.128) Fortunately we are not limited to his word and can use a picture. Esarhaddon the Assyrian King, had a Negroid portrait of him carved on a stele at Sinjirli, now located in the Berlin museum.

From the reign of Kashta (c. 760-747 BC) onwards, they chose to portray themselves as Egyptian style pharaohs, and their royal culture was founded in the cult of Amun, relying on his oracle at Gebel Barkal to make their most momentous decisions.[33] (Manley, P.106)

They celebrated many aspects of Egyptian culture and even influenced a revival of art, architecture and religious practices. One example of this is by Pharaoh Shabaqa, who saw a papyrus being devoured by worms in the Temple of Ptah and ordered it to be incised in stone, this became known as the Shabaqa stone. Dr York also writes "Long After The Introduction Of Christianity, The Nubians Remained Faithful To The Cult Of Isis On The Islands Of Philae And Agilka,"[34] and the temples are there to prove it. Piye was the first to build a pyramid and later much of the Nubian Kings would also do the same and would be buried underneath their respective pyramids. However they adapted this by burying them in beds rather than coffins. (Ivan Sertima, p.129)

They were eventually overthrown by the Assyrians in 667 BC who were an extremely strong force at that period. The 25th Dynasty pharaohs are labelled by Egyptologists as 'The Black Pharaohs', however this projects an image that they were the *only* black pharaohs, otherwise why aren't any of the other pharaohs referred to as black pharaohs especially in light of all the evidence we have just seen. It seems as if they know there is no way of hiding the Nubian identity of the 25th dynasty so they casually mention them but leave the other black Egyptian pharaohs out of the equation. But maybe I'm just a conspiracy theorist. I thought the identity of a black 25th dynasty was accepted since the beginning of Egyptology, that is until I heard of 'A history of Egypt Under the Pharaohs' by Dr. Brugsch-Bey. He advanced the theory that the Nubian and Kushite Kings "were not really black at all, but came from outside to give leadership and guidance to these imperfectly developed people." (Ivan Van Sertima, p.127)

Brugsch-Bey also claimed that the Kushite Kings were descended from a Libyan High Priest of Thebes Herihor in the 21st dynasty, this idea was later supported by others. However the evidence for these claims were disproven by Reisner's discovery of the King's graves. The objective of this chapter was not to prove the blackness of the Nubian pharaohs, but rather to show and examine the links and similarities between Egypt and Nubia. It is unbelievable, that even the identity of the Nubians had been mismatched. Ivan Van Sertima asks "Why then are they not represented as black or, even when so conceded, relegated to a footnote in the conventional theories of the ancient world?" (Sertima p.126)

12th dynasty of Nubian pharaohs?

Each dynasty in Ancient Egypt was ruled by members of the same family line, typically the title of pharaoh was passed from father to son. If the son was too young to rule someone would take their place as regent e.g. (Ahhotep I regent for Kamose 17th D) or if no sons were present another family member such as a cousin would be elected. Another dynasty would start when someone from a different family would rise to the throne thereby starting their own dynasty. If Amenemhet I was the first pharaoh of the 12th dynasty and we have good evidence to make this claim (Prophecy of Nefertari), then the pharaohs in the 12th dynasty were also Nubian. This is overlooked in most cases, even by Afrocentrists, however in light of such evidence this should prompt an in-depth study to check the Nubian origins of the 12th dynasty pharaohs. 'Egypt and the Egyptians' have no problem saying Amenemhet I was from the South or Nubian (Spencer p.43) and if they know the order of kingship how come they don't recognise the 12th D as one of Nubian origin? Frank Yurco is one of a few people to mention this:

> ...the XIIth Dynasty (1991–1786 B.C.E.) originated from the Aswan region. As expected, strong Nubian features and dark colouring are seen in their sculpture and relief work. This dynasty ranks as among the greatest, whose fame far outlived its actual tenure on the throne. Especially interesting, it was a member of this dynasty that decreed that no Nehsy (riverine Nubian of the principality of Kush), except such as came for trade or diplomatic reasons, should pass by the Egyptian fortress and cops at the southern end of the Second Nile Cataract. Why would this royal family of Nubian ancestry ban other Nubians from coming into Egyptian territory? Because the Egyptian rulers of Nubian ancestry had become Egyptians culturally; as pharaohs, they exhibited typical Egyptian attitudes and adopted typical Egyptian policies. (Yurco 1989) [35]

Although Yurco recognizes the Nubian 12th dynasty he still says the idea that the Ancient Egyptians were black is false speculation. Mentuhotep I was ruler before Amunemhet I and according to 'A History of Egypt' was a Nubian Southerner. (Ivan Sertima p.121) This Nubian relationship could have made it slightly easier for Amunemhet I to ascend to the throne, though Mentuhotep III and Amunemhet I were not related. Who knows if any other pharaohs or dynasties were Nubian?

Queen Sobekneferu was the last pharaoh in this dynasty, this is even more reason to suggest this dynasty was Nubian. Nubia had its own independent line of kings adjacent to that of the Egyptian dynasties, a large amount of women ascended to the throne and would often lead armies into battle. One of the fiercest Queens was Kandace Amanirenas, in 24 BC while Egypt was under Roman Rule the Kushites invaded Aswan and dismantled a bronze statue of the Emperor Augustus. She buried the head underneath the stairs of one of their temples as an act of disrespect to mimic people stepping on the head every time they entered the temple. She and her Nubian army fought against the Roman governor Gaius Petronius and she would lose an eye in the battle (just like the battle between Haru/Horus and Sutukh/Set). They strongly opposed the foreign Roman rule of Egypt and would often paint figures of Roman soldiers pierced with swords or arrows. The name Kandace/Candace appears in original Nubian records as 'Kedeke', this is where our modern name Candice comes from. Candace was a Queenly title used to refer to the mother of a king.

Modern Nubian/ Sudanese tribes

Modern Sudan is now home to a mixture of Nubian and Arabs. Since the Arab takeover of Egypt in 642 AD, they then gradually infiltrated into Sudan and took over the country. North Sudan has an arid landscape which is inhabited by mostly Arabs making up 48% of the population. The South being much greener, is home to the majority of Nubian tribes who live a more agricultural and pastoral lifestyle. The North is richer than the South. The largest non-Arab ethnic group is that of the Dinka, who constitute 11% of the population, followed by the Nubians at 8% and the Beja at 6%.[36] It is important to know the tribes and different people living there now if we are to trace their history and relationship with Ancient Egypt. The adjacent positioning of both countries means that they must have a long and intertwined history together. In the minds of the Nubian Kings, Egypt and Nubia were northern and southern halves of an ancient original territory of Amun. They believed these two lands had been united in mythological times and eventually grew apart. The Egyptians also claimed that Nubia had always been a part of Egypt. Whether this was a genuine belief based on oral tradition and fact or just a way to encourage settlement is another story. The mistreatment of the Nubians leads me to think the Egyptians didn't believe this, but at the same time they told Diodorus that they were sent out by the Nubians. The evidence would point to me that both parties knew they were once originally joined however over the years they

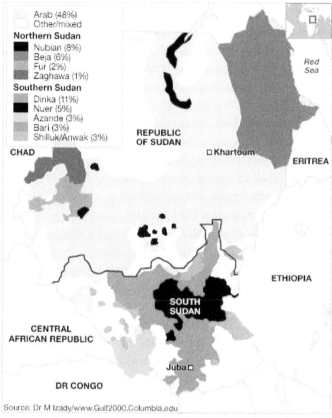

Sudan's arid north is mainly home to Arabic-speaking Muslims. But in South Sudan there is no dominant culture. The Dinkas and the Nuers are the largest of more than 200 ethnic groups, each with its own languages and traditional beliefs, alongside Christianity and Islam.

Picture 4.17 – Sudanese Tribes

battled for wealth and supremacy or joined forces to drive out common enemies.

For example Eugene Prittard (quote 1.4) mentioned the physical similarities of 3 Sudanese tribes (Beja, Bishari and Barabra) with those of Egypt. (EB Egypt) say "The southern section of the Eastern Desert is inhabited by the Hamitic Beja who bear a distinct resemblance to the surviving depictions of predynastic Egyptians."[37] This is good, they might not have spotted or chose to mention the similarity with the *dynastic* Egyptians, but in any case we have their own testimony given to Diodorus. In the video 'Lost Kingdoms of Africa – Nubia' the team go to the Nuba people among the Nuba Hills in present day Sudan. The Nuba people believe they are descended from the ancient Kingdom of Nubia. A leader of a traditional Sudanese ruling family says that they come originally from an area near Meroe. Shaza Rahal, translates the following from her uncle, the leader of the village community: "They are all the same people they just separated, so there's some that stayed in Egypt, some came to Sudan the rest stayed in Meroe. The only difference between here and there, you'll see is the colour of the skin but in terms of the language it's the same, the traditions are the same." [Lost Kingdoms of Africa: Nubia] (See Picture 4.2) Nubianet confirmed previously that the ancient name of Medjay is still preserved by the Beja people of today.

The languages spoken in Sudan belong to three families of African languages: Afro-Asiatic, Nilo-Saharan and Niger-Congo. The most popular Afro-Asiatic languages are Arabic and the Bedawi language of the Beja. The Nilo-Saharan languages, such as Dinka, Nuba, Nuer, and Shilluk, account for the next largest number of speakers. The Egyptian language as well as Bedawi fall into the Afro-Asiatic class, which might indicate both groups spoke the same language at one point. Due to 'Arabization', a strong component being the spread of Islam, the use of Arabic as a language and other cultural aspects most of the Nubian tribes now culturally refer to themselves as 'Arabs'. Thus the demographics above of the different tribes are to be taken with a pinch of salt. EB say "Moreover, ethnic identity may not actually coincide with a particular racial character. Those Sudanese who consider themselves Arabs are, for the most part, ethnically mixed, and many of them are physically indistinguishable from dark-skinned southerners." Sudan.net say "they descended primarily from the pre-existing indigenous populations; that is, the ancient Nubians." Robin Walker. P55 has this to say on the subject, "Most North Africans refuse to call themselves Africans preferring instead to be recognised as Arabians. Strictly speaking though most of them are actually 'Musta'rab,' that is Arab by adoption and not descent." We must stop referring to ourselves by alien names and outside forces or we will lose our cultural identity. What happened to Egypt, Nubia and South Africa should serve as a warning to the rest of the Africa. Walker continues about the Arabians, "They are no more indigenous to Africa than the Dutch conquerors of South Africa who call themselves Afrikaners." Kimani Nehusi explains the misuse of the term African. "There are basically 3 groups of people living in Africa. There are Africans, there are Europeans and there are Arabs and what the Europeans and Arabs have been saying that they are African when it suits their purpose. We must be careful that we distinguish nationality and citizenship from identity in this question. "[38] These statistics are notable in the religious choice of the country. Approximately 70% are Muslims, 5% are Christian and 25% practice indigenous beliefs known as animism.[39]

Animism according to the Oxford Dictionary, is the belief that inanimate and natural phenomena have souls. It can also refer to the idea of a life force present in nature.[40] This has equal footings with the Ancient Egyptians. "None of them were sun worshippers, but rather a respect for the universe and the planet and its life for it was the provider." [The Holy Tablets 13:11:112] 'The All Prayer' in the Nuwaubian culture also recognize this aspect "I am in the love of all, and all is in me. I am a part of all and all is a part of me." We have seen examples of Nubian reverence with the Egyptian religion and they had their own local gods as well such as Apedemak, and Hoeus Mandulis. These were eventually displaced by Christianity and Islam.

Lost Kingdoms of Africa suggest that it wasn't Egyptian domination but climate change which contributed to most of Nubia's problems. The desert climate of Sudan makes it one of the harshest environments on Earth. The dessification of the Sahara made many migrate to other areas and even recently the Aswan Dam has caused many problems. It is important to remember that Nubia was once a major civilization that should be included with Egyptology, for they are often mentioned independently. Perhaps this is no coincidence and was intentionally done to omit any aspects of a black Egypt. Despite their historical battles the history of Egypt and Nubia is by far the biggest source of evidence to link Ancient Egypt with a black Africa and the legacy of both should be celebrated by Africans worldwide and in the historical and Egyptological field.

Summary

- We have seen evidence that kingship derived from Nubia, which places them as The First Egyptians confirming the Egyptian accounts to Diodorus that they were immigrants sent to Egypt by the Nubians.
- Both Egyptians and Nubians seem to know their land and people were once originally joined but over time they battled for wealth and power and became fierce rivals, or allies in Ancient times.
- More research would need to be done into the six or seven types of Negroid. The Sudanese and people from Punt (Eritrea) can claim Egyptian ancestry
- There were even cases of a blatant cover up to conceal the Nubian (black) heritage of the 25th dynasty pharaohs. Modern scholars agree the two were ethnically linked but still do not project the image of black Egyptians.

• The Nubians and Egyptians (inter-married) at several periods throughout history. First the Medjay coupled with Egyptian women in the Old Kingdom, followed by an Egyptian migration into Nubia in the 19th dynasty encouraged by the pharaohs. The 25th dynasty is also likely to have been a period of mixture between the two groups.

Notes and References

1. York-El, Dr Malachi Z. Scroll #?? *Lets Set the record straight.* ISBN#?. Egipt Publishers. Athens, Georgia, P.348.

2. Virginia Maxwell, V. Fitzpatrick, M. Jenkins, S. Sattin , A (2006) *Egypt* (Lonely Planet Country Guide) Lonely Planet Publications. 8th Revised edition. p.322

3. *Lost Kingdoms Of Africa – Nubia.* (2010) Video. BBC Four. Presented by Dr Gus Casely-Hayford. Directed by David Wilson.

4. *Prehistory of the Sudan*
http://www.ancientsudan.org/history_01_prehistory.htm Accessed 14/5/2010

5. "Sudan, history of the."Encyclopædia Britannica. 2011. Encyclopædia Britannica 2006 Ultimate Reference Suite DVD.

6. Ibid (4)

7. Ibid (4)

8. Ibid (2) p.322

9. Ibid (4)

10. Davidson B, (2001) *Africa in History.* Weidenfeld & Nicolson; New edition. p.26.

11. Walker, R (2008) *Before the Slave Trade.* African World History in Pictures. Black History Studies Publications. p.31

12. Storm, R (2007) *Mythology of Ancient Egypt: Myths and Legends of Egypt, Persia, Asia Minor, Sumer and Babylon.* London: Southwater. P.36

13. Spencer A, (2007) *The British Museum book of Ancient Egypt.* P.288 British Museum Press.

14. Brewer D, Teeter E, (2007) *Egypt and the Egyptians.* Cambridge University Press; 2nd edition. P.110.

15. King Merenptah (2004) *The Artefacts speak: Ancient Qustul (Ta-Seti) - Egypt's Origin.*
http://www.historykb.com/Uwe/Forum.aspx/ancient/550/The-artifacts-speak-Ancient-Qustul-Ta-Seti-Egypt-s-Origin [Accessed 10/9/2011]

16. Shaw I (2009) *Building the Great pyramid.* Available from: http://www.bbc.co.uk/history/ancient/egyptians/great_pyramid_01.shtml [Accessed 5/9/2010]

17. Brophy, T.G. and Rosen, P.A., 2005, 'Satellite Imagery Measures of the Astronomically Aligned Megaliths at Nabta Playa', *Bulletin of the American Astronomical Society*, Vol.35

18. York-El, Dr Malachi Z. *The Cycles* #240. Egipt Publishers. Athens, Georgia P.32

19. Bauval R, T Brophy (2011) *Black genesis: The Prehistoric origins of Ancient Egypt.* Bear and Company.

20. York-El, Dr Malachi Z. Scroll # *Science of the pyramids.* ISBN#? Egipt Publishers. Athens, Georgia. P.23

21. Diop C (1974) *The African Origin of Civilization: Myth or Reality.* A Capella Books. P.150

22. *Upper Nubia in the late Third Millennium B.C.: the early Kerma Culture and the Kingdom of Yam.*
http://www.nubianet.org/about/about_history3_2.html [Accessed 8/10/11]

23. *Swiss Archaeological Mission of Sudan*
http://www.kerma.ch/index.php?lang=en [Accessed 9/10/11]

24. Alberge D (2003) *Tomb Reveals Ancient Egypt's Humiliating Secret.* The Times London. July 28. http://wysinger.homestead.com/article10.html [Accessed 10/10/11]

25. *Ancient Nubia: map and History of rulers.*
http://wysinger.homestead.com/mapofnubia.html [Accessed 5/9/2011]

26. *The Napatan State: Nubia as an Egyptian-style Kingdom: 661-300 BC.*
http://www.nubianet.org/about/about_history7.html [Accessed 4/8/2011]

27. *Egyptian and Nubian Cultural and Religious Assimilation*
http://www.nubianet.org/about/about_history5.html

28. (Video) *Nubia: The Forgotten Kingdom* (2003) Directed by Amy Bucher. USA 60m.

29. 'Great Pyramid tombs unearth 'proof' workers were not slaves'.
http://www.guardian.co.uk/world/2010/jan/11/great-pyramid-tombs-slaves-egypt [Accessed 21/9/11]

30. *A Group and C Group Cultures.*
http://www.nubianet.org/about/about_history3.html [Accessed 15/10/11]

31. Between late predynastic times and the 4th dynasty—and probably early in the period—the Nubian A Group came to an end. There is some evidence that political centralization was in progress around Qustul, but this did not

lead to any further development and may indeed have prompted a pre-emptive strike by Egypt.

32. Sertima, I (2003) *They came before Columbus.* Random House USA. p.128

33. Manley B (1996) *The Penguin historical atlas of ancient Egypt.* Penguin reprint edition. p.106

34. Ibid (20) p.113

35. F. J. Yurco, "The ancient Egyptians..", *Biblical Archaeology Review* (Vol. 15, no. 5, 1989)

36. Ibid (5)

37. "Ancient Egypt."Encyclopædia Britannica. 2010. Encyclopædia Britannica 2006 Ultimate Reference Suite DVD

38. *Motherland.* Documentary DVD. (2010) by Owen Alek Shahadah. Quote by Dr Kimani Nehusi, scholar author university of East London.

39. CIA. *The World Factbook Sudan.*
https://www.cia.gov/library/publications/the-world-factbook/geos/su.html - [Accessed 24 Sept 2011]

40. Iannone A, (2001) *Dictionary of world philosophy.* Routledge. P.54

Chapter 5

Ancient Egypt and African tribes - Nigeria

D r Malachi York states on p.242 in Lets Set The Record Straight "The original Yoruba's lived in Nubia and Egypt."[1] So one can say the Nubians and Egyptians *became* Yoruba people. The Yoruba's are an ethnic group from Nigeria in West Africa. The land of Nubia includes Southern or Upper Egypt and Northern Sudan so Sudan/Nubia can be used interchangeably. The Yoruba people and culture only goes back to a certain point in history, in fact life in Nigeria also has a time restraint which means that before this culture was established they would have been known as something else; according to the above quote Sudanese and Egyptians. Make note he says Nubia and Egypt which means that this one group or tribe of people, Yoruba's, occupied these 2 areas. He then adds, "The Yoruba Kingdom was founded in the 8th Century about 785. This was a vast empire which included Nigeria, Benin, Angola, Chad and Sudan" later he adds Togo and Ghana to the list. All of these countries follow the same trail from East to West apart from Angola, located further south (See Picture 5.1). An article written by Yoruba language program students at the University of Georgia, states "It is believed that their primary ancestor, Oduduwa came from Egypt".[2] Encyclopædia Britannica say, "They seem to have migrated from the east to their present lands west of the lower Niger River more than a millennium ago"[3] and Lucas says "Yoruba's migrated southwards and westwards from Egypt."[4] Directly to the East of Nigeria is Sudan/Nubia and Egypt is North-East. The Egyptians themselves admitted they came from the south i.e. Sudan with references already mentioned in Chapter 1 and 4. If they did live in Sudan and Egypt then something would have urged them to migrate to Nigeria such as a foreign invasion, environmental reasons, or simply to explore new lands. There are likely to have been some inhabitants already living there, so a cultural exchange and process of intermarriage would have taken place between the Nigerians and Egyptians. The general consensus among African scholars is that the Yoruba's come from a higher religion and civilization, but they have no definite knowledge of their origin. This makes the present study that more crucial. Sertima says, "It now seems perfectly clear that the vast majority of predynastic Egyptians were of continental African stock, and even of central-west Saharan origins."[5] Lucas says, "there can be no doubt that the Yoruba's were in Africa at a very early date. A chain of evidence leads to the conclusion that they must have settled for many years in that part of the continent known as Ancient Egypt." (Lucas 1948, p.18) Sudan currently seems to be the origin of both Egypt and Nigeria, but more importantly we see a relationship between all three. Where are these statements coming from? One would be an anomaly but the high frequency makes it ever more likely. Recent discoveries in Africa suggest studying African history should undergo a new methodology, most notably oral traditions, as story telling is a major pastime in African populations. If these statements are true then how come it is not mainstream knowledge, not accepted by Nigerians and scholars and only mentioned by a few people? Shouldn't such quotes prompt a serious investigation to prove it and educate the black population on their true origins? If they are true, then there must be historical and cultural proof, so this chapter will explore the similarities between Ancient Egypt and Nigeria.

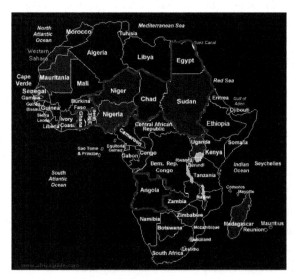

Picture 5.1 – The Yoruba kingdom

Yoruba is a West African tribe and language in Nigeria, West Africa. According to Lucas Yoruba means 'the living rpa' or 'the creator of rpa' where rpa was known as Geb. (Lucas p.222) The capital is Abuja, which took over from Lagos in 1991. It has an area of 351,310 square miles, a population of 167 million incorporating 250 ethnic groups, making it one of the most densely populated countries in the world. The most populous tribes are Hausa/Fulani (29%), Yoruba (21%) and Igbo (18%) who occupy the North, South and West respectively. The religious denominations consist mainly of Muslims 50%, Christian 40%, and indigenous beliefs 10%. Tribal and religious differences have created long term tension in Nigeria.[6] Muslims from 'Boko Haram' (against Western Education) bombed a church on Christmas Day 2011 so there is an urgency to understand, teach and practice our own culture rather than practice alien religions which only causes division. (Read Actual Fact: Who you are, Not what you accept' by Malachi Z York). Religious difference is nothing new, even in Egypt the pharaoh Amenhotep IV or Akhenaten tried in vain to convert the country to monotheism via the worship of only Atun. However the other Gods were too intertwined with their culture for that to last, and after his death they went back to polytheism.

There is evidence the Yoruba kingdom once extended to Dahomey and the Gold coast where Gods which originated in Yoruba land are still worshipped. (Lucas p.8) The Yoruba language is also spoken in Togo and Benin, and goes by Oku in Sierra Leone. "The Yoruba history begins with the migration of an East African population across the trans-African route leading from the mid-Nile river area to the mid-Niger."[7] Archaeologist's findings show that the Nigerian region was inhabited more than 40,000 years ago, or as far back as 65,000BC. (Omoleya, 1986 cited in Karade, p.2) EB say the oldest skeleton is dated to about 9000BC.[8] The earliest civilization of the Yoruba's is the Nok culture; there is debate of the time it was established, Davidson says 900BC by using carbon 14 dating,[9] Omoleya says between 2000BC - 500BC (Omoleya p.15) and EB say 500BC to 200AD. This is followed by Ile Ife, 12thC to 15thC considered to be the spiritual home of the Yoruba's and Oyo from 1400 to 19thC which extended into Togo. The Yoruba's have a rich history and are famous for Nollywood movies, arts and terracotta sculptures, oil and iron smelting. The previous chapter mentioned Meroe was famous for smelting iron; this suggests a possible influence on the Yoruba's from Nubia.

Lucas: The Religion of the Yoruba's

Joseph Olamide Lucas wrote a book 'The Religion of the Yoruba's: Being an account of the religious beliefs and practices of the Yoruba people of Southern Nigeria. Especially in relation to the religion of ancient Egypt'. He finds a connection between Egypt and Nigeria.

> "CONNECTION WITH ANCIENT EGYPT. A chain of evidence leads to the conclusion that they [Nigerians] must have settled for many years in that part of the continent known as Ancient Egypt. The facts leading to this conclusion may be grouped under the following heads: A. Similarity or identity of language. B. Similarity or identity of religious beliefs; C. Similarity or identity of religious ideas and practices; D Survival

of customs and names of persons, places, objects etc." [Lucas p.18]

The Yoruba History

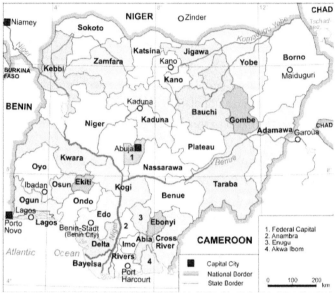

Picture 5.2 – Map of Nigeria

I have mentioned several sources above including Lucas, York, EB and Sertima that mention a migration of Egyptian peoples into Nigeria or Yoruba land. An article 'Yoruba: the Egyptian connection'[10] reveal some of the early history of the Yoruba civilization. The author suggests the Yoruba came in waves of different migrations and many oral traditions confirm this. The Awujale of Ijebu land has shown that the Ijebu's are descended from ancient Nubia. He was able to use the evidence of language, body, scarification, coronation rituals that are similar to Nubians' etc, to show that the Ijebu's are descendants of the Nubians. "Many traditional Yoruba's have always claimed Egypt as their place of original abode, and that their monarchical tradition derives from the Egyptians'. Apostle Atigbiofor Atsuliaghan, a high priest of Umale-Okun, and a direct descendant of Orunmila, claimed that the Yoruba's left Egypt as a result of a big war that engulfed the whole of Egypt. He said the Egyptian remnants settled in various places, two important places being Ode Itsekiri and Ile-Ife." Chief O.N Rewane narrates part of the oral tradition which says the Yoruba's came from the South of Egypt and settled in various places including

Illushi, Asaba area – Ebu, Olukumi Ukwunzu and Ode-Itsekiri. Aderibigbe suggests a migration from a civilization on the banks of the Nile estimated at (2000BC – 1000BC) as a result of some upheavals in Egypt. This corresponds with the invasion of the Hyksos in 1660 BC. A historical figure known as King Oduduwa or Odudua meaning 'Lord of the other world' is said to be the mystical founder of the Yoruba race. (Lucas, p45) Between this time he and a group are said to have settled and mixed in with the indigenous people of the Nok culture in Nigeria. A scientific study mentions that a Bantu expansion occurred ~4,000 years ago, originating in Cameroon or Nigeria and expanding throughout sub-Saharan Africa. The clustering of the Xhosa, Fang, Bamoun, and Kongo populations, all of which are Bantu Niger-Kordofanian speaking populations, likely reflects a Bantu migration from Nigeria/Cameroon expanding toward the south.[11] (Bryc p.4) York gives an account of the early history of the Yoruba's in 'Let's Set The Record Straight' p.243. The Yoruba's encountered the Arabs of Arabia in (5th C) Mecca, which was the world trade centre at the time. Yoruba was introduced to Mecca by Lamurudu aka Obatala, it was not known as Yoruba at the time, just idolatry or polytheism. The offspring's of Lamurudu were Oduduwa, the King of Gogobiri and Kukuwa, tribes in the Hausa country. The Hausa were Yoruba people who spoke the Yoruba language but converted to Islam and combined the two to breed their own branch of Islam, dialect and script called Hausa today. Oduduwa was heir to the throne of Mecca and went back to the religion of his forefathers during the reign of his father and both of them were determined to revert back to ancestral worship. They were permitted to be polytheists in Mecca however while in Mecca a lot of them converted to monotheism or Islam. One night the priest of Lamurudu, Asara put idols in the Ka'aba which at the time was attributed to Allat, who is the female crescent deity, symbol of Isis. However Asara's son was a monotheist and disagreed with the thought of idols residing in the Ka'aba, so destroyed the idols. A civil war broke out between the polytheists and monotheists, the monotheists were victorious and the polytheists were expelled from Mecca. Oduduwa went northwest from Arabia back to Sudan (which suggests they went from Sudan to get to Arabia in the first place). Yoruba practices, customs and traditions are still in Sudan to this day under different names. Some gods in Sudan are called Amma (Dogon), Yurugu, Nommo (twins), ngkola, Tere, Nuba, Nzeano, Tsode, Wantu-Su. Davidson also states the Sudanese migrated southward and were ancestors of the Yoruba of western Nigeria. (P.96 Davidson.) As time passed they were once again confronted with monotheism and Sudan became uncomfortable for them so they went to Ile Ife Nigeria. When they first reached there Oduduwa became King of the Yoruba. Many independent kingdoms were established in Ile Ife 'The House of Expansion' by the 12th C. As we have seen West African history is relatively limited. A review of an exhibition, The Kingdom of Ife at British museum (4 March – 6 June 2010) claims that the art was so different, unexpected and "un-African", that one of its first students thought it was lost art from Atlantis! They also admitted Ife remained mysterious and there is still so much to learn about the art and the world which created it.[12] Walker also points out a Nigerian artefact in Ile Ife was so astonishingly high in quality that it was disputed to have come from a black race.[13] And this is in Nigeria which has one of the highest amounts of black people in the world. (See Picture 5.3). This proves the primitive view of Africa by the western world.

Picture 5.3 - Kingdom of Ife (Nigeria)). Magnificent head of an Oni (i.e. king) 12th/15th century AD. Copper. Height 29 cm.

Oyo in the north became dominant from the 1600's over the other Yoruba kingdoms until the 19th C. The seven grand children of Oduduwa became the kings and queens of the seven original Yoruba states. In the 1400's Sudan was invaded by European tribes such as the Portuguese who brought spices and other goods in return for their so called friendship. They even brought some of these Sudanese to the point where they sold their own brothers, mostly the Muslims and Yoruba's who were mounted on European ships and taken to the New World. And so the African kidnapping business was in effect, what is called slavery. The first of those to be kidnapped were taken to Portugal in 1441 AD. The Portuguese Prince Henry sponsored many African exploration programs and Europeans began scanning the African coast in search of souls to kidnap. Though these Sudanese might have been in Arabia it doesn't mean they are Arabian. Some have used this to suggest an Arabian origin of the Yoruba people however the Holy tablets records a story in the early history of the Yoruba people where they encountered Cuthites and refused to mix in with them. The story goes that after a great scientist Yaaquub died, his head prophet Haggai aka Sheshbazzar, Zerubbabel or Oduduwa, and his group of 59,999 followers sailed around the whole coast of Africa. Sheshbazzar means sun or fire worshippers. Nigeria was the 16th country they visited.

> "3:4:217 Oduduwa, which is another name for Sheshbazzar, he led the tribe Shabazz on a pathless journey. 218 The journey was to a place called Oyo. 219 The people there referred to his followers as Yoruba. 220 They called him Obata'alah. His priesthood was called Orisha; each was an Oba or a Papal. He was the first pope."

> 3:4:249 So they took residence and named the place Nigeria, home of the Yoruba tribes. 250 But the woolly haired people of that land refused to mix with them. 251 So they were forced to depart only leaving their religious system of Orishi, 252 A system of ancestral worship, 253 Which they brought from Arabia, called Yoruba. 254 The land where Teraphims have always been worshipped. Such as the moon deity Allah... The three daughters, Al-Iat, Al Uzza and Manat are sometimes depicted together with Allah, the Moon-god, represented by a crescent moon above them. 255 Their religious system was created with the ability to adapt to anyone else's culture. 256 As in the case of Santeria, or Brujeria, or Voodoo, also called Jou-Jou, 257 Where the Yoruba Gods Shango, 258 Oshun, 259

Yemeyah, 260 Oya, 261 Ogune, 262 Eshu-Elegrbara, 263
Shopona-Sonoponno-Olode-Ilegbig bona, 264 Yemonja-
Okokun, 265 Olu-Gbo, 266 Osanyin, 267Orisha-Oko, 268
Agemo, 269 Orunsen, and 270 Oduduwa. 271 This was taught
by their great ancestor and god Yaaquub. 272 The religious
system was created to be able to supplant itself over others, 273
And absorb them like a dying star consumes other stars. 274 It
vamped down on Judaism to create Islamism. 275 It vamped
down on Christianity to create Santeria. 276 It vamped down
on Satanism to create Voodoo. 277 Then the ships continued
up the Atlantic Ocean to Sierra Leone..."

"3:4:293 Those that remained behind, by jumping ships at
different ports in Ganawa, stayed and oppressed the original
woolly haired NUWBUNS, 294 Introducing them to
mythological religious beliefs such as New Yoruba, New Islam,
Judaism, Christianity, and a host of others, which later became
the enchantment or the spell."
[Dr Malachi Z York, The Holy Tablets]

The Holy Tablets 3:4:191 describes Yaaquub, Haggai and their people as
Asiatic Black Men/Women, black people with 6 ether straight hair of Hindu
descent. The Arabian theory is false, rejected by most such as Lucas p.18, Ojo
p.8 and genetic studies (See Chapter 10). Only the Fulani tribe show high
signs of admixture with Arabians. The account of the Yoruba's by Dr York
does not include the original story of the original journey from Sudan into
Mecca. Yoruba as we know it has its earliest roots in Nok, ~900BC, so we are
to assume that the journey from Mecca to Ile Ife was another migration,
possibly after the invasion of the Hyksos. If the 500 BC date by EB is to be
believed, this also corresponds to the Persian invasion in 525 BC, so wars are
likely to have been a major factor for migration.

The Yoruba religion – Orisha

Picture 5.4 Yoruba African Orisha's

1. **Port Of Sudan**
2. **Assab**
3. **Djibouti**
4. **Gulf Of Aden**
5. **Eil In Somalia**
6. **Massawa, Ethiopia**
7. **Somalia**
8. **Kenya**
9. **Tanzania**
10. **Mozambique**
11. **Madagascar (Mauritius)**
12. **Cape Town**
13. **Walvis Bay, In Namibia**
14. **Luanda**
15. **Angola**
16. **Nigeria**
17. **Sierra Leone**
18. **Mauritania**
19. **Morocco**
20. **Port Of Tangia**
21. **Algeria**
22. **Bizerte In Tunisia**
23. **Alexandria, Egypt**
24. **Zanzibar**
25. **Libya**

Picture 5.4 - Map showing the stop points of Haggai and his followers during the journey around the continent of Africa. [Taken from Diagram 23, p274 The Holy Tablets].

Olodunmare/Olokun was the king of the gods, known collectively as the Orisha from the words "ori" the very Source of Being and "se" a verb meaning to originate, thus the Source-Being which gives origin to all Beings" (Oloyoye, pg.13). Georgia students say the word *ori* is the 'reflective spark of human consciousness embedded on human essence', and *sha* which is the 'ultimate potentiality of that consciousness'. Others say Orisha seems to derive from the Latinized form of Horus.[14] Orisha's are anthropomorphic; personified aspects of nature gods and ancestral spirits. Yoruba Gods of the Orisha include Olodumare, Obatala, Oduduwa, Shango, Ogun, Oshosi, Eschu-Elegbara, Oshun, Oya, Yemonja-Olokun, Olurun. These supreme beings or deities are the ancestors of the Yoruba. (York, p.242) As far as dealing with the actual origin of the religion itself, it is referred to as a surviving religion of a "higher" religion. That religion is said by Lucas to be from the Ancient Egyptian– Religion otherwise known as Khamet or Kemet or by York as an Arabian religion.

The Yoruba's are said to have 401 deities, the following list shows their order of importance:

1. The supreme deity – Olorun
2. The Major Orisas, of whom Esu and Ifa are the most important
3. The Deified Spirits of Ancestors and other Spirits, of whom Oro, Eluku, Agemo and Egungun are the most important.
4. The Minor Orisa

This uncertainty requires special attention to be paid on the origin and characteristics of the Orisha. Lucas already stated that most Egyptian Gods were 1) well known, at one time, to the Yoruba and 2) had exact equivalents in Yoruba e.g. Olorun and Osiris. He gives excellent reasons, word associations and cultural similarities to explain the link between the equivalent Gods of each culture in his book. I will summarise the characteristics of the supreme deities here with their equivalent representative on the Egyptian side with the help of 'Encyclopaedia of Gods'.[15]

Table 5.1: Lucas' God Associations

Olorun	Osiris
Olorun is a supreme deity among the Yoruba's meaning 'Lord of the sky or of the heavens'. Osiris was originally the Lord of the dead and later was associated with the sky. In Egypt he was worshipped at Abydos. Olorun is too high for primitive people so must come from a higher source. Olorun is the impartial judge, linked to the Osirian judgement hall. One Osirian title is Lord of Zaddu 'dead' a modified form Sadu identified with death. Worship of Olorun is scarce. Yoruba term *gba Osiri re* or *da osiri bo o* means to plot against an innocent person with a view to murdering him.	*'All seeing eye'*. God of the underworld and vegetation. One of the most significant and widely revered deities. Son of Geb and Nut, brother to Isis, Seth and Nepthys. Linked to Anubis. Was set up by his brother Set to step into a coffin then thrown into the Nile, was swallowed by a fish and cut into 14 pieces. Isis found it got the magic word from Re and was able to breathe life into his body and impregnate herself with his semen to make Horus.
Esu	Sutukh (Set)
Supreme power of evil, and the prince of darkness, his worship arises from fear. Described as buruku wicked to death. Has a knobbed club known as Agongo Ogo. Offerings are made to avoid his malevolence and secure his favour against enemies. Has 16 lines on his back so is linked to Esu the god of divination. Is also called Elegbera. A saying *Esu li ota orisa* 'Esu is the enemy of Orisa' or Olorun links him to Set being the enemy of Osiris. Esu was represented by a stone and so was Set. Esu is fusion of Set and Shu. Shu became a sun god by fusing into Ra.	*'He who shines'*. God of chaos and adversity. Represents hostility and violence. Linked to an aardvark. Represented by the crocodile. Was jealous of his brother Osiris and conspired to kill him. Book of the dead accounts Seth as the 'lord of the northern sky' who controls the storm clouds and thunder.
Ifa	Osiris
The oracular deity, the most popular and important deity in Yoruba land as he is worshipped and consulted by all. Ifa is derived from nefer the title of Osiris in the Yoruba language. Titles of Ifa show	*See above.*

similarity with Osiris in Book of the dead.	
Obatala	**Khnum**
Name translated as 'King of whiteness' or 'Lord of the white cloth'. His worshippers must wear white clothes, eat white food e.g. shea butter, white or bitter kola nut. Described as the great god. The God of purity. Titles include Orisa popo 'Orisa who kneads clay' or Orisa Oj Enia 'The Orisa who causes man to live' that is to breathe life into him and give him existence. The ala in his name can also mean King of the Nile. Khnu-mu in Yoruba word derivation leads to Okuri or Okinrin meaning man. The use of white relating to Obatala is suggested by the white colour of the River Nile.	*'Moulder and creation'.* Earth God. Said to create human life on a potter's wheel. Usually seated before a potter's wheel on which stands a naked figure in the process of moulding. Khnum supervises the annual Nile flood which is physically generated by the god Hapi. The Khnum cult is at Esna, north of the first cataract, his consort is the goddess Menhyt. Described at other sites as the 'ba' or soul of various deities including Geb and Osiris. Depicted with the head of a ram.
Oduduwa	**Mut or Nut.**
'Lord of the other world'. The chief female Orisha, wife of Obatala the chief male Orisa. Reputed as progenitor of Yoruba race hence why they call themselves *Omo Oduduwa* 'Descendants of Oduduwa'. Was regarded as a leader and hero hence some think she's male. Associated with Olorun in the work of creation. Regarded as union between earth and sky which would be Geb and Nut. Other name is *Yemuhu* meaning 'the living Mut' or 'Mother Nut'.	*Mother.* The patron goddess of Thebes. The counterpart of Sakhmet in Upper Egypt. Superseded the goddess Amunet she became the consort of the sun god Amun, and mother to moon god Khonsu. Regarded as the divine mother of the Theban kings. Wears a vulture head-dress surmounted by twin crowns of upper and lower Egypt. Dressed in a bright red or blue patterned gown. Also with a lion head. Cult centre at Thebes where her sanctuary was known as the Iseru.
Aginju and Yemoja	**Aginju (??); Yemoja - Mirit Qimait**
Offspring's of Obatala and Odudua. Aginju means 'desert' a male represents land. His worship ceased as Yoruba's migrated south. Yemoja female represents water means 'The mother of fishes'. They married and had a son Orungan. He committed incest with his	"Two goddesses, corresponding to the two Hâpi's—Mirit Qimâit for Upper, and Mirit Mîhit for Lower Egypt— personified the banks of the river."[16] History of Egypt Volume 1 Part A p.48 In Nuwaupu Merit means 'one of music' and is female.

mother, she ran and fell into the ground. Streams of water poured from her body into a lagoon where 15 deities emanated. Links these names to Egyptian deities or words. Mirit Qimait and Mirit Mihit together with the Hapi's described as guardian deities of the fishes.	
Sango	Ptah
Sango is the deity of lightening and thunder, his name incites fear. Lucas couldn't trace a deity in Egypt with the name or derivation of Sango. However Sango is also known as *Jakuta* 'fighter with a stone'. *Jakuta* can also mean 'living soul of Ptah'. Ptah was regarded as incorporate with a stone. The Yoruba word for stone is *Okuta* 'soul of Ptah'. Also *apata* a rock consists of *pa* 'house' and *ta* 'Ptah'.	*'Opener'.* Creator god and god of craftsmen. Cult centre at Memphis. After Atum is the main rival claimant as creator God. Consort is the lioness headed God Sakhmet. Son is Nefertum the god of the primeval lotus flower. Wears a skull cap, and holds the waas or rod of dominion and a staff with an ankh. Sacred animal is the bull. Said to have spoke and thought the cosmos into existence. Came from primeval waters of Nun hence Ptah-Nun. Title is khery-bakef 'he who is under his tree'. Created Dwarfish craftsmen (pygmies) or Ptahites work at various trades including jewellery. Envisaged as moulding mankind out of base materials.
Ogun	Horus
Ogun is the God of Iron and War. Those who make use of iron such as hunters, soldiers and blacksmiths make offerings to him. The dog is sacred to Ogun. One of the offspring of Yemoja, Ogun is a modified form of Khu. Horus was known by his worshippers as Khu. Horus was a warrior God and his followers worked with iron. Prof. Sayce says Horus of Edfu was served by Smiths.	*'Mountainous one.'* Sky God. One of the most universally important gods in the Egyptian pantheon. Symbol is the falcon or hawk. Had a 80 year battle with Sutukh to avenge the death of his father Osiris. His eye got lost in the battle thus a symbol the eye of Horus was formed. A form of the sun god aka *herakhti* 'Horus of the horizon' sometimes depicted as a sun disc mounted between flacon's wings. Performed the opening of the mouth ceremony on his dead father Osiris.
Orisa Oko	Osiris
God of the farm agriculture and harvest. Represented by iron staff symbolizing	Same above

strength. Happy honey bees are his messengers. Arbiter of disputes. Osiris is the god of vegetation. Said to have taught the Egyptians the art of making agricultural implements. Worshipped at the annual harvest festival. Fresh fruits and yams are first offered to the Gods before general sale. Linked to Osiris as he is god of vegetation. Orisa Oko is a phallic deity. Osiris worshipped with elaborate phallic rites. Also linked to Horus and Min.	
Sopono	Shu of Punt
God of smallpox. One of the most dreaded. The only God whose worship has been forbidden by the British government. One of the deities said to have sprung from Yemoja. Known as *Aladupe* 'one who kills and is thanked for killing.' Sopono derives from Shu and Pua-nit (Punt). Appears to denote Shu of Punt probably the title of Atthar the Southern Arabian god of Punt. The title survives among the Yoruba's, who use it in naming a strange god who came into existence after their migration into West Africa.	I will not attempt to link Shu to Sopono as Lucas only translated the name and did not give reasons. Punt is said to be the land of the Gods in Eritrea.

Lucas also linked Moremi to Isis and Ela/Olurogbo to Horus. Catherine Acholonu, wrote a book called 'They Lived Before Adam' which also revealed a connection between Nigerians and Egyptians.

> "The repeated intonation of the name of the Egyptian god 'Ra' and the use of the Egyptian letter /r/ on the monoliths of Ikom, Cross River State, all point to the thesis that Egyptian culture and religious tradition was invented and nurtured in ancient Nigeria, and that the names Thoth and Ra were inventions of the names of a god-man, an ancestor who must have lived in ancient Nigeria long before recorded time. In fact what we found in the course of our search, is that the Egyptian gods Thoth, Ra, Ptah and Horus assumed the identities of ancient Nigerian gods

Obatala/Idu, Oduduwa, Ela, and Orunmila respectively, in order to ensure for themselves global status and influence, for these West African gods were the first rulers of the Pre-Deluge world." [17](Acholonu, 2009, p.54)

Table 5.2: Acholonu's God Associations

(The Orisha side contains references from Lets Set the record straight, GodChecker.com[18] and Orishanet[19] to provide a second opinion of the Orisha's)

Tehuti (Thoth)	Obatala
'Wisdom'. God of the moon and of wisdom. Patron deity of scribes and of knowledge incl. scientific, medical, maths and said to have given man the art of hieroglyphic writing. Wears head of an ibis or baboon. Also a crown with a crescent moon and moon disc. Described as benign and fair, keeps record of souls who pass to the afterlife and adjudicates the Hall of two truths. In pyramid texts he decapitates adversaries of truth and wrenches out their hearts.	Or Orishanla. God of the North. Son of Olorun and Yemonja-Olokun. Also said to be the son of Olodumare. Obatala is the father of Dada, Shango, Ogun, Ochosi and Schankpannan. The father of all the Orisha, other Orisa must pay homage to him. His special colour is white, all things associated to him must be white. The source of all that is pure, wise peaceful and compassionate. Also has a warrior side. The so called master of **wisdom** and creator mentioned in the story of creation. Olorun is said to have built the universe and assigned him the task of building the Earth. However he got drunk on palm wine and Oduduwa did it instead. Obatala was then assigned the task of making man. Said to be responsible for human's imperfections.
Ra/Re	Oduduwa
One of several manifestations of the sun god and creator of Egypt. Created himself out of the mound that emerged from the primeval ocean. Generally depicted as a falcon wearing the sun disc on its head surrounded by the serpentine form of the cobra-goddess Wadjet. Also perceived as the god of the underworld. Often rides in his barque as a human figure with a ram's	Created dry land. The first ruler of Ife and all of the Yoruba. Son of Yemonja-Olokun and Olorun. Brother of Obatala, God of the south. Oduduwa made the Earth instead of his brother when he fell drink and was promoted to God of the Earth. I suspect the North south could be in respect to Lower and Upper Egypt. Said to be both male and female.

head surmounted by a sun disc and accompanied by the cobra goddess. Re's cult centre is at Heliopolis. The eye of Re is an important notion in magic.	
Ptah Same as above	Ela
Haru/Horus Same as above.	Orunmila God of Destiny. He accompanied the creator God Oludumare at the creation of the world and when the destinies of mankind were decided. He is consulted in an oracular capacity at Ifa and makes decisions on such matters as choice of sacrificial animals. He is also a god of healing.

There is a big difference in opinion between Lucas/Acholonu and York. Lucas/Acholonu both state that some of the Egyptian Gods have their exact equivalent in the Orisha, while Dr York says they got this system of worship from Arabia. Meanwhile Lucas and Acholonu's match up of Gods do not fit. I summarised Lucas' god associations from chapters he wrote especially for the first few Gods. If we compare the first set of Gods Osiris and Olorun by Lucas there are differences between them that make the probability of a joint persona less likely. The first is the question of supremacy. Olorun is a supreme deity, and Osiris is not (depending on your viewpoint). Brewer sees Osiris as the first king of Egypt (Brewer p.102) and so does Kueshana in reference to their escape from Atlantis. However he is superseded by Re, Amun, Atun, Atum and Ptah as a creator deity. The next is reality of actually existing? As we have seen Gods can be in human form and don't have to be the figment of your imagination. Olorun is a pure spirit too remote to be worshipped so therefore has no representation in any shape or form. (p.51) Sources say Osiris was the first king of Egypt and even identified his body. Then next is worship. Lucas raises an excellent question, 'If they were the same being then why was worship of Olorun almost non existent? He suggests that Osiris worship was almost entirely done by the priestly class, and Olorun probably also had a small priestly class which vanished with the transference and limitation of his worship to lesser deities. There is an expression *gba osiri re or da osiri bo o* which means 'to plot against an innocent person with a view to murdering him'. This points directly to Osiris and the name is almost identical. There is a *possibility* for this to be the same being, over time religious ideas do get altered however at this point I cannot make a definite conclusion. The only link I can agree on is between Obatala and Khnum as the title of moulder and their relation to white seems too close to be co-incidence. In Acholonu's connections both Tehuti and Obatala are associated with wisdom. Lucas also pointed out earlier that Obatala was described as a moulder hence confirming his role in making man.

York's says in *'Let's set the record straight'* that the Orisha are ancestors who went to the other side. In a recorded lecture class he explains that some of the Yoruba Gods were so great and accomplished so much in their lifetime that they became deified. However the earlier explanation in the Holy Tablets is unclear because verse 271 says that Yaaquub was their great ancestor and god then the Nigerians refused to mix with Yaaquub's legion. The Holy Tablets needs to be updated so this should not be fully believed. First of all Yaaquub's people are described as Asiatic Black Men and Women, black people with 6 ether, straight hair of Hindu descent (3:4:191) and this hardly describes the Yoruba's. For him to be their ancestor would mean he existed centuries before and he died from a brain tumour aged 150 before reaching them. (3:4:200) It was Sheshbazzar/Obatala who became leader after him that encountered the people of Nigeria and they refused to mix with them so they left their system of ancestral worship from Arabia called Orishi which now seems perfectly fused with their culture. The suggestion it came from the Arabs, deserves an inside look at the Orisha. Under the system of Orisha certain practices such as spiritual awakenings, appeasing the Gods or asking for help (e.g. monetary or good health) require blood sacrifices of animals and even humans. An article in The Grio 'Are Blacks Abandoning Christianity for African faiths?' reported an element of 'Afrophobia' fear about things related to African culture. Dianne Diakité, an associate professor at Emory University's religion department who participates in Yoruba and other African-based religions had this to say, "But perhaps that fear, or at least a hesitation, may be justified when investigating what is involved in West African-derived religions. Animal sacrifices, secret initiations, the chanting of the names of ancestors in libations, the personification of spirits in masquerades, shaving of body hairs, spirit possessions and refrain from eating tabooed foods are some of the aspects associated with the African religions that may be difficult for some people to accept."[20] The need of blood sacrifices to appease the Gods is present in many cultures and of course the Bible (Genesis 22:2, 1 Samuel 1:3) when Abraham was told to sacrifice his son Isaac under the command of the Lord. It is extremely likely the Orisha are in fact direct ancestors of the Yoruba people and should be revered. It seems that their worship was influenced by visitors from Arabia which is why they require blood sacrifices, a 6 ether trait. In which case Orisha worship should abandon the negative practices. As we experienced problems linking the Nazderu and Annunaqi it is also problematic to link the Nazderu with the Orisha and they should not be grouped as equivalents.

Other links between Ancient Egypt and Nigeria

The authors above who found links between Ancient Egypt and Nigeria may be considered 'unconventional' Egyptologists, however there are many clues in the public domain which reveal a link. A principal trademark of Nok is their terracotta figurines, first found in 1928 in a tin mining village. Nok is located in the Niger-Benue region of Nigeria and artefacts are found in an area covering 600 square miles. British archaeologist Thurstan Shaw conducted work excavating the Nok figurines. They produced many clay figurines of animals and humans with particular focus on the heads and eyes. They were highly skilled in working iron and stone. This same practice was done in Egypt. In Ancient Egypt from the late middle kingdom to the Ptolemaic period, figures called shabti's were placed in burials to carry out any such communal labour in the afterlife. (Spencer p.16) They are mentioned in Genesis 31:19 as 'images'. The word in Hebrew is listed in KWSB #8655 as Teraphim, described as a family idol in the shape of persons.[21] Terracotta's or shabtis were

found in burial tombs of Egyptian pharaohs including Tutankhamun, as a representation of themselves and their family. Picture 5.5, shows a clay terracotta figure found in Nigeria, dated back to around 500BC in the Nok period on show at the Minneapolis Institute of the arts. Part of the description next to it reads, "This work depicts a person of high status wearing elaborate beaded jewellery, and with a crooked baton on his right arm and a hinged flail on the left. These are symbols of authority also found in ancient Egyptian depictions of the Pharaohs and the god Osiris."[22]

Picture 5.5 – Seated dignitary

Osiris is seen holding the crook and flail in picture 5.7. The crook is used to write the word Heqa 'ruler', so the crook symbolises rulership, and the flail symbolises direction, as mankind is seen as cattle to by tended by the God/pharaoh. The influence of Egypt in religion is seen in Psalm 23:1 The Lord is my shepherd; I shall not want. The crook and flail are not clearly visible on picture 5.5, the inscription doesn't say they are withered away, but we are told the figure has these items by a museum, which is a trusted source. So unless the museum is telling an outright lie and we assume this to be true, the question we need to ask ourselves is:

WHY ARE THE NIGERIANS MAKING FIGURES OF MEN HOLDING A CROOK AND FLAIL, SYMBOLS OF EGYPTIAN ROYALTY AND KINGSHIP?

Picture 5.6 – Shabti box of priestess Henutmehyt

Painted shabti-box of the Theban priestess Henutmehyt, which shows her adoring two of the Canopic deities. Her painted shabtis are intended to carry out agricultural activities for her in the afterlife. 19th to 20th Dynasties. C. 1250-1150 BC; wood. H.34.5cm.

Picture 5.7 – Osiris, Deity of vegetation and agriculture and later death. Wall painting from the grave of Sennutem, 14th C, BC.

MIA also comment on 'the elaborate coiffure and beard' in picture 5.5 which is extended just like Osiris. The beard is called a 'khebes' worn by Egyptian pharaohs and gods to symbolise royalty. Diop pointed out how the coiffure (hairstyle in Picture 5.8) is similar to the uraeus in the comments below. Credit is given to Diop for finding this and noting the similarity, however it is not the hairstyle we should be concerned with, it is the specific spiral shaped horn found on the forehead, just like a unicorn. You might be thinking what does a horn have to do with a snake in comparing the Nigerians to the Egyptians? The horn found on a unicorn is said to neutralize poison. Snakes are poisonous, and pharaohs wore the uraeus as a symbol of medicine and purity. The snake worn on the left side of the forehead, symbolised Wadjet, the cobra goddess of lower Egypt and the vulture worn on the right symbolized Nekhbet, the vulture goddess of Upper Egypt. For both of them to be worn together meant that pharaoh had control of Upper and Lower Egypt. The Egyptians propriated the lethal character of the snake and used it as a protection from their enemies and as a symbol of medicine, which later became the caduceus, staff of Hermes, the medical symbol used today with two snakes curled round one stick. The horn in Picture 5.8 also indicates a high rank, as found in seals of the Indus Valley.

The notes on Picture 5.5 finish to say, "The Nok culture existed during the late Pharaonic period and intra-African trading could have spread Egyptian influences into many other parts of Africa." This is seconded by Basil Davidson who mentions that the Egyptians sent traders into the fertile lands of the South West in the 4th dynasty as well as the 6th dynasty towards the fringes of the Congo forest. (Davidson p.30) As I mentioned earlier the time of migration from Egypt to Nigeria is said to be (2000BC – 1000BC) resulting from possible upheavals. The Hyksos invasion of 1660 BC could have brought about the first Egyptian migrants to Nigeria, followed by other major invasions such as Assyria 667 BC and Persia 525 BC. Once first contact had been made others were sure to follow. The Nok culture started from 900-500BC, the latter date of 500 BC falls into the Late Period (dynasties 26-31, c. 656-332BC). If we take the Persian invasion of 525BC minus 25 years, we get 500 BC the start of the Nok culture according to EB in the 27th dynasty. (Refer to Timeline Figure 1.1) Cambyses defeated Psamtek III at Pelusium. Egyptians held many rebellions to overthrow them and with the help of Greece Persian rule was stopped in 404BC. The Persians reconquered Egypt in 343 BC, however this was short lived due to the arrival of Alexander the Great in 332 BC. That date is signified as the end of Dynastic Egypt! So from 525BC – 332BC Egypt was primarily dictated by a foreign power. It is possible that a large number of migrations happened within this time period and after the end of the dynastic period when they became uncomfortable with the Greeks and Romans. Could various wars in Egypt's history have been the catalyst for a wave of migrations into the region of North Africa? After the fall of Egypt which obviously resulted in battles and servitude to their new rulers, the Egyptians are documented to have moved into other areas as they were not allowed to practice their culture and were being persecuted. Did they start a new culture called Yoruba over time and combine their Egyptian ways with people already there? York's account earlier mentions a few things worth noting. The first being Obatala or Sheshbazzar introduced Yoruba into Nigeria in the 5th C. Is this 5th C BC or AD? This Sheshbazzar was the leader of Yaaquub's followers who were Asiatic black people that they refused to mix in with. Then Oduduwa who was Obatala's wife or brother depending on which version you accept went from Mecca into Sudan after a civil war, and then into Nigeria when Sudan became uncomfortable. This could be why the Awujale of Ijebu says the Ijebus are descended from ancient Nubia.

Picture 5.8 - Ife Nigeria Head (Lagos Museum) Compare the coiffure with the Uraeus of the Egyptian pharaoh.

Picture 5.9 - Head from a statue of Amenhotep III showing the king wearing the so called Blue Crown with a prominent coiled uraeus. 18th dynasty c.350BC; quartzite. H. 22cm. Taken from Picture 29 Britsh MBE

York sides with an Arabian influence of religion in all his accounts of Yoruba history. From the fourth century BC, caravan trails are found coming from Meroitic Kush going to several places; and there is much to suggest that other trails may have led westward towards the Niger. (Davidson p.40) Brewer also confirms these caravan trails went to sub-Saharan Africa; "The oases served as military garrisons and as stopping points along the caravan routes that connected Egypt with the deserts and with sub-Saharan Africa." (Brewer p.22) Sertima mentions the use of horses and carts that have been found along two main trails between North and West Africa. (Sertima P.114) These trails are perhaps the first real piece of evidence to prove a migration between these two lands. As suggested by others a major migration must have occurred during the dynastic period so we have at least 5 migrations from Egypt/Nubia at which point an intermarriage would have occurred between them and the indigenous people of Nigeria who have been there since ~65-38k years ago, as we cannot expect Nigeria to have been uninhabited.

Davidson explains the frequent process of southern migration which accounts for the great variety of cultural forms existing in Africa. When one group of people (lets say People A) choose to move to a new country or location they would usually take men, and a handful of women, in small and strong groups. They would settle in either by conquest or agreement, and then take wives from their new but indigenous fellow country folk (People B), here traditions become intermingled. Within a generation or two there'd be a profound intermingling of the two cultures. At this point I suspect that some of People A would go back and bring more of their clan/tribe since the danger and uncertainty of travelling has been diminished. The mothers, not the fathers would be the ones to decide what language the children spoke (People C); most often they would choose their own language, and People's A language/culture would gradually disappear. Some caution is due to this explanation, as in the case of the Fulani; who conquered Hausa land in 1804-11 and afterwards adopted the Hausa language. (Davidson p.110). Could this framework of intermarriage be used to explain a cultural diffusion between Egypt and Nigeria? If so, this would explain the presence of Egyptian language and religion in Yoruba that has been highlighted by many. Certain tribes in Africa have a long history of being nomadic, and moving around due to the seasons and new land for their cattle to herd. Apart from the Sahara desert there were no other natural formations limiting travel which made the Bantu expansion mentioned above a reality.

The Igbo's – Catherine Acholonu

One of Nigeria's other major ethnic group 'the Igbo's' also have a very interesting history which can also be linked to Egypt. Catherine Acholonu is an author of Igbo descent who has revealed some profound information on the subject. 'They Lived Before Adam' p.2 says "The Igbo civilization came from the homo erectus. They went by various other names such as, bushmen, san/shan, twa, pygmies and eshi/nsh." The evolution of humans is as follows: Genus Homo, Homo Erectus, Homo Saurus, Homo Sapien. A lot of similarities exist between York and Acholonu. They constantly arrive at the same conclusion, and because they have not cited each other's work, the results are more credible. For instance, Acholonu says "the Igbo's lived in caves and underground in mounds, with tunnels leading into the bowels of the Earth, many of which have been discovered." (Acholonu 2009, p.3) York states in,

'Are There Black Devils' p.173 "The Gods dug holes into the centre of the Earth where there were air pockets and taught the Pygmies how to get there after a meteorite shower killed off most inhabitants of the Earth 2,250,000 years ago".[23] They are both referring to 'Shamballah and Aghaarta' *cities in the centre of the Earth*! Pygmies are small in stature, several tribes reside in tropical Africa, including the Kalahari, the Ituri Forest in Congo, the Twa, Tswa and the Babinga. They are known to be hunters and gatherers, practicing neither agriculture nor cattle raising. The pygmies of Ituri consist of four groups, Sua, Aka, Efe and Mbuti, called collectively the Bambuti. The Mbuti are the shortest group of Pygmies in Africa, averaging 4"6 inches (137cm) in height. Iteru was the Egyptian word for river which suggests the Congolese borrowed this from Egypt. They differ in blood type from their Bantu and Sudanese speaking neighbours. Bantu is a sub branch of the Niger-Congo languages which originated in Nigeria and Cameroon. The biological affinities between both sets of pygmies is a topic for further discussion. Egyptian records show that the Bambuti were living in the same area some 4,500 years ago.[24] Why would Egyptians keep a record of this group of Pygmies? Could it be that they descended from them? York calls them Ptahites, descendants from the God Ptah, and describes them as black haired, nappy, dark-eyed olive brown skin, (IJG p.98). The Holy Tablets 1:9:132 says "They went directly to the original Pygmy tribe of Bushmen in South Africa who were the Kishites, Cushites and the Hawilahites." Leviathan Part 1 explains how the Adamites also known as Pygmies were bred to work gold mines for the Annunaki in Zimbabwe, or the ancient name for Southern Africa Raphali/Mondopa.) This would make everyone on Earth including the Egyptians descendants of the Pygmies. Verse 137 of the Holy Tablets continues "The Pygmies called these supernatural beings Bahur Malukaat, or "River Angels". 138 They lived in underwater castles." I have an Igbo friend who lived in Nigeria and told me about these river gods. Human life as we know it, from bone evidence did not start in Egypt, the earliest human traces in Egypt goes back to 250,000BC (Lonely Planet) so the Egyptians must have an early ancestor which as stated before is the homo-erectus or pygmy according to Acholonu. The Dogon also believe that the first humans were dwarfs. This places them into the same original ancestry and cosmology with the Igbo. The Egyptians attributed the origin of Pygmies to the land of Punt who they identified as 'nehsi' another name for Nubian. (Chami, 2006, cited in Acholonu 2009, p.108) Acholonu explains "This shows that the Egyptians knew the Igbo word Nshi and actually used it to describe Black dwarfs, just as the Igbo did. It also shows that there were Pre-historic cultural affinities between the Igbo and the Egyptians, and that the

Egyptians might have imported their gods from Igbo land." In year 6/7 of Hatshepsut's reign a trade mission was sent to Punt and brought back many foreign delights including the Queen of Punt. (Brewer, p.52)

Picture 5.10 – The Queen of Punt showing 'Hottentot' body proportions, a common trait of African women.

These black dwarfs were noted to possess longevity such that they could live for hundreds of years and still appear like children. (p.118) It's no surprise to find that York says that the Annunaki's Nergal and Arishkegal were scientists who found the cure for death by being able to manipulate chromosomes to such an extent that aging doesn't occur.[25]

The Igbo worshipped a ram headed god, equivalent of Egyptian Ammon/Osiris. (See picture 5.13) Storm (2007) p.15, says, Amon the Egyptian King of the Gods, was often depicted wearing the head of a ram." Lucas associates Amun with the Yoruba, he says "The Egyptian *amon* means 'to conceal'. The word exists in Yoruba with the same meaning e.g. *fi p amon* 'conceal it'." In Nuwaupu Amun is known as 'the hidden one'. Christians say Amen, at the end of every prayer, Jews (Amin) and Muslims (Amiyn), they all sound phonetically the same as Amun. Revelation 3:14 reads "And unto the angel of the church of the Laodiceans write; these things saith the Amen, the faithful and true witness, the beginning of the creation of God." In Egyptian doctrine Amun was a self created God, and was the beginning, so we can clearly see the significance of Amun in Nigeria and modern religions.

Picture 5.11 - Isis and son Horus.

Picture 5.12 - Mother and son in Whispering Palms. Lagos, Nigeria.

Much of Acholonu's work revolves around excavating a set of stone inscriptions at Ikom, Cross River State and monuments at Igbo Ukwu. The bronzes found at Igbo Ukwu, have been dated to about AD 900. It is believed that the bronzes were part of the furniture in the burial chamber of a high personage, a priest-king, probably a forerunner of the Eze Nri, the king of Nri, a highly ritualistic monarchy that still survives in northern Igbo territory. (EB) Among the Igbo Ukwu monuments the word REN, appears commonly, which we know means name.

WHAT ARE THE NIGERIANS DOING WITH STONE FIGURES THAT HAVE EGYPTIAN WORDS?

In fact she finds Nuwaupu in the Igbo language as 'Nuwaokpu' which means 'In the Most Ancient Original First World'. Rather than just link the Igbo's and Egyptians together Acholonu goes one step further to suggest the "Igbo bushmen were at the centre of the story of Adam and Eve and the march of civilization from West Africa to into Sumer and Egypt." (Acholonu p.30) There is evidence that original Egypt before Menes was first Igbo land and Niger Delta, then Yoruba land (Ife) then back to Igbo land from where Menes took off to conquer North Africa and annex it. Moses' flight from Egypt was from Yoruba land across the Niger to Igbo land, not the Red Sea. These events took place in Upper Egypt, but the records are preserved in Lower Egypt (North Africa). These are in her new book 'Eden in Sumer on the Niger'. For this to be true would place West Africa at a pivotal position in human history! The biblical story of Adam and Eve was not a singular event but rather a mixing of tribes with Eve from the Pygmies and Adam from the Cuthites, black skinned, 8 ether wavy haired East Indians. It was these two tribes that interbred not just two people. A description of the pygmies from records of the New Kingdom refers to them as pig tail wearers, the scar bearers, the Nehusyu with burnt face (referring to their skin colour) and frizzy or curly hair (an afro). This description locates them within the Igbo cultural environment as Igbo Nwa-Nshi dwarfs also bore facial scarification's called *ichi* and wore a pig tail/Nza worn by to symbolise authority. This similar use of the word *nshi* shows that the Egyptians and Igbo's shared pre-historic cultural affinities. P.108. On the subject of Ichi, MDW Jeffrey's a British anthropologist had studies showing a type of ichi as having 2 'eagle wings' and a 'hawks tail'. (Picture 5.14) He drew similarities between this and the winged solar disk of ancient Egyptians (Picture 5.15) and asserted the Igbo and their kwa brethren borrowed this from the Egyptians, concluding that this is proof of cultural diffusion from Egypt to West Africa.

According to Acholonu who cites Sitchin (2004), Re reigned in Egypt by 11,000BC, his son Osiris ruled briefly by 10,000 BC and Horus came into power in 9000BC. Re is said to be Eri, a sky being who landed in a space craft among the forest people of Igbo land and with his Hamite followers and taught them to use weaponry. Prior to 11,000 BC the Igbo as the pygmy, lived in a state of divine grace separate from the rest of the world. 11,000 BC is the time alternative historians speak of nuclear wars between the Gods or Nephilim which led to a deluge that sunk Atlantis. By 9000 BC Horus involved the Kwa people, probably the Bini warriors of Benin in this war of the gods. He is said to have taken refuge in southern Nigeria to prepare for the ultimate battle with Seth and set up a metal foundry there to develop weapons. As well as frequently visit Nigeria/Cameroon with Ra, Edfu pyramid records describe the flight of the god Re, to the land of Khennu in the district of UaUa to escape the conspiracies of his enemies. He landed in the throne place of Horus located in West Africa. Khennu was a royal friend of Horus and his father Re, who probably resided in Nigeria. Khennu coincides with the Igbo clan Nkannu and UaUa coincides with WaWa, which are both clan names that belong to residents of Enugu state not far from Awka. She makes strong connections to him as an Awka black smith who had a role in spreading the use of metal technology and agriculture to the Bantu who

Plate 19 - Ornate Ram head, Igbo Ukwu

Plate 20b - Ram headed Ikenga - Igbo symbol of personal power, equity and justice

Plate 20c - Numerous ram-headed Ikenga wood carvings, courtesy Igbo Ukwu Museum

Picture 5.13 - Ram ornaments at Igbo Ukwu, Nigeria.

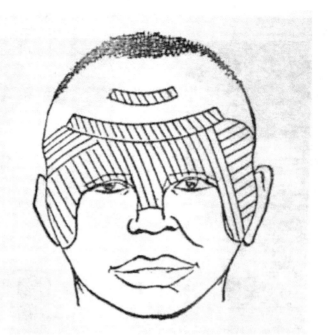

Picture 5.14 - Ichi head depicting a sun and a moon and a winged disc, Naga symbols and symbols of Egyptian god Tehuti/Thoth.

Picture 5.15 - Maat- goddess of justice and truth.

colonized most of sub-Saharan Africa. (P.148.) In fact, UNESCO report that Termit in eastern Niger became the first iron smelting people in the world around 1500 BC.[26] Sertima mentions the 'lost wax technique' used in Egypt and Nubia diffused to the Yoruba and Bini of Nigeria via Meroe, capital of the black kings after their retreat from Egypt. (Sertima p.171) Menes was most likely imposed upon Egypt by Ra from among his human friends from Ancient Nigeria/Nok/Biafra, the horsetail shown in the Narmer palette probably makes him Igbo in origin. Re had built himself an underground kingdom within the bowels of the Cameroon mountain range, known in Egypt as the Duat meaning underworld, a heaven for the pharaohs to spend their afterlife.

That Re/Horus might have went to Nigeria/Cameroon I don't dispute but there is more evidence suggesting Orion/Sirius was heaven to the Egyptians. In fact this underworld might have been a reference to Shamballah and Agaartha, although there aren't any known entrances from that area specifically. (Acholonu 2009 p.145)

Ifa tradition also mentions *Ela* a creator god of the sky, earth and mankind, who is given hero status in his battle against evil. It is said his first embodiment was Obatala and Orunmila the second. Obatala aka Orishanla (god of gods) was seen as the Igbo ancestor a god of the natives whilst Oduduwa the Yoruba ancestor was leader of the foreigners. Ela had 16 divine companions (16 duads - eight gods with their consorts) known as Odu on a mission to save the world. These are the 16 odus used in Ifa divination. (Lucas p.75) The eight twin gods (Archangels/Manu) of Ifa tradition coincide with the 8 great immortal ancestors of Dogon mythology who were said to have brought salvation and knowledge to mankind through death and resurrection. (p.218) The Nag Hammadi scriptures mentions the Son of God an Immortal human, an androgynous being who created out of himself eight other androgynous beings, numbering a total of sixteen. She then explains as Meji also means half the 16 saviours of Ifa could also mean a total of 8 beings. This recurring theme of twins is present in Egypt, Nigerian, Dogon and Nag Hammadi (Jewish) doctrine. The Nigerians (Yoruba) have the most amounts of twins in the world and could reveal a link to Egypt.

Apart from the Yoruba's and Igbo's the Urhobo people also claim Egyptian ancestry. A Urhobo website says they are AKKA people. This is their account of their history and Ancestors. The origin of the name Uhobo which eventually became Urhobo is possibly related to the name of the patriarch General Horemhobo; the last Pharaoh of the 18th dynasty (ruled 1348-1335 BCE). He was assigned to the former most senior Akka ethnic group as Urhobo people. The Urhobos once lived in Zevbaka and Amono in ancient Egypt, the Benis in Bini, the Itsekiris in Goshen, all on the right side of the river Nile while the Yoruba's lived in Sakara and other places on the opposite side of the Nile, all living together amicably. However upheavals during the Arab, Greek and Roman conquests forced them to migrate in a mass exodus from Egypt, as well as the search for fertile lands. Incidentally they dominated as leaders in the Delta of Egypt where the Akka people comprising the ethnic groups listed above once lived. After moving, these various tribes and people lost their history of Egypt and of the so-called Edo region which they know as Akka region. Akka; a name the Urhobos brought from Egypt is very significant in the lives of mankind today.[27]

The Twin Connection

The Yoruba have among the highest rates of twin births in the world, at 45-50 sets of twins per 1,000 live births.[28] There are two types of twins identical and non identical. Identical twins are referred to medically as monozygotic (mono 'one' zygote 'sex cell') because one sperm fertilizes one egg and splits into two separate embryos. Non identical twins are referred to as fraternal or dizygotic because they develop from two separate eggs that are fertilized by two separate sperm that make two separate embryos. They are called in Yoruba 'Ibeji' which means twins. The first born is Taiwo (having the first taste of the world) and the second born is Kehinde (arriving after the other). Coincidentally twins are a common theme in Ancient Egypt, because the Gods of the Ennead and Ogdoad were born as twins.

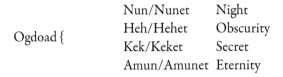

Ogdoad {

Nun/Nunet	Night
Heh/Hehet	Obscurity
Kek/Keket	Secret
Amun/Amunet	Eternity

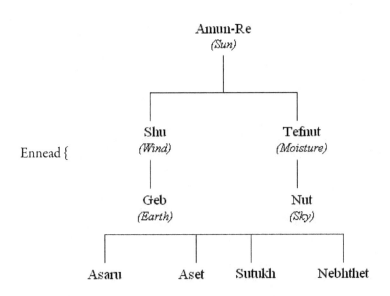

DO THE OGDOAD AND ENNEAD (DEITIES) OF ANCIENT EGYPT WHO WERE BORN AS TWINS HAVE ANYTHING TO DO WITH YORUBA PEOPLE PRODUCING THE HIGHEST AMOUNT OF TWINS IN THE WORLD?

Some have suggested that the high occurrence of twins in is due to their high intake of yams and cassava which leads to chemicals that release more than one egg. However this has not been scientifically proven. But one thing is for certain. Families *with* twins have a higher chance of producing more twins than families without twins. This suggests a link between these supreme Egyptian gods and the Yoruba people by way of genetic inheritance (See chapter 9). The Ogdoads are four pairs of two gods and goddesses symbolizing primeval waters. (Storm p.58) They can be attributed to Adam and Eve representing the first beings created every the time the Earth was destroyed. The sinking of Atlantis, Noah/Gilgamesh, and the dinosaurs all confirm the Earth went through such catastrophes. Each set of the Ogdoad represented genetic shifts every four generations giving birth to various types of humims.[29] York explains in 'Great Women of the Scriptures'[30] that Eve had 23 sons and 22 daughters and each time she gave birth she would bear a male and female child together. Are there black Devils p.196 and 197 gives a complete list of the names of their 45 children. The other group are the ennead (Sedjet). Atum the self created deity is said to have sprang forth from the primeval waters of Nun. He then created from himself Shu and Tefnut. They in turn made Geb and Nut. They made two sets of twins Aset (Isis) and Asaru (Osiris) and Sutukh (Set) and Nebthet. As well as brother and sister, each set of twins was also husband and wife, for instance Aset and Asaru conceived Haru (Horus).

Picture 5.16 – 'Ibeji' statues.

In early Yoruba land and other parts of West Africa it was common for twins to be killed at birth because they were feared or considered abnormal. Now twins are paid respect and honour in Yoruba land receiving a degree of reverence almost amounting to worship. This is due to the fact that they are thought to have protection by twin gods and to some extent are seen as the real representatives of the Orisa Ibeji. In Ijebuland twins are regarded as a special gift of the gods and the personification of the orisa, Ibeji (Oladele, 1980 cited in Ojo p.43). They were thought to have extra-human powers (Barrett, 1977 cited in Ojo p.43). If one of the twins happens to die, a wooden image is used as a substitution for the child to balance the equilibrium. Failure to do this will incur the displeasure of the Twin Gods who may punish the parents by causing the remaining child to die. Periodical sacrifices or offerings of cooked beans or vegetables are made to the twin gods during the lifetime of the twins. Sometimes a mother can even beg on behalf of the twins, by saying Ibeji nki o- "Twins are saluting you" to passers by, who when saluted have to give a present large or small as a token of their respect to the representatives of the twin gods. A species of monkey called Edun Dudu, or Edun Ori-okun is sacred to the twin gods. In Badagry there is a temple sacred to the twin gods. There is a praise song sang to celebrate the birth of twins shortly after they're born. The Holy Tablets says that originally all babies were born in pairs as twins.

> 1:2:13 "When the Anunnagi, Aluhum of 360 degrees, split into two beings of 180 degrees each, meaning the disagreeable is on the outside; if the male child is agreeable, the female twin counterpart is disagreeable. If the female is agreeable, the male twin or counterpart is disagreeable. 14 The one must conquer the other, to become agreeable or to become a child of light, imperfection, that was clicked on in the darkness of perfection. 15 In this way, was the disagreeable being created, calling them twins. Every person born was a twin. One defeated the other and that is how each of you were born."
> [The Holy Tablets, Dr Malachi K York]

Summary

• The evidence collected shows that instability in Ancient Egypt and Nubia urged people to migrate to Nigeria and other parts of West Africa. A process of admixture occurred between them and the native people. Elements of pharaonic civilization such as language, religion and customs survived in Nigerian culture.

• I cannot say conclusively the exact origin of the 'Orisha' but they are so intertwined with Yoruba history/life and linked to their creation suggesting they were our ancestors.

• However their worship should be restricted to Ifa divination and prayer. Any form of blood sacrifice is barbaric and should be stopped.

• After over two millennia of religion and many other atrocities, Africa struggles with poverty, disease and wars and famine. The first step to a problem is first admitting it. It's time to drop the cultural and religious titles and unite as one people if we are ever to grow.

• African oral traditions such as Dogon and Ifa tradition reveal our origin and should be taken more seriously.

Notes and References

1. York-El, Dr Malachi Z. Scroll #360, *Let's Set The Record Straight?* Egipt Publishers, Athens, Georgia. P.242

2. Ojo A, (1999) *Yorùbá Omo Odùduwà.* Papers on Yoruba People, Language, and Culture 1999 Yoruba language program students. University of Georgia.

3. "Yoruba." Encyclopædia Britannica. 2010.Encyclopædia Britannica 2006 Ultimate Reference Suite DVD 8 Sept. 2010.

4. Lucas J (1948) *The Religion of the Yoruba's.* CMS Bookshop. Lagos.

5. Sertima I (2003) *They Came Before Columbus.* Random House Trade Paperbacks; New title edition (Sep 23 2003) p.113

6. BBC News Africa. *Nigeria: A Nation divided.* Available from: http://www.bbc.co.uk/news/world-africa-16510922 [Accessed 14/1/2012]

7. Karade B, (1994) *The Handbook of Yoruba Religious Concepts.* Weiser Books. P.1

8. "Nigeria." Encyclopædia Britannica. 2010. Encyclopædia Britannica 2006 Ultimate Reference Suite DVD 29 Sept. 2010.

9. Davidson B, (2001) *Africa in History.* Weidenfeld & Nicolson; New edition. p20

10. Olomu and Eyebira. (2007) *Yoruba the Egyptian Connection.* Available from: http://www.raceandhistory.com/cgibin/forum/webbbs_config.pl/noframes/read/2139 [Accessed 21/11/2011]

11. Bryc et al (2009) Genome-wide patterns of population structure and admixture in West Africans and African Americans. *Proceedings of the National Academy of Sciences of the United States of America.* 107 (2) p.786-791

12. Faces of Africa: Kingdom of Ife at the British museum. Available from: http://www.guardian.co.uk/artanddesign/2010/feb/26/kingdom-of-ife-british-museum-review [Accessed 13/10/2011]

13. Walker, R (2008) *Before the Slave Trade.* African World History in Pictures. Black History Studies Publications.

14. Diop C (1974) *The African Origin of Civilization: Myth or Reality?* A Capella Books. P.186

15. Jordan M (2005) *Encyclopaedia of Gods: Over 2500 Deities of the World.* Great Britain: Kyle Cathie.

16. Maspero G (2003) *History of Egypt.* Volume 1 Part A p.48. London The Grolier Society of Publishers. Available from: http://www.gutenberg.org/files/19400/19400-h/v1a.htm

17. Acholonu-Olumba, C . (2009) *They Lived Before Adam, Prehistoric Origins of the Igbo - The Never-Been-Ruled.* CARC Publications, Abuja.

18. *African mythology: The Gods and Spirits of Africa.* Available from: http://www.godchecker.com/pantheon/african-mythology.php [Accessed: 11/9/2010]

19. Orishanet Articles. *The Orisha's.* Available from: http://www.orishanet.org/ocha.html Accessed 14/2/2012

20. Zodhiates, S (2009). *Hebrew-Greek Key Word Study Bible-KJV.* AMG. 2nd revised edition. Old Testament dictionary. #8655

21. The Grio. *Are blacks abandoning Christianity for African faiths?* Available from: http://www.thegrio.com/news/african-religions-gain-following-among-black-christians.php?page=2 [Accessed 14/05/2011]

22. *Minneapolis Institute of the arts.* Available from: http://www.artsmia.org/viewer/detail.php?i=2&v=12&dept=8&op=1449 See Image 20: Seated Dignitary. [Accessed 15/07/2010]

23. York-El, Dr. Malachi Z. Book No #1. Are there Black Devils? (Revised) ISBN# 1-, Egipt Publishers, Athens, Georgia, 2000 AD.

24. "Bambuti."Encyclopædia Britannica. 2012. Encyclopædia Britannica 2006 Ultimate Reference Suite DVD 8 May 2011.

25. York-El, Dr. Malachi Z. Book No #192. *Great balls of fire cast at the Earth?* ISBN#? Egipt Publishers, Athens, Georgia, 2000 AD.

26. *Motherland.* Documentary DVD. (2010) by Owen Alek Shahadah.

27. *Urhobo World.* Available from: http://www.urhobo-world.webs.com/ [Accessed 8/8/12]

28. BBC World Service. 2001. *The land of twins.* Available from: http://www.bbc.co.uk/worldservice/people/highlights/010607_twins.shtml [Accessed 17/2/2012]

29. York-El, Dr. Malachi Z. Book No #203 *Questions to Dr. Malachi Z. York-El about The Beginning?* ISBN#1-59517-116-9., Egipt Publishers, Athens, Georgia.

30. York-El, Dr. Malachi Z. The truth Bulletin. Edition #2 *Great Women of The Scriptures.* Egipt Publishers, Athens, Georgia.

NUWAUPIAN GALLERY

ASARU

THE ANCIENT EGIPTIAN ORDER , MIR #9   ATHENS,GA

The Ancient Egiptian Order

Chapter 6

Egypt and other African countries

A part from Sudan and Nigeria, the original home of the Yoruba's, Dr York mentioned that the Yoruba kingdom included Chad, Benin, Togo, Ghana and Angola. "Egypt is in Africa and there is no scientific reason to think that Egyptians would not share some biological origins with other Africans."[1] This chapter will look for clues of an Egyptian presence in these countries and the rest of Africa. The first country I will mention is Benin, Nigeria's neighbour to the East. York noted a similarity between Benin and Ancient Egypt. "A Statue Made Out Of Basalt, Of The Earliest Known Egyptian Found, Showed Him With A Beard And A Short Kilt Covering His Private Parts. The Remarkable Thing About This Statue Is, It Looks Like One Of The Male Servants Of The Benin Culture's Statues, Of West Africa, Proving Again They Are All The Same Family. I Say That Because, Every Time You Look In An Encyclopaedia, You'll Find They Never Mention Egypt With Africa, As If It Is Not Part Of The African Continent. How Racist And Ridiculous In 1998 A.D."[2]

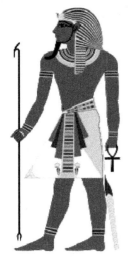

Picture 6.1 - Egyptian wearing a kilt

Picture 1 shows an Egyptian wearing a kilt, which confirms the wearing of kilts spread to other countries. When the British invaded Benin in the 19thC and found sculptures, they were so impressed by them that they claimed, "The sculptures must have been made by the Portuguese, the Egyptians, or the lost tribes of Israel"[3] What was done here which we see repeated from Chapter 5 is to totally dismiss the high skill level of West Africans to another group of people or grudgingly admit it based on their preconceived notions of undeveloped people. But by saying this they are unknowingly linking them with the Egyptian civilization which adversely counteracts the efforts of non-black supporters. Chapter 5 mentioned Dahomey and the Gold Coast worship Gods originating from Nigeria. However there is also evidence linking Ghana to Egypt. Lucas mentions a spirit of a Nigerian ancestor 'Agemon' who he links to Egyptian deities Geb and Amon. Lucas writes,

"The God Amon is also worshipped by the Ga's of the Gold Coast (Ghana) in West Africa. There he is known as Nyon-mon; that is, "the living Amon," and worshipped as the Supreme Deity. He is also regarded as being connected to the sky. He causes rain to fall, the lightening to flash, and the thunder to sound."[4] A Nuwaupian update 'Gateways and their Guardians' mentioned Ghana by saying:

> *"so your ancestors will come forth for you, and raise you up in the*
> *heavens with the help of your heavenly family. Khamanu, Sabatu,*
> *Natharu winged reyay, disk <u>a symbol of their crafts</u> as found on*
> *the walls of the temples such as Karnak the golden disk symbol of*
> *Mafkuzet of nebet golden children pure ones saints. The bowl or*
> *basket shaped symbol. The fine woven baskets are symbolic of*
> *ancient cloths weaved to become kente or a dinka cloth as well as*
> *the weave on the shield of Netharet Neith and dress of Nethartet*
> *Mut as found in gana Ghana which is also called the gold coast of*
> *the tribes of Akan and Iwi. And you can study the tribe of Ghana*
> *called the gara or Burkina Faso also in Nigeria's east and Ghana's*
> *north keepers."*
> [Mursultat Bastet Yaa Nafurtet Sent Atum Re]

The Holy Tablets expands on the second or new migration mentioned in Chapter 5. Mizraim also known as Egypt had seven sons who inherited certain parts of Africa.

> 13:11:75 We migrated. And as we migrated we spread to
> <u>Senegal, Mali, Chad and different places.</u> 76 The Midianites
> escaped the massacre of Gideon and the Israelites; 77 Settling in
> what is called Mali today, amongst the Dogons, the original
> Nuwbuns. [The Holy Tablets, Dr Malachi Z York]

We have already seen the significance of Mali especially as descendants of the Egyptians, their association with the Nommos and knowledge of astronomy. Now it's time to throw Chad into the equation. Chad surprisingly has a rich history which may throw the question of Egyptian origins into further disarray. Black Genesis reveals how Chad, one of the world's poorest countries may be an even earlier source of lineage before Nubia, which as we learnt from Chapter 4 gave rise to the Egyptian civilization.

In 1923, Ahmed Hassanein Bey a desert explorer came across the Tebu people, pastoral nomads in Jebel Uwainat. There were 150 of them supposedly led by a King Herri. King Herri showed him mysterious rock carvings of animals not known in that part of the Sahara such as lions, giraffes, ostriches and gazelles. A Sahara historian J L Wright claimed the people that Hassanein encountered were Tebu refugees from the Goran tribe who originally had come from the Tibesti Mountains in northern Chad. Hassanein spoke of other tribes in the Libyan Desert the Goran and Bidiat. There is an abundance of rock art in the Tibesti-Ennedi highlands in Chad similar to the ones found at Uwainat which suggests a prehistoric Origin. The Ancient Egyptians made reference to a group of people called *Temenu*, a possible source of the word Tebu. A German explorer Gerhard Rohlfs describes the Tebu people. "Their stature is svelte, their members fine, their disposition light and swift; they have lively eyes, their lips are a bit tough, their nose is small but not snubbed, and their hair is short but less wiry than the Negroes... All other travellers who made contact with the Tebu have noted that their physical traits tend more towards the Negro... their customs and traditions are also nearer to that of the Negro... the land of the present day Tebu is located south of Fazan, in the north of Lake Chad.' [Black Genesis p.182]

Bauval/Brophy introduce a scenario where the early modern humans of East Africa moved northward into Chad and settled in the Tibesti-Ennedi highlands. Around 9000 BCE they started moving North again into the then tropical area of the Sahara going first to Gilf Kebir and the Uwainat mountain region, then slowly spreading east and northeast toward the Nile. Starting at about 8500 BCE Libya, Egypt, Chad and Sudan experienced hospitable ecosystems involving rains and warm weather. Then starting around 5000 BCE, as the Sahara became drier these people began moving out of the desertified regions. Finally by 3500 BCE the desert became super arid and forced them to migrate eastward into the Nile Valley. If this is true and it does very much appear to be the case-then the origins of the ancient Egyptians are rooted in a black skinned race of sub-Saharan pastoralists that had themselves likely come

from the Tibesti-Ennedi highlands and, going further back in
time, had their source in eastern Africa.[5]
[Black Genesis p.167]

It was climate change which forced migration and this ultimately led to the rise
of the Pharaohs and the Egyptian civilisation. That the ancient people of Chad
were ancestors of the Nubians, who then started Egyptian civilization, is a
topic which needs further study. With this evidence, together with Acholonu's
statement in Chapter 5 that the Igbo's led civilization from West Africa to
into Sumer and Egypt, especially since Chad borders Nigeria, means the
significance of West Africa is seriously underestimated.

Senegal is mentioned by Diop later in this chapter as well as Chapter
10. An American anthropologist George Murdock showed that the Mande
people of West Africa created a centre of plant domestication around the
headwaters of the Niger River circa 4500 BC. They contributed crops such as
the bottle gourd, the watermelon, the tamarind fruit and cultivated cotton to
Egypt in a NE direction across the African continent.[6] In Arkells excavation of
Khartoum he found the charred fragment of an oil palm fruit whose original
home would be amongst the Mande, going in an Egyptian direction. In fact
trade of agriculture has also been linked between Egypt and Ethiopia. A
genetic study of Ethiopian mtDNA heritage found that the beginning of
agriculture in Ethiopia is usually attributed to increasing contacts with Egypt
and the Near East, from the middle of the 5th millennium B.C. Records
concerning the trade of myrrh between Egypt and Ethiopia, along the Red Sea
coast, go back to the 3rd millennium B.C. (p1 Kisivild) The Oromos and Afars
speak Cushitic languages and are purported to have connections to ancient
Egyptians, since the land of Cush—the son of biblical Ham—is generally
considered to be in the vicinity of the ancient cities of Meroe¨ and Napata,
located in present-day Sudan.[7] Diop made reference to a statue of a falcon and
crocodile found in Zimbabwe suggesting a link with Egypt via the Gods Horus
and Sobek. The Egyptian suffix *wa*, e.g. bak-w meaning 'servants' in Egyptian,
can be linked to Sumba-*wa*: the Sumbs, and Zimbab-*we*.[8] The evidence is
mounting piece by piece and we are beginning to see just how inter-related the
whole thing is.

Picture 6.2 - Zimbabwe: The falcon and crocodile are echoes of Egypt.
The falcon is associated with Horus and the crocodile Sobek.

Black scholars such as Diop and Walker have noticed the exact replication of Ancient Egyptian head shape and hair styles by other African groups.

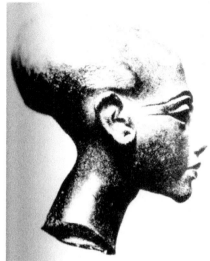 

Picture 6.3 - Profile of Akhenaten's daughter showing a markedly long or hyperdolichoce-phalic skull probably caused by a deliberate deformation of the skull in infancy. This is thought to have been done by collecting and plaiting the hair very tightly towards the back of the head for prolonged periods as is done among the Fang of Gabon and the Mangbetu of Congo. This same cranial shape has also been found in some Phoenician burials. Taken from Walker 2004, fig 60, p.65

Picture 6.4 - Profile of a Mangbetu woman from North East Congo showing the same hyperdolichocephalic cranial shape.[9] [Taken from Walker 2004, fig 61 p.65.]

Sertima also mentions that skull deformation was deliberately practiced by the Egyptians and Ancient American Upper Class to distinguish them physically from their subjects. (Sertima P.172)

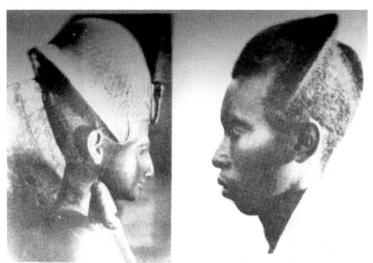

Picture 6.5 - Pharaoh Ramses II and a modern Watusi. The Watusi hair do can be conceived only for woolly hair. The small circles on the Pharaoh's helmet represent frizzy hair (as noted by Denise Cappart in her article in Reflet du Monde, 1956). [Taken from Diop 1974, fig 11, p.19.]

Picture 6.6 - Left. Wooden doll. XI dynasty. Picture 6.7 - Right. A native woman of Der in nubia, with her hair dressed like the XI doll. Originally published in The Egyptian Expedition, 1930-1931. p.363 by H.E Winlock, with his original captions.) Winlock adds: Most of the Eleventh Dynasty tombs at Thebes contained dolls....with great mops of hair made of strings of little beads of black mud ending in elongated blobs. Strange as they may look they ....not one whit more uncouth than a modern doll bought this year at Amada in Nubia which ahs each thin plait of hair tipped with a blob of clay. And these blobs of clay ....no childish fantasy, for the well dressed woman of Der, the capital of Nubia.

Picture 6.8 - Detail from the sarcophagus of Queen Kawit, Eleventh dynasty showing typical African hair. Taken from Walker 2008. figure 71 from p.71. Photo courtesy of Runoko Rashidi.

Diop suggests we probe more deeply into the origin of the Laobe, Yoruba, Peul, Toucouleur, Serer, and Agni who he links back to the Nile Valley.

Peul

The Peul probably came from Egypt because *Ka* and *Ba* are typical totemic names of the Peul which correspond with Egyptian metaphysical beliefs of the ka (spirit) and ba (soul). Bari another totemic Peul name is a combination of Ba and Ra. The Peul as well as Serer tribes (Sar, Sen etc) are one of the numerous tribes which produced pharaohs in the course of history. Several pharaohs bore the name of *ka* and *ba* such as King Ka of the protodynastic epoch which is in line with a Peul branch called Kara. Uganda-Rwanda also have the Kara tribe. The Peul were originally blacks but from the 18th dynasty in Lower Egypt mixed with a foreign white element.

Toucoleur

According to their own tradition the Toucoleur now living on the banks of the Senegal River had probably resided in Anglo Egyptian Sudan, an area called Nyoro. Language similarity exists between them and the Nuer.

"Anglo-Egyptian" Sudan	Senegal (Futa-Toro)
Kan	Kann
Wan	Wann
Ci	Sy
Lith	Ly
Kao	Ka (Peul)

There is a tribe of people in Ethiopia called Tekruri. In the event the Toucoleur are a fraction of that tribe, the name Tekruri was probably derived from Tekrur; the capital of the state on the lower Senegal river instead of Toucoleur. According to historical and archaeological sources, the kingdom was founded by the Serer people.

Serer

The Serer probably came to Senegal from the Nile basin: their route perhaps marked by upright stones found at the same altitude from almost as far away as Ethiopia to Sine-Salum. The stones possibly correspond to an agrarian cult symbolizing the ritual union of sky and Earth. The Serer bury their dead as the Egyptians did however abandoned mummification because of the scarcity of cloth. They used a cone shaped tomb that covered the soil instead of a pyramid. The dead were buried with objects just like the Egyptians believe that life continues after death just as it unfolded on Earth.

Agni

The Agni also seem to be of Egyptian origin considering the first name that always accompanies that of King Amon. E.g. Amon Azonia was a Ani king who lived in the 16th C, Amon Tiffou an Ani ruler from the 17th C and Amon Aguire an Ani monarch of the 19th C. Ani is similar to Oni the name of the Nigerian King of Ife, Oni is also a name of Osiris mentioned in the Book of the Dead and can be linked to Anu, the name of a pre-dynastic black race of Egypt.

MDW Jeffreys points to a connection between the Bamum and the Egyptians because of the vulture and serpent on the namuz (Egyptian headpiece). He was convinced that the Bamum cult of the King derives from a similar Egyptian cult. A legend reports that the King of Cayor in Senegal had a vulture which fed on the human flesh of slaves. There are language similarities between the Egypt and Senegalese Wolof.

Ch-6: Ancient Egypt and other African countries

Egypt	Senegal
Atoum	Atu
Sek-met	Sek
Keti	Keti
Kaba	Kaba, keba, kebe
Antef	Anta
Fari- the Pharaoh	Fari: title of emperor
Meri, Meri	Meri
Saba (Kush)	Sebe
Kara, Kare	Kare
Ba_Ra	Bara, Bari (Peul)
Ramses, Reama	Rama
Bakari	Bakari

Notes and References

1. Keita S (1993) Studies and Comments on Ancient Egyptian Biological relationships. *History in Africa* Vol. 20, published by African Studies Association. P.128

2. York-El, Dr Malachi. Scroll #191. *Science of the Pyramid.* ISBN#? Egipt Publishers. p.114

3. *Rebirth of Africa: Art of Benin Nigeria.* Available from: http://www.rebirth.co.za/sculpture/bronze.htm [Accessed 5/1/2012]

4. Lucas J (1948) *The Religion of the Yoruba's.* CMS Bookshop. Lagos. P.136

5. Bauval R, T Brophy (2011) *Black genesis: The Prehistoric origins of Ancient Egypt.* Bear and Company.

6. Sertima, I (2003) *They came before Columbus.* Random House USA. P.118

7. Kivisild et al. (2004) Ethiopian Mitochondrial DNA Heritage: Tracking Gene Flow Across and Around the Gate of Tears. *The American Journal of human genetics.* 75:752–770.

8. Diop C (1974) *The African Origin of Civilisation: Myth or Reality.* A Capella Books. P.183

Chapter 7

Ancient Egypt and South America

The Rizqiyians assert that they are the fathers of various other cultures of South America. When you consider there are pyramids across South America, the advanced and controversial Mayan calendar, giant stone heads by the Olmecs, and some of their cultural ceremonies, you might get an inclination of a Nubian/Egyptian influence. This *for me* is enough reason to take this quote seriously and explore a possible link between Egypt and South America.

The Olmec Civilisation

The first group we will look at are the Olmecs. The Olmecs are said to be founders of Meso-American civilisation (Mexico and Central America), their homeland located in the modern states of Tabasco and Veracruz. Archaeologists have dated human presence in Mesoamerica to as early as 21,000 BC.[1] Human development in Meso-America is grouped into several periods.

Period	Time
Pre classic	Before 6500 BC
Classic	6500 – 1500 BC
Early formative	1500-900 BC
Middle formative	900-300 BC
Early classic	100 – 600 AD
Late classic	600–900 AD
Post classic	900 -1519 AD

Table 7.1 - Periods of development in Meso-America according to EB pre Columbian civilizations.[2]

They are famous for making colossal stone heads in a time that can be classified as 'ancient'. The size of the heads and the time they built them are very impressive, but what really sets them apart is their Nubian features. The heads caused controversy in the archaeological world because most people couldn't explain an African presence in South America before Christopher Columbus, who is credited with 'discovering America'. Ivan Van Sertima's book, 'They Came Before Columbus' explores this topic in brilliant fashion which we will discuss during the course of this chapter. In a video interview he gives the following summary of the Olmec civilisation.

> "This civilisation occurred in the gulf coast of Mexico, when we speak of Mexico however you must get it very clear in your mind that we are not speaking of the stringent Mexico of today, we speak of Mexico when it was the very core and heartland of native American civilisations, a Mexico that included parts of Colorado, parts of Texas, part of California going right up to La Plata in Canada. This civilisation known as Olmec was to touch all other civilisations in America; the Maya, the Toltec, the Aztec e.t.c. it was even to stretch right out into South America. What is very unusual about this civilisation was that not only was it the mother of American civilisations but it contained elements that were not just native to America but was a fusion between the native American and people coming from outside. The most significant of these outsiders were the Africans, we have very clear evidence in stone heads, in terracotta's that are clay sculptures as well as skulls and skeletons of an African physical type entering that native population somewhere between 948 and 680 BC..."[3]

The heads appeared across the Olmec heartland. San Lorenzo is the oldest known Olmec centre dating to 1150 BC, which (EB Mesoamerica) say was far ahead the rest of Mesoamerica which was at a Neolithic level. 10 out of 17 of these colossal heads are located are at San Lorenzo, 4 at of La Venta, 2 at Tres Zapotes and 1 at Rancho la Cobata. The first head was found in 1862 in the Canton of Tuxtla. The heads at La Venta are given a date from 800-700 BC, range from 6-9 feet tall and 25-40 tonnes. The heads are described as having flat faces, thickened lips and helmet like headgear. (EB)[4] Dr York linked the headgear with an Egyptian helmet shown in Picture 7.1.[5]

Picture 7.1 – Left: Olmec head, Right: Egiptian Helmet.
Notice the similarities with the helmet, the emblem on the front, and the ear plugs.

Picture 7.2 – Head of Nuwba Chiefs from Africa,
with Olmec Stone Head

The heads were said to represent players in a sacred rubber ball game, but are now generally accepted to be important rulers or part of a religious priesthood. This is because some of the heads have a flat top and were used as an altar to be worshipped.[6] (Sertima video) A lot has been said to deny the Nubian features of the giant heads and they range from the ridiculous to the incredible! Some suggested that the heads are of children because most children exhibit such physical features and that children were held in high esteem in the Olmec culture. Others have suggested that the carvers only had blunt tools so could not carve the facial features precisely, and some like always have given it the silent treatment.[7] Actually black children have less Negroid features than black adults such as light skin, and baby hair which is straight and less thick. They start to get to their true colour as their bodies produce more melanin and is activated by the sunlight. (See Chapter 9) When the 'baby hair' is cut off and their bodies have more protein their hair then grows back as proper woolly, kinky and curly hair. I'm not a midwife, nursery worker nor a paediatrician so I can not comment on the noses of babies; however the full set of lips displayed on the heads look more like adult lips rather than children's.

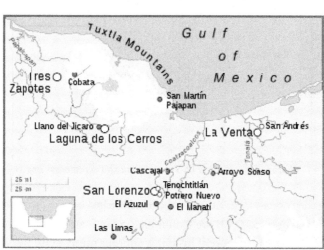

Picture 7.3 – The Olmec heartland

Picture 7.4 – Map of La Venta a civic and ceremonial site

Regarding the carver's *skill,* EB and others say the heads were carved with 'great technical prowess,' (EB pre Columbian civ.) so the strong Nubian features were done on purpose. This is just another funny example of desperate attempts to discredit the facts. To add to the equation, a Mediterranean figure described with a long beard, Semitic nose and turned up shoes is also found in La Venta.[8] This makes things even more interesting, why would there be figures of both parties here together, especially since they weren't supposed to have arrived at a much later time in history? What we need to determine is, what was the racial identity of the Olmecs, and were the heads made in the image and likeness of the Olmecs, or out of respect to possible visitors? This will be answered later.

Pyramids

Apart from Nubia and Egypt there are a number of pyramids around the world including Mexico and South America. Chichen Itza in Mexico and Machu Picchu in Peru are two of the New wonders of the world. The statues in Easter Island are also marvelled. We know that pyramids were first built in Mars followed by Egypt and Sudan, so was there a Martian or African influence on pyramid building across South America or did it develop independently? Something as unique as pyramids which are located in small concentrations around the world seem less likely to be the result of random 'eureka moments'. I say this because to build one you will most likely need:

1) Influencing by someone else (word of mouth, project assignment)

2) a specific reason (pyramids were used as much more than tombs for Pharaohs in Ancient Egypt. The time and effort it takes to build one, you better have a good reason to do so!

3) the technique. Building structures made from stone some hundred metres in the air especially in ancient times is no easy feat, this requires great knowledge of geometry, mathematics, engineering and astronomy.

Dr York offers caution in the dating of the South American pyramids and stone heads by saying the scientists don't have instruments to date solid stone, so they guess, and the monuments are actually thousands of years older than what scientists say they are. He gives a good case study. "Take For Example, The Pyramid Temple Of Tikal, Guatemala, Dedicated To The Olmec Jaguar Deity. It Was Dated 600 B.C, And Said To Be Built By The Mayan, However The Mayan Revered Quetzalcoatl, Not The Jaguar, Who Was A Deity To Their Ancestors The Olmec, Thousands And Thousands Of Years Before The Mayans Came On The Scene."[9] EB say the Maya had settled in villages in 1500 BC which is a good 300 years before the first Olmec site, however the Mayan cities weren't established till 200 AD. This does not fit in with the above quote. Even the Encyclopaedia of the God's say's Quetzalcoatl's origin was with the Aztecs and they worshipped him circa 750-1500 AD and probably much earlier.[10] With this information I would say Dr York was wrong on this occasion. Unless he meant to say the Aztecs instead of the Maya, who appeared in Mesoamerica in the 12th Century AD. [11] (See Notes) and established Tenochtitlan in 1325 AD. This would make a 2000 year gap, so he was right with the time difference but the wrong civilisation. Judging from the evidence we have seen in Chapter 2 that the pyramids of Giza were built 8000 years earlier than previously claimed, I would also think twice about the datings. However with regards to the stone heads found at La Venta dating 800-700 BC, this date was derived from carbon 14 testing of wooden charcoal platforms the heads were rooted in. (Sertima p.147) Quetzalcoatl is the heroic creator God of the Aztecs, described as 'the feathered serpent'. (Jordan p.212) He would be the Central American counterpart of Osiris because he also was crucified making him one of the 16 crucified saviours. (Read 'The World's Sixteen Crucified saviours' by Kersey Graves.)

There is a 110 foot/33m high mound pyramid found at La Venta made of stone dubbed the Great pyramid. There is no stone in La Venta, most agree the stones were formed from volcanic or meteoric activity. The nearest such location is Cerro Cintepec, a volcanic flow in the Tuxtla Mountains 50-80 miles away. How did they carry massive stones in Tuxtla across such a large distance to La Venta to build their pyramids and stone heads made from basalt? EB believe the stones were somehow 'dragged' to the nearest stream and from there transported on rafts up the Coatzacoalcos River to the San Lorenzo area. This poses several problems. According to Van Sertima the heads were sculpted out of gigantic balls, because there aren't any jointed parts or built up layers of stone. In this case the chances of dragging a stone 50-80 miles even if it was in a perfectly rounded ball shape would be drastically limited. There could be a slight possibility that the stones were built up from jointed pieces with advanced joining techniques but all the heads show no visible signs of this, especially on the back of the heads which all exhibit a smooth surface. In this case it is almost certain that they were carved from individual giant balls. Thus it would be very unlikely that 40 tonne stone would be dragged and then transported on a boat without sinking. We have seen in Chapter 2 the true story of the pyramids which offer more credibility than the engineering fallacies commonly cited, and judging by the weight of cultural evidence between the two groups would it be reasonable to suggest the Olmecs were influenced either by the Egyptians or ET's to build their own pyramids. Van Sertima pointed out the significance of the 8-700 BC time period and the extraordinary parallels between ancient America and Africa in a way I cannot better, by asking?

> Is it not strange that it is in this very period when the Negro African begins to appear in Mexico and to affect significantly the Olmec culture that the first pyramids, mummies, trepanned skulls, stela, and hieroglyphs begin to appear in America. Is it not strange that it is during this very period that a Negro-African dynasty gains ascendancy in Egypt and black pharaohs (Negro-Nubians) don the plumed serpent crown of Upper and Lower Egypt? No mummies, no pyramids, appear in this hemisphere during the heyday of these things in the Egyptian world, but suddenly they spring up in full flower at the same point in time as the Negro Nubians usher in an Egyptian cultural renaissance, restoring these features that had long lapsed in Egypt and for which there are no evolutionary precedents in America.

(Van Sertima, 2003, p.34)

In Teotihuacán, (the place where men became gods') there are three pyramids dedicated to the Sun, Moon, and to Quetzalcoatl, an Aztec god. This city was established for modern reasons not a city in the modern sense. (SOP, p.15) The Pyramid of the Sun measures 246 feet, 75m high and 738 feet 225m across making it the third largest pyramid in the world after the Pyramid of Khufu at Giza and the pyramid of Cholula.

These South American pyramids served as tombs, temples, altars and astrological sites and were dedicated to their various Gods and deities. (SOP p.13) They, along with the Egyptians and Nubians aligned their religious structures on earth to the cardinal points in the heavens, (p.44 LSRS) for example many of the pyramids in Mesoamerica were built at 32/33° degrees in line with the Tropic of Cancer which also lines up with Orion. (SOP p.7) These Temples Were Built By Intelligent Beings Called 'The Ancient Ones' Or 'The Elders'. All You Have To Do Is Look At The Measurements Of The Temples And You Will Know That This Is No Coincidence. [SOP, P.16] In fact this is common in the oral tradition of the Aztecs who believe that their God Xelhua built the Great Pyramid of Cholula.[12] As Teotihuacan means 'the place where men became gods' some archaeologists attribute this to giants who we know as deities, gods, elders and the ancient ones. (p.15) Many cultures speak of their origin from star people or ET's; the Bible mentions 'Sons of God' Genesis 6:2/4 which proves that the Annunaqi/Eloheem's influence reached every part of the world. (SOP, P.16)

Picture 7.5 – Pyramid of the Sun

Picture 7.6 - Pyramid of the Moon

Picture 7.7 – Chichen Itza, present-day Mexico, one of the
New Wonders of The World.

More striking similarities between both groups are pointed out by Dr York:

- One of the Nubian stone heads and a statue of a smiling man have an ankh, called in the Mexican language Teotihuacan or Tonacaquahuiti. This means tree of life which is the same Egyptian meaning 'key to eternal life'
- The priesthood dressed the same
- They both wore beards as an index
- Olmec temples and one of the stone heads are made from purple; purple is used by Egyptian royalty and as an emblem of powers of their supreme beings
- They have the same use of hunting dogs; Columbus recorded finding a hunting dog in his journals called Basenji when visiting the Caribbean, also used by the Egyptians. A toy dog was found in Vera Cruz Mesoamerica.
- The Olmecs wore a serpent and featherhead serpent the same as the double crown of Lower and Upper Egypt. One of their four calendars 365.25 days is identical to the Egyptian calendar
- Paper made from wood pulp was found within the Olmecs. Apart from Mexico this is only ever found in Egypt.
- Signs of hieroglyphs are found in Mexico.
- Boats made from papyrus reeds used by the Egyptians are found used in central and South America today. (P.46 LSRS)

Picture 7.8 – Toy dog found in Vera Cruz

Picture 7.9 – Olmec Terra cotta figures showing Negroid and Mongoloid elements

There are hundreds of figures of hybrid jaguar-human motifs found on clay, stone and jade figures represented as deities, which EB say was a central theme of their religion. Haven't we already seen this in Egyptian gods such as Sakhmet and Mut who wore the masks of a lion to show they had the same animal like characteristics? Frederick Peterson suggests this feline was imported from tropical regions, from where is the question, but certainly leans in favour of an outside presence. [Peterson 1959, cited in Sertima, 2003, p.33) All these similarities between the Olmecs and Egyptians are no co-incidence. The statistical probabilities of both groups sharing so many cultural similarities without contact is *very* low, almost impossible. Even if the Olmecs were influenced by Egyptian or Nubian people we still need to answer the question posed before, about the racial identity of the Olmecs and whose image and likeness the heads were made in.

> The Olmec Are The Original Nuwbuns, Who Travelled To
> This Hemisphere Millions Of Years Before The Continental
> Drift. They Became Known As The Olmecs, Meaning People
> Of The Rubber Land, By Their Descendants, The Aztec,
> Because Of The Rubber Trees That They Transported To This
> Land, Which They Cultivated Into Balls, Shoes, Raincoats Etc.
> They Were Dark Skinned, Wide Nosed, Full Lipped Nine-
> Ether, Woolly Haired People.
> [Dr Malachi Z York, Science of the Pyramids, p.21]

In Let's Set the Record straight he mentions several groups of Nuwbuns who journeyed across to the Americas at various times. They are Nuwbuns from Southern Sudan, South and central Africa, Southern Africa (Ethiopia, Uganda and Kenya) as well as Nuwbuns who were the Dogon of Mali. It is the last set of Nuwbuns we will concern ourselves with here because these Nuwbuns he says, travelled Westward to America and their descendants the Cushites, Hamites, Mizraimites, Shemites and Phutites migrated here after the flood and set up their own empires. The Holy tablets confirm "As a matter of fact, the Dogons were the descendants from the Egyptians." [HT 3:5:114]

Furthermore, Nuwbuns travelling to America millions of years ago is outside the scope of this project, we only need to be concerned with recent times i.e. Adam or after the flood. Although Dr York has stated the Olmecs were originally black he also quoted the work of Van Sertima on p.60 of LSRS. In the words of Van Sertima the Olmecs were a mixture of Mongoloid, Negroid and Mediterranean Caucasoid. After the various mixing between the three groups they blended into one unique look and were called Olmec. He adds the Negroid features do not rule out the absence of other races. Dr York had no problem referencing this; however he changed the order to Negroid, Mongoloid and Caucasoid in order of the strongest genes. (See Chapter 9)

Now we have a situation where the descendants of the original black or ancient Olmecs came to America after the flood to set up empires. After a long time they became mixed in with the Mongoloid and Caucasoid race to make what we now term as modern Olmecs dating around 1200 BC. If this is so, the colossal heads are still predominantly Negroid so cannot be in the image and likeness of modern Olmecs, it would probably be in remembrance to their original black ancestors or another group of Negroids they may have come in contact with.

Van Sertima suggests that Nubian Egyptian armies were on a metal run after the Assyrians blocked Asian sea routes. Among them was what Sertima and Constance Irwin deduce to be a Phoenician merchant captain. They were skilled sailors during that time (p.138) and it would account for the Mediterranean type figure mentioned earlier. They set out to acquire iron however they could have been knocked off course by a storm of North Atlantic currents, taking them from the North or West African coast right into the Gulf of Mexico. P.33 (See Picture 6.11) Jairazbhoy noted that Tanis was the place where Egyptian ships went out on distant expeditions, Negroid colossal stone heads were found there similar to those found amongst the Olmecs and Tanis was co-incidentally made the capital by the Nubian pharaohs. [Sertima p.269]

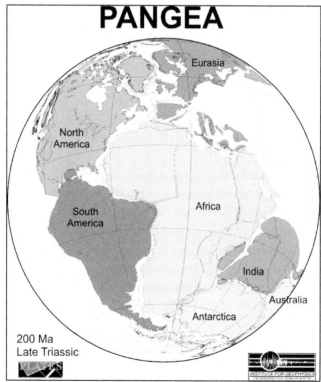

Picture 7.10 – Pangaea Supercontinent before the Continental Drift.

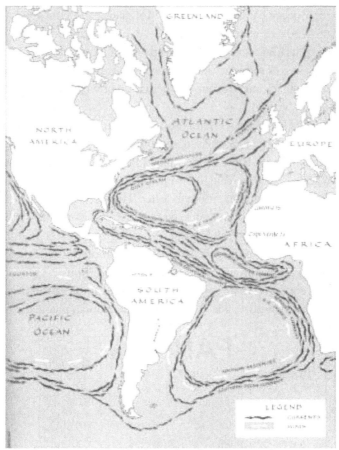

Picture 7.11 - Worldwide winds and currents, emphasizing
Atlantic drift routes from Africa to America.

When they encountered this group of shipwrecked Nubian-Egyptian sailors
they constructed huge heads to show their level of respect and reverence
towards them, they were *Gods* among the Olmecs. These outsiders are said to
have entered the Gulf of Mexico anytime between 800 – 680 BC a period
which roughly spans the 25th dynasty of Egypt. (Sertima P.147) This is crucial
especially when noting that the first period of American pyramid overlapped
the last stage of Egyptian-Nubian pyramids being built. [LSRS p.44] After this
time they borrowed many of their cultural practices such as winged disc, dogs,
calendars, pyramids, and the use of purple which are traceable today. Winged
discs were used in pre-Columbian America the same way they were used in
ancient Egypt, to symbolise unity between Upper and Lower Egypt. The
gateway of the sun in Tiahuanaco has an Egyptian winged disc symbol over the
gate as well as a frieze depicting three rows of birdmen attendants. The use of

birds with Gods in Egypt such as Haru and Tehuti and Quetzalcoatl with the Aztecs is very significant. (Sertima p.76&77)

Sertima mentions Jairazbhoy who highlighted an oral tradition in the Popul Vuh, the bible of the Quiche Maya. I will repeat it exactly here to avoid any discrepancies or miscalculations. "It appears from this oral tradition (if it relates to the Egyptian flotilla lost off North Africa) that they were blown off course into the North Atlantic current and made their landfall at a place called Panuco (north of Veracruz) in seven wooden ships or galleys." The Popul Vuh also mentions "black people and pale skinned people as among the people who came to this land from the sunrise." [Jairazbhoy, cited in Sertima p.269] The pale skinned people mentioned here along with the black people accounts for the Caucasoid element of the Olmec racial trinity quoted by Sertima.

Another oral tradition reported by Nicholas Leon says that according to the Native Americans "the oldest inhabitants of Mexico were Negroes. The existence of Negroes and giants he continues is commonly believed by nearly all the races of our soil and in their various languages they had words to designate them." Several archaeological objects such as a colossal granite head and axe of Hueyapan in Vera Cruz, Ethiopian type heads and paintings of Negroes in Teotihuacan, also found in Michoacan and Oxaca help to confirm this. [Leon, cited in Sertima p.266]

At the Temple of Danzantes (dancing figures) in Monte Alban are over 140 bas-relief figures on large stone slabs, mostly Negroid or with Negroid-Mongoloid elements. (Picture 8) (p.150) Apart from stories and African looking figures is there any physical evidence to prove this? Von Wuthenau reported Negroid skeleton's in early pre-Christian and medieval layers. (Wuthenau 1969, cited in Van Sertima p.27) A polish craniologist Wiercinski also pinpoints Negroid characteristics present in the skeletons of the ancient Mexicans. Of the skeletons examined in pre-classic Olmec cemetery of Tlatilco 13.5% were Negroid. In the Classic period at Cerro de las Mesas the figure shortened to 4.5%. This indicates that the Negroids intermarried until almost fully fusing with the native population. (Sertima P.270)

Sertima pinpointed the resemblance of a woman from pre-Columbian America with the Egyptian Queen Tiy, the Negroid mother of Tutankhamun (Picture 7.12). Sertima also points out Jairazbhoy's mention of almost identical ritual practices and funerary customs shared by both cultures most notably in the phallic cult (Picture 6.14) and the Opening of the mouth ceremony (Picture 6.12), as well as similar names for religious objects and concepts. For example:

Sun is Ra in Mexico and Peru, in Egypt it is Re or Ra.
sacred incense is copal in Mexican and kuphi in Egyptian,
paradise is yaru in Peruvian, Egyptian iaro or yaro,
sacred crocodile barque is cipak or cipactli in Mexican, sibak in Egypt.
[Sertima p.269/270]

The later civilisations of Meso-America are agreed to have been influenced by the Olmecs such as the Mayans, Aztecs, Mixtecs, Toltecs, and Zapotecs. There aren't vast differences present in the visual makeup of these civilisations, (See Pictures 7.16 & 7.17) they existed in succeeding time periods, inhabited roughly the same areas of Meso-America and had many cultural similarities.

We will now look at what happened to produce the Olmecs of today and the various civilisations of Meso-America from the original Nuwbuns in Africa.

HT 13:11:139 When he arrived to the shores he had encountered a new people, the Edomites of the Zu Aztecs, who were descendants from the Olmecs. 140 These Edomites had mixed their seed with the original Mayans, who were of Hindu mixture, extraterrestrials, from the planet Nirvana. 142 These are your original Mayas. They were living in what's called Middle or Central America. The Mayans disregarded the Olmec traditions and kept on to their Chinese traditions, of virgin, blood, and children, sacrifices to their gods who were the Reptilians of the Dogons, called Dogir, meaning "Ugly Water Beings," by the Sudanese from Nubia today. So the Olmecs told them they are not having that. They made boats for them and sent them back across with the next tides to the area of what is now Vietnam, Phnom Penh, Guam, Malay Etc. When they got there, there were people already there that had mixed in with the Malian, the Chinese and the East Indian on this side. The Mayans mixed in and settled with these people. They set up vast civilizations, one most commonly known is the Angkor, in the Central Plain of Cambodia, also called Kampuchea.
[The Holy tablets, Dr Malachi Z York]

Picture 7.12 – Left. Negro-Egyptian head of Queen Tiy, mother of Tutankhamun. Right. Negroid Sun dancer from Vera Cruz. Classic. [Taken from Sertima p.135]

Picture 7.13 - Opening of the mouth ceremony in Mexico and Egypt. Compare (a) Egyptian papyrus painting from the Book of the Dead depicting the Opening of the mouth ceremony with (b) wall painting in cave at Juxtlahuaca, with gigantic figure wearing lion skin. He holds two ceremonial objects, similar to the Egyptian, before the kneeling man. Both priests wear skins of beasts whose tails hang between their legs, and both proffer a snake-headed instrument to the kneeling bearded man. [Sertima]

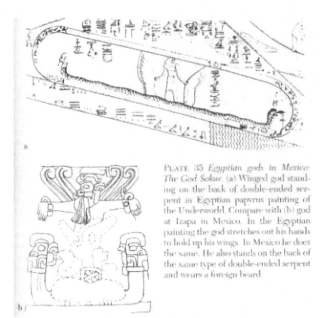

PLATE 35 *Egyptian gods in Mexico: The God Sokar.* (a) Winged god standing on the back of double-ended serpent in Egyptian papyrus painting of the Underworld. Compare with (b) god at Izapa in Mexico. In the Egyptian painting the god stretches out his hands to hold up his wings. In Mexico he does the same. He also stands on the back of the same type of double-ended serpent and wears a foreign beard.

Picture 7.14 – Winged gods of Egypt and Mexico

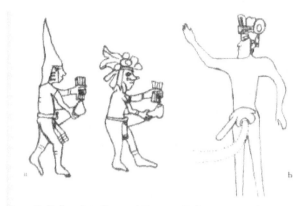

PLATE 33 *Phallic cults in Egypt and Mexico* a: Phallic procession in Mexican Codex Borbonicus holding artificial phalli; b: Olmec painting of phallic figure from Oxtotitlan with right arm upraised; c: Egyptian god Min from Medinet Habu holding phallus and raising right hand; d: Mexican terra-cotta figure with man holding phallus in the manner of the Egyptian god Min

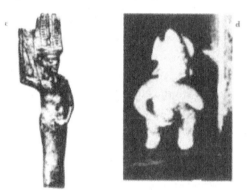

Picture 7.15 – Phallic cult in Egypt and Mexico

The above quote says the Mayans were of Hindu mixture and had Chinese traditions. Let's Set the record straight confirms this: "The Mayans were descendants of the Hindus and the Chinese. The word Maya itself is a Hindu word, which comes from the Sanskrit word, and means "Illusion'." [LSRS p.62] The Mayans set up civilisations in a city Angkor or Nuwaupic ankh-hor 'may Horus live' in Cambodia. Horus is recognized and worshipped here. Monuments of Angkor model the sinuous coils of North constellation of Draco.[13]

There are 5 races of humans, white, black, red, brown and yellow.[14] [Coon, cited in Cayce, 2000, p.55]. Diop wrote that only 3 well defined races exist, the white, the black and the yellow and the so called intermediate races probably result from crossbreeding.[15] White and black are self explanatory, red would be Indian, brown the Mexion or Aztec/Native American and yellow the Chinese. The Holy tablets 1:1:20 which we saw previously from Chapter 3 said there were "3 species of Mongoloids, and 2 species of Caucasoid, all growing out of the original Nuwaubians." So how did these races come about? The Holy tablets 1:1:16 say that '9 ether is the combination of all the existing gases of nature' and in HT 1:1:20 'Nine ether then personified themselves as flesh and blood beings; they became human beings from Atoms to Adam' by sound and electrical energy. It is therefore possible that the other ethers 6 (white), 7 (Mexion) and 8 (Cuthite/Watusi e.g. Adam) also personified into humans and each made man in their own image and likeness. This is not mentioned in Nuwaupu, however the white races are linked with beings from the Ashtar command from the Pleiades and Andromeda star constellations (Job 9:9, 38:31) and the Indian races from the planet Nirvana which came here 56 million years ago. (See Chapter 9) A period of mixing is described in Let's Set the record straight.

The Nuwbuns originally came here millions of years ago before the continental drift and set up colonies. A group of Mongolians mixed in with these Africans and produced ab-originals. Then Chinese descendants of the Teros (Picture 7.16) or Hexians, under Hsu Shen of the Shang dynasty, the yellow seed, or in Egiptian sciences the Namu, came here looking for more land and they mixed in with the Nuwbuns to produce the Mexions. The Mexions consist of Aztecs and the likes, Native Americans, ab-originals, and are referred to as Hamu, the brown seed. The actual Teros (not the Chinese descendants) came to California and bumped into the Olmecs. They lived amongst each other and produced what became known as the Native Americans. Later a period of mixing between the Native Americans and the Olmecs produced the Hopi's, who Dr York says came to America 16,000 years ago.[16] Hopi means 'peaceful people' their symbol was the falcon suggesting an Egyptian origin. When tracing language or word similarities vowels can be interchanged so the 'a' in Hapi can be substituted with the 'o' in Hopi suggesting that the Hopis are descendants of the Egyptian God Hapi, a god of the Nile. Another name for them is Navajo or Lemanites. The Hopi was chosen to create a mystic order that protected the original Dogon customs. This is why the Hopi to this day have the same exact rituals and ceremonies of the Dogon. The Nubas gave them secrets of the stars, which are held by the Dogons today, about the Sirius star constellation and the alignment, that happens every 60 years, called the Sigui. This is why they have been compared with the heads of Nuba chiefs by York and Sertima in Picture 7.2. Perhaps we can probe even deeper into the racial composition of people in Mexico using biological factors. A racial and ethnic blood type analysis of a Mexican population produced these results: Mestizo (Indian-Spanish) 60%, Amerindian or predominantly Amerindian 30%, Caucasian or predominantly

Caucasian 9%, other 1%.[17] Chapter 10 gives a greater breakdown of genetic and biological affinities.

If we take a closer look at these civilisations we will see a link. For example Sertima mentions that terra cotta portraits, golden pectorals and pipes among the Maya display an African presence. (Sertima p.27). EB say the Maya excelled in the intellectual pursuits of hieroglyphic writing, calendar making, and mathematics.

Weren't these defining characteristics of the Ancient Egyptians, also present in the Olmec culture? Religion is one of the defining aspects of a civilisation. Pictures 7.14-16 show a clear and undeniable spread of Egyptian religious practices into Olmec tradition. Upon closer examination can we find more clues into the origin and practices of these civilisations?

Mesoamerican civilizations all had their own group of Gods, we have already mentioned Quetzalcoatl and Xelhua. With this in mind, is there a possibility that their gods of 7 ether (the brown seed) manifested into physical form and made them in their image and likeness, rather than them being the product of 3 human racial mixtures? This by now 'becomes a puzzle' and each clue needs careful consideration. One of the Aztecs Gods is Tezcatlipoca who according to (Sertima p.29) and (Jordan p.211) was black. It is important to differentiate between black as a ceremonial colour and black as in Nubian features. Another god of the Mexicans is a black god of jewellers Naualpilli who is described as having kinky hair and trader God Ekchuah. Black gods with Negroid features can be found among the American Indians. [Sertima p.29] Taking consideration of the first line of this chapter, the Rizqiyians claim that they fathered various cultures in South America so this can account for a Nubian presence in those populations from a very early date. The oral tradition mentioned by Nicholas Leon is not startling; perhaps there is even a relationship between the black Rizqiyians and the black gods of Meso-America? I said this just as a simple hypothesis. However days later it seems this question was answered by 'possible telepathic suggestion', which led me to a live audio CD that I have heard countless times but always overlooked until I wrote this chapter. "Yaanuwn is one of the masters of the school of the bird, they call him the feathered bird, this is why in South America when they look over the sky they see this image of the bird, that is his school. So certain arriving masters to this plane knew what school they would go to, each galactical (what they call it?) body, had their own school on this planet."[18] He also mentions the importance of birds in another book. "The Eloheem (gods) referred to as the peacock belonged to the school of the peacock. In Nazca, Peru, South America there are several landing sites of all these schools which were drawn with one stroke. The landing sites are visible from above the ground and are hundreds of feet wide ad long. There are 18 bird figures from 30 to 300 yards long. The wingspan of the largest is 140 yards across. The different shapes of these landing sites represent different schools of the masters."[19] Yaanuwn according to Dr York is an ET being, the 19th of 24 elders in the Intergalactic Confederation who has been assigned to wake us up. The above text in no way says that there is a link between Yaanuwn and Quetzalcoatl, he clearly mentions a feathered bird instead of serpent. However the use of a feathered animal in South America narrows the probabilities and leads me to think that Yaanuwn is in fact linked to Quetzalcoatl, the Aztec God. Quetzalcoatl might be called the feathered serpent by the Aztecs however his name comes from the Quetzcalli bird who arrived in Mexico courtesy of the pochteca via South America. This bird is not native to Mexico it comes from the tropical South. The pochteca as they were known in Mexico came from the Hot Lands, a black tribe of merchants originally from the Mandingo tribe who arrived in 1310. So the people of Mali who we already know are related to the Egyptians just happen to bring in this bird who Dr York claims was associated with Yaanuwn? What seals the deal for me is the legend of a battle between an eagle and a serpent, this site was used by the Aztecs to build Tenochtitlan. If the Aztecs called Quetzalcoatl 'the feathered serpent' when the name derives from a bird then it is highly probable the serpent won the battle and they called him this thereafter. What's more, the Dogon tribe of Mali are known to have been in contact with the Nommos a Reptilian race mentioned in Chapter 2 so this could have also impacted the naming. I cannot overlook these things as mere co-incidences so I deduce one of these possibilities, 1) Yaanuwn and Quetzalcoatl are the same being but the Aztec's mistook/renamed Yaanuwn by the name Quetzalcoatl, 2) Quetzalcoatl was an inducted member into the school or (ancient brotherhood) of the bird owned by Yaanuwn and could have even received tutelage form him directly. Such things as the Intergalactic federation or 24 elders can be researched in New Age circles (See dolphins in Chpt 2) but is to be classified as 'outformation' not 'information', (knowledge from the Earth, one situation where as Dr York says 'you either believe me or you don't!'

One of these masters was Rahmah or Qaddisin, the 13th out of 24 elders.[20] His physical description is white hair, red eyes, caramel complexion, fairly thin and he lives in Shamballah (an underground city within the core of the Earth). Rama and a group of enlightened individuals led an ancient Indian empire, which according to the Ultimate Frontier was the fourth greatest on Earth. They also were said to have salvaged some of their culture from Atlantis.[21] Rama being the leader of this Indian empire was probably Indian himself so he would be a likely link for the Hindu branch of later Olmec ancestry which later produced the Mayans. If the Rizqiyian father quote is true, then who would be the mothers? They would have to be non-black to produce the later Olmecs etc. This leads me to think of two possible scenarios. The first; is that the Rizqiyians bred with a group of female Mexican Gods, the second; that like in Genesis 6:4 they had sexual relations with daughters of men and bore children. These daughters could have been created from their original Gods i.e. Genesis 1:2 in their image and likeness. Sertima even mentions "the wedding of gods and of women." [Sertima p.95]. The answers to these questions, '*I simply don't know*' but the evidence presented suggests that crossbreeding took place at some point in time between the gods and human counterparts of these groups.

Picture 7.16 – The Teros from the Planet Jomon in the star constellation Arcturus. [Taken from 1996 calendar p.1]

Picture 7.17 - Mayan 'natives' in Mexico's Disney-like Xcaret amusement park.

Picture 7.18 – Aztec people.

Picture 7.19 - An Olmec scene. The style is very similar
to the many temple reliefs in Egypt.

It is interesting that among the several groups of Nuwbuns to have entered America mentioned by Dr York, the last ones after the flood were the Dogon of Mali. Their chiefs from Nuba have appeared alongside the colossal heads (Picture 7.2) to show the matching traits and also as the ancestors of the Hopi to whom they passed on their knowledge of astronomy. We have already seen the religious influence brought by the Mandinka from Mali in relation to the God Ekchua. A similarity among the languages of Mesoamerica and the Mande people of West Africa has been noted by linguists. Sertima mentions the use of *na* among both groups. Na is at the root of words in these languages meaning mystical knowledge, intelligence, prophecy sorcery and magic. For example, *Na-at* (intelligence in Maya), *na-ul* (medicine man in Zapotec), *na-ual-li* (magician in Nahuatl). Now in African languages *na-biu* (to prophesy in Peul and Dyula) *an-na-bi* (prophet in Soso) and *na-bi-na* (intelligent in Wolof). In Malinke *nama koro* (hyena wise men) is an exact translation of the Nahuatl Coyotli-naual meaning 'coyote wise men'. D.G Brinton in his book 'Nagualism' says these Na words were brought into Mexico by foreign medicine men and was borrowed by the Natives into their language. Na or its derivatives are not found in the Mexican languages in its simplicity and true significance. (Brinton 1894, cited in Sertima p.98)

Another researcher Clyde Winters found that some of the Olmec monuments had a script which was identical to the Mende script amongst people living in West African countries Sierra Leone and Liberia.[22] There is another group of people called Mandé who are spread across 14 African countries and belong to various tribes. One of these tribes are the Mandinka, so because of this and the evidence put forth by Sertima to suggest they arrived in 1310 I can only assume that the language similarity pointed out by Winters referred to the Mandé people not Mende people. We have not seen any other evidence to suggest a Mesoamerican link from Sierra Leone. For further information read Winters 2011, 'Olmec (Mande) Loan Words in the Mayan, Mixe-Zoque and Taino Languages'. In this paper he outlines the evidence from the Otomi and Mayan languages which indicate the borrowing/copying of Manding/Mande lexical items by speakers of these languages in Pre-Columbian times.

Rainmaking rituals occur in Central America and West Africa [Sertima p.87] as well as pictures of facial scarification's which were used in olden days to mark tribal origins. (Sertima, Plate 6, p.138) In this case the Olmecs would have two recent groups of African lineage, the first by Nuwbuns from Mali to cross into America and the second by a group of shipwrecked Nubian sailors from Egypt sometime in the 25th dynasty.

Summary

We have a story which would pretty much read something along the lines of:

The ancient Olmecs were Nuwbuns full blooded black African people who migrated here millions of years before the Continental Drift. A much later group of Nuwbuns from the Dogon tribe of Mali migrated here after the so-called flood of Noah. Over time and due to the geographical location of Mexico they mixed in with American Indians till their features changed from black African to a mixture of Mongoloid, Negroid and Caucasoid. Sometime around the 25th dynasty of Egypt an Egyptian crew ended up in the Gulf of Mexico and were so important to the Olmecs they constructed huge heads in the image and likeness of these Nubian visitors. Thus a period of cultural exchange began and the Olmecs borrowed many Egyptian practices.

Notes and References

1. "Mesoamerican civilization."Encyclopædia Britannica. 2011. Encyclopædia Britannica 2006 Ultimate Reference Suite DVD 3 Nov 2011.
2. " pre-Columbian civilizations."Encyclopædia Britannica. 2011. Encyclopædia Britannica 2006 Ultimate Reference Suite DVD 18 Oct 2011.

3. *They came before Columbus* - Dr Ivan Van Sertima, Part 1 (TV Documentary)
http://www.youtube.com/watch?v=IywJ1DGuecY&feature=related [Accessed 22/10/2011]

4. "Olmec."Encyclopædia Britannica. 2011. Encyclopædia Britannica 2006 Ultimate Reference Suite DVD 1 Oct 2011.

5. York-El, Dr. Malachi Z. Scroll #360 *Let's Set the Record Straight* (Revised) ISBN#?, Egipt Publishers, Athens, Georgia.

6. *They came before Columbus* - Dr Ivan Van Sertima, Part 1 (TV Documentary)
http://www.youtube.com/watch?v=IywJ1DGuecY&feature=related [Accessed 26/10/2011]

7. *Connecting the dots the Olmecs* http://www.wafrika.com/?p=24 [Accessed 24/10/2011]

8. Sertima, I (2003) *They came before Columbus.* Random House USA. P.138

9. York-El, Dr Malachi Z. Book #191 *Science of the Pyramids.* ISBN# Egipt Publishers, Athens, Georgia. p.16.

10. Jordan M (2005) *Encyclopaedia of Gods: Over 2500 Deities of the World.* Great Britain: Kyle Cathie. P.211

11. *Aztec Arrival in Mexico.* 1) Wikipedia Aztec - In the 12th century the Nahua power centre was in Azcapotzalco, from where the Tepanecs dominated the valley of Mexico. Around this time the Mexica tribe arrived in central Mexico. 2) EB - The origin of the Aztec people is uncertain, but elements of their own tradition suggest that they were a tribe of hunters and gatherers on the northern Mexican plateau before their appearance in Mesoamerica in perhaps the 12th century;

12. Crystalinks. *Pyramids of Mesoamerica.*
http://www.crystalinks.com/pyramidmesoamerica.html [Accessed 19/11/2011]

13. York-El, Dr. Malachi Z. Scroll No #197. *The Luciferian Conspiracy* (Revised) ISBN# 1-59517-145-2, Egipt Publishers, Athens, Georgia. AD. p.321

14. Cayce E (2000) *Edgar Cayce On Atlantis.* Little, Brown and Company. P.55

15. York-El, Dr Malachi Z. Book #? *Sacred Egiptian Initiation.* ISBN#? Egipt Publishers, Athens, Georgia.

16. York-El, Dr. Malachi Z. Book No #1. *Are there Black Devils?* (Revised) ISBN# 1-, Egipt Publishers, Athens, Georgia, 2000 AD. p.270

17. Bloodbook. *Race and Ethnic Blood Type Analysis.* Available from: http://www.bloodbook.com/race-eth.html [Accessed 16/10/2011]

18. Diop C (1974) *The African Origin of Civilisation: Myth or Reality.* A Capella Books. p.43

19. York-El, Dr. Malachi Z. (Live Audio CD) *Who and What are you.* Tape excerpt at 2m.

20. York-El, Dr. Malachi Z. Scroll #15. *666 Leviathan The Beast as the Anti-Christ. Leviathan pt 1 of 4.* ISBN #1-59517-144-4. Egipt Publishers. Athens, Georgia. p.101.

21. Eklal Kueshana (2000) *The Ultimate Frontier.* The Adelphi Organisation. USA. 10th edition. p.88

22. Afrocentric World. Afrocentric e-zine. *The Afrocentric Controversy* http://clyde.winters.tripod.com/junezine/ [Accessed 10/11/2011]

Chapter 8

The modern Egyptian Population

After the many settlements and invasions of Egypt by foreigners since ancient times it is important to take a look at the ethnic composition of the people living there today. The following pictures show some of the present Egyptian population.

Picture 8.1 - Men smoking water pipes, Egypt

If one were to venture to Egypt or see Egypt in the news, sporting events, holiday advertisements, historical documentaries and other media, they would get their own personal view of an Egyptian type. Let's see what other writers have to say of this:

"The Modern Egyptians today are descended from the successive Arab settlements that followed the Muslim conquest in the 7th C, mixed with the indigenous pre Islamic population. 60% of population are Fulani or Peasant. 5% are Egyptian Copts, a Christian minority. Nubians live south of Aswan." [1]
['Lets Set The Record Straight' York (2004), p.359]

A Diverse Culture

"Most Egyptians will proudly tell you that they are descendants of the ancient Egyptians, and while there is a strand of truth in this, any Pharaonic blood still flowing in modern veins has been seriously diluted. The country has weathered invasions of Libyans, Persians, Greeks, Romans and, most significantly, the 4000 Arab horsemen who invaded in AD 640. Following the Arab conquest, there was significant Arab migration and intermarriage with the indigenous population. The Mamluks, rulers of Egypt between the 13th and 16th centuries, were of Turkish and Circassian origins, and then there were the Ottoman Turks, rulers and occupiers from 1517 until the latter years of the 18th century. Beside the Egyptians, there are a handful of separate indigenous groups, with ancient roots. The ancestors of Egypt's Bedouins migrated from the Arabian Peninsula. They settled the Western and Eastern Deserts and Sinai. The number of Bedouin in Egypt these days is around 500,000, but their nomadic way of existence is under threat as the interests of the rest of the country increasingly intrude on their once-isolated domains (see p499). In the Western Desert, particularly in and around the Siwa Oasis, are a small number of Berbers who have retained much of their own identity. They are quite easily distinguished from other Egyptians by, for instance the dress of the women - usually the *meliyya* (head-to-toe garment with slits for the eyes). Although many speak Arabic, they have preserved their own language. In the south are the tall, dark-skinned Nubians. They originate from Nubia, the region between Aswan in southern Egypt and Khartoum in Sudan, an area that almost completely disappeared in 1970s when the High Dam was created and the subsequent build-up of water behind it drowned their traditional lands."[2]
[Lonely Planet: Egypt. Maxwell et al (2007) p.66]

Ethnic composition

"The population of the Nile Valley and the Delta (comprising about 99 percent of Egypt) forms a fairly homogeneous group whose dominant physical characteristics are the result of the admixture of the indigenous African population with those of Arab ancestry. The peasant, or fellah, is less racially mixed than the town dweller. In the towns—the northern Delta towns especially—the foreign invader, Persian, Roman, Greek, Crusader, and Turk, has left behind a more heterogeneous mixture. The inhabitants of the middle Nile Valley up to Aswān are the Sa'idi (Upper Egyptians). Nubians differ culturally from other Egyptians in that their kinship structure goes beyond the lineage; they are divided into clans and broader segments, whereas among other Egyptians of the Valley and Lower Egypt known members of the lineage are the only ones recognized as kin. The deserts of Egypt contain nomadic, semi nomadic, or sedentary but formerly nomadic groups, with distinct ethnic characteristics. Apart from a few tribal groups of non-Arab stock and the mixed urban population, the inhabitants of Sinai and the northern section of the Eastern Desert are all fairly recent immigrants from Arabia. They bear some physical resemblances to Arabian Bedouins. Their social organization is tribal, each group conceiving of itself as being united by a bond of blood and as having descended from a common ancestor. Originally tent dwellers and nomadic herders, many have become semi nomads or even totally sedentary, as in northern Sinai. The southern section of the Eastern Desert is inhabited by the Hamitic Beja. They bear a distinct resemblance to the surviving depictions of predynastic Egyptians. The Egyptian Beja are divided into two tribes—the Abābdah and the Bishārīn. The Abābdah occupy the Eastern Desert south of a line between Qinā and al-Ghurdaqah; there are also several groups settled along the Nile between Aswān and Qinā. The Bishārīn live mainly in The Sudan, although some dwell in the Elba Mountain region, their traditional place of origin. Both the Abābdah and Bishārīn people are nomadic pastoralists who tend herds of camels, goats, and sheep. The inhabitants of the Western Desert, outside the oases, are of mixed Arab and Berber descent. They are divided into two groups, the Saʾādī and the Mūrābitīn. The Saʾādī regard themselves as descended from Banū Hilāl and Banū Sulaymān, the great Arab tribes that immigrated into North Africa in the 11th century. The most important and numerous of the Saʾādī group are the Awlād Alī. The Mūrābitīn clans occupy a client status in relation to the Saʾādī and may be descendants of the original Berber inhabitants of the region. Originally herders and tent dwellers, the Bedouin of the Western Desert have become either seminomadic or totally sedentary. They are not localized by clan, and members of a single group may be widely dispersed. The original inhabitants of the oases of the Western Desert were Berber. Many peoples have since mixed with them, including Egyptians from the Nile Valley, Arabs, Sudanese, Turks, and, particularly in the case of al-Khārijah, black Africans—for this was the point of entry into Egypt of the caravan route from Darfur, the Darb al-Arbaīn. In addition to the indigenous groups, there are in Egypt a number of small foreign ethnic groups. In the 19th century there was rapid growth of communities of unassimilated foreigners, mainly European, living in Egypt; these acquired a dominating influence over finance, industry, and government. In the 1920s, which was a peak period, the number of foreigners in Egypt was in excess of 200,000, the largest community being the Greeks, followed by the

Italians, British, and French. Since Egypt's independence the size of the foreign communities has been greatly reduced." [3]
[Encyclopaedia Britannica 2006, Egypt]

The CIA World Factbook based on the 2006 census class Egyptian as the main ethnic group at 99.6%, and other at 0.4%. [4] These sources are all in agreement that the majority of the population are descendants from an admixture of an Arab and African (indigenous) type. Followed by, recent immigrants of Arabian descent such as Bedouins and Berbers, while Nubians occupy Aswan and the Southern Egypt. It is interesting to note that the writer of the Egypt Lonely Planet guide whose motives are in no way similar to mine says there is a strand of truth that the modern Egyptians are descendants from the ancient Egyptians.

Notes and References

1. York-El. Dr Malachi Z. Scroll #360 *Lets Set the record straight.* ISBN#?
Egipt Publishers, Athens, Georgia. P.348
2. Virginia Maxwell, V. Fitzpatrick, M. Jenkins, S. Sattin, A (2006) *Egypt* (Lonely Planet Country Guide) Lonely Planet Publications. 8th Revised edition. p.322
3. "Egypt."Encyclopædia Britannica. 2011. Encyclopædia Britannica 2006 Ultimate Reference Suite DVD.
4. CIA: *The World Factbook, Egypt.* Available from:
https://www.cia.gov/library/publications/the-world-factbook/geos/eg.html
Accessed 19/3/2012

Chapter 9

Introduction to Physical anthropology and archaeogenetics of Africans

The previous chapters have presented historical and cultural evidence of a dynastic black race being the main inhabitants of ancient Egypt as well as linking several African/black South American tribes to Egypt. Written historical evidence is useful, but to 'seal the deal', prove without a shadow of a doubt, one would have to use physical and scientific evidence. Chapter 9 will give a short introduction to race, genetics and the unique traits of African peoples. Chapter 10 will examine results of physical and genetic testing of Egyptian and African peoples. A recent 'outformation class' said, *"You must know your workings Nuwaupians as Ontologists. That is the inside of you and the outside of you. Know your organs and how they work, you must know thyself!"*

Anthropology is the study of mankind especially its societies and customs. [The Oxford Dictionary of Current English] "Physical anthropology is the study of biological features of ancient and modern humans, including health, nutrition, mortality, genetics and physical variability in the past and present, and of humans' primate relatives and fossil ancestors."[1] This and other various scientific disciplines will be used for evidence. "And what better culture is there to study archaeology than Egypt?", because they practiced the art of mummification which prevented bodies from decay, a large number of bodies were buried in tombs so they are easily accessible and the desert sands of the Sahara naturally preserved bodies. The author Herbert Wendt mentioned in Chapter 1, noted that Egyptian skeletons show the same racial characteristics as Nubian tribes. What are these racial characteristics? To an untrained individual, one might not notice the difference between a Negroid or Caucasoid skeleton but biologists recognize that the races exhibit different physical and genetic traits.

Background on race and genetics

A dictionary definition of **race** is; "race2 n. each of the major divisions of humankind, each having distinct physical characteristics." [The Oxford

Dictionary of Current English] I don't know who came up with this definition but it is said that "races are distinct genetically divergent populations within the same species with relatively small morphological and genetic differences." The head of the human genome project and a former president of the USA mentioned that we are all, regardless of race, genetically 99.9% per cent the same. Sarich and Miele wrote a book on race where they argue that human racial differences are both real and significant and provide powerful evidence of the significance, not the triviality, of those differences.[2]

Some see race as biologically invalid categorizations and social constructs which at times may be the cause of racism. Others see the races as subspecies; geographically isolated and genetically differentiated populations.[3] In a modern day crime investigation, the police will normally have a description of a suspect which includes their race identified by black, white or Asian. Whether or not we like the terminology or argue its scientific faults, it *does* exist, and there are underlying biological reasons for this variation among humans which we will see in the course of this chapter. The misrepresentation of the Egyptians warrants a thorough understanding of race and the science behind it. We have seen in chapter 6 that some prefer to split the races into either 3 (white, black, yellow) or 5, (white, black, red, brown and yellow). Each race has physical differences, these are determined by biological factors such as genes and DNA. However, most of the variation in human genetic makeup can be attributed to differences within these so-called races than between them.[4] So to begin with, what is a gene?

Gene, a hereditary unit that occupies a specific location on a chromosome and determines a particular characteristic in a organism. [The American heritage dictionary]

Put simply a gene is a section of DNA. 'Genetics is the study of the inheritance of biological characteristics... genetics is also the study of genetic information itself and the way in which it functions at a molecular level.'[5] One subject of study here is cell reproduction. There are two types of cell reproduction; mitosis for growth and repair and meiosis for sexual reproduction. In meiosis a cell splits to form new cells with half the number of chromosomes to produce gametes (egg or sperm) for sexual reproduction. This only occurs in the ovaries or testes, and the gametes contain different genetic information to each other and to the parent cell. In mitosis a cell divides in to two cells which are identical and exact replications of the parent cell.

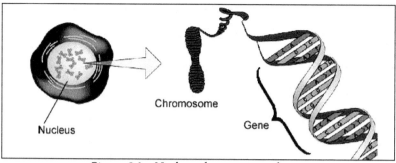

Picture 9.1 – Nucleus, chromosome and gene

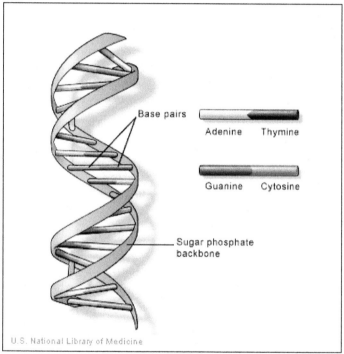

Picture 9.2 – DNA Structure

Chromosomes are rod shaped bodies found in the nucleus of cells, they contain long strands of genetic information called, DNA. DNA is the common material for inheritance in all living things and is at the centre of genetics. DNA (deoxyribonucleic acid) carries the genetic code that determines the characteristics of an organism, such as skin colour, height and sometimes even behaviour. Each gene has the code for creating a specific protein. The sequence of bases in the gene controls which amino acids are created and joined to make a specific new protein (or enzyme) molecule.

A nucleotide consists of a combination of the sugar deoxyribose, a phosphate group and one of four nitrogenous bases, (Adenine, Guanine, Cytosine and Thymine). C and G can be paired in any order, the same goes for A and T. There are 24 different ways to group these four nucleotides in every possible order.[6] The significance of this number is mentioned in the Holy Tablets.

> 1:9:226 The Chimpanzee and Gibbon evolved into Humims, and they became your Nubuns, the original Pygmy tribe. 227 Their woolly hair comes from the Supreme Beings with _24 strains of genes coated in melanin_. 228 These are the original Anunnagi, Aluhum. 229 The guardians of the Nubians with nine ether. [The Holy Tablets, Dr Malachi Z York]

One key component of a Negroid's biochemistry is that we have the most amount of melanin, other races have it in lesser quantities. (For more information Read: The Melanin-ite Children Scroll #133 and People of the Sun Scroll #147 by Dr Malachi Z York.) Melanin is a pigment which causes the dark colouration of skin in Africans and is produced in the pineal gland. It is produced by cells in the epidermis called melanocytes. A melanocyte is an epidermal (skin) cell capable of synthesizing melanin. The pituitary gland secretes Melanocyte Stimulating hormone, this regulates skin colour in human beings by stimulating melanin synthesis in melanocytes and melanin granule dispersal in melanophores (pigment cell containing melanin in animals). Melanin is found throughout the human body,[7] but each race has different levels of melanin production which accounts for the variation in skin colour. Tyrosine (TYR) an amino acid is converted to melanin by the enzyme tyrosinase. This is what gives your hair its colour and keeps it from turning grey until old age.

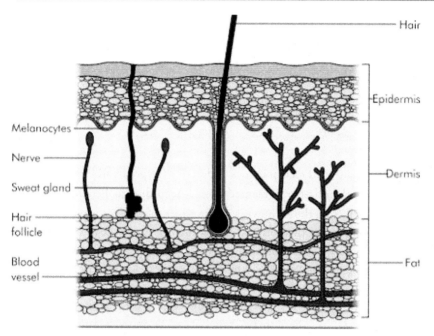

Picture 9.3 - The Structure of the skin

1:1:38 When you see full spectrum light in its physical state, it manifests as blackness. That is, all light and colour combined are blackness. And the manifestation of the solid form of light is melanin. [The Holy Tablets, Dr Malachi Z York]

Melanin does more than add colour to the skin and is extremely important. The sun emits 3 types of UV light (UVA, UVB and UVC) UVA and B is the main environmental cause of most skin cancers. UV radiation is a part of the electromagnetic spectrum, such as radio waves, microwaves and X-rays. Each has different frequencies and wavelengths, and can cause genetic mutation or chemical changes to DNA.[8] UV is absorbed by water in living tissue so can't damage organs. According to MacMillan Cancer Support, a leading charity for Cancer patients in the UK:

"Black- or brown-skinned people have an extremely low risk of developing skin cancer because the pigment melanin in their skin gives them protection."[9]

According to GCSE Biology:

We cannot see or feel ultraviolet radiation, but our skin responds
to it by turning darker. This happens in an attempt to reduce the
amount of ultraviolet radiation that reaches deeper skin tissues.
Darker skins absorb more ultraviolet light, so less ultraviolet
radiation reaches the deeper tissues. This is important because
ultraviolet radiation can cause normal cells to become
cancerous.[10]

Herodotus mentioned melanochroes to describe Egyptians and Ethiopians, in
recognition of their darkly pigmented skin.[11] According to 'People of the Sun',
melanin is a gift from the Annunaqi.[12] The white race are more prone to
developing skin cancer than other races because they have the least amount of
melanin, this is evident in their skin and hair. The most at risk are fair skinned
people with red hair and freckles. Episodes of overexposure to the sun e.g.
people who work outdoors for a living are at an increased risk of developing
skin cancer. It is the UV light/radiation which causes the chemical changes
and damage to DNA. There are two types of cancer caused by sun damage, *non
melanoma*, a less serious type of skin cancer or *malignant melanoma* a more
aggressive form. This makes them physically unsuitable for the hot climate of
Africa, and less likely to have been the original inhabitants. Nature generally
puts each organism, (plant, animal or human life) not only in an environment
they can survive in, but can thrive in! These are not racist statements but
scientific facts. An article by FOX news reported that black Americans are
genetically stronger than white Americans.[13] The study showed that
Europeans have less genetic variation as a result of experiencing two
population bottlenecks. This allowed "bad" mutations to build up in the
European population, something that the more genetically varied African
population had more success in weeding out.

Africans *according* to that study proved to be genetically stronger, and
there are certain genetic conditions that can affect each race of people, and
other health conditions that run in families such as diabetes and breast cancer.
One genetic condition that affects people of African and Caribbean descent is
sickle cell anaemia or sickle cell disease (SCD). Someone with SCD has two
sickle haemoglobin (HbS) genes inherited from their parents, different from
the normal haemoglobin (HbA). If they have one HbA gene this makes them a
carrier and not affected by SCD. Haemoglobin is a protein that carries oxygen
from the lungs to all parts of the body. The HbS gene causes an abnormality of
haemoglobin in red blood cells, and as a result of giving up oxygen to the
tissues, it sticks together to form long rods inside the red blood cells, making

these cells rigid and sickle-shaped. Normal red blood cells can bend and flex easily. Because of their shape, sickled red blood cells can't squeeze through small blood vessels as easily as the normal cells. The small blood vessels get blocked by the cluster of cells which then stops the oxygen from getting through to where it is needed. This in turn can lead to severe pain and damage to organs. In Britain (at least 1 in 10-40 has the sickle cell trait and 1 in 60-200 has Sickle cell disorder, SCD). It is estimated there are over 6,000 adults and children with SCD in Britain at present. It is actually beneficial for Africans living in Africa to be a carrier because they are more tolerant to malaria and show less severe symptoms when infected. SCD is an evolutionary mutation in Africans. The shape of the blood cell is less effective in taking or releasing oxygen, and therefore malaria parasites cannot complete their life cycle in the cell. African Americans are also susceptible to diseases such as prostate cancer, hypertension and diabetes, this is environmental and genetically related.[14]

Most DNA is located in the cell nucleus (nuclear DNA), but a small amount of DNA can also be found in the mitochondria (mitochondrial DNA or mtDNA).[15] mtDNA are structures within cells that convert the energy from food into a form that cells can use. mtDNA contains 37 genes, 13 of these provide instructions to make ATP the cells main energy source. "The remaining genes provide instructions for making molecules called transfer RNA (tRNA) and ribosomal RNA (rRNA), which are chemical cousins of DNA. These types of RNA help assemble protein building blocks (amino acids) into functioning proteins."[16] The best way to trace ancestral relations is by mtDNA. The HTs 1:9:265 says "The Mitochondria DNA is only given from the mother to daughter, the male species does not have any Mitochondria DNA." However the ancestry website says that both males and females have mtDNA, and either sex can take a mtDNA test because during fertilization mtDNA from the father is destroyed so a child (whether male or female) can inherit mtDNA from its mother.[17] For if males had no mtDNA they wouldn't be able to test their maternal lineage. It seems the HT's are wrong on this occasion. Male mtDNA is thought to not be transferred because it is located in the tail of the sperm, which is lost during the fertilization process, whereas a female's mtDNA is in the centre of the egg. New evidence has shown ubiquitin tagging (which tags a molecule for destruction) of paternal DNA if it enters the egg.[18] Only males can take Y-chromosome tests because only males have Y chromosomes, females have XX.

The following scientists contributed well to the study of mtDNA. Douglas Emory of Emory University conducted a study of the mitochondria of 800 women in the 1980's. His conclusion at a scientific conference in July

1986, was that the mitochondria in all of them appeared to be so similar that these women must have all descended from a single female ancestor. Wesley Brown of the University of Michigan then picked up the research and compared the Mitochondria of 21 women from diverse geographical and racial backgrounds. He concluded that they owed their origin to "a single Mitochondria Eve" who had lived in Africa between 300,000 and 180,000 years ago. Rebecca Cann of the University of California at Berkeley, had obtained the placentas of 147 women of different races and geographical backgrounds who gave birth at San Francisco hospitals, she extracted and compared their Mitochondria. The conclusion was that they all had a common female ancestor who had lived between 300,000 and 150,000 years ago. [Read HT 1:9:257]

The conclusion of these studies reached by Dr York is that women existed before men. [The Holy Tablets 1:9:266] "This is just further proof that the first person to walk on the planet was a female." Although this might seem strange and adverse to the bible which so many believe, there are many scientific facts to prove this. (Read Genetic Kiss and The Black Book) Truth is stranger than fiction. I will not mention them here to save going off topic!

The Egyptians practiced 'xenophobia', the practice of not allowing female members of the royal family to marry foreigners. This makes the female Egyptian or at least those from the royal family a perfect specimen to find their true origin. Together with the female fossils of Ardi found in Ethiopia in 1994 puts females ahead of males in testing for genetic affinities. If the earliest human ancestor came from Africa then Egypt in Ancient times would be less likely to have been populated by a non-black race.

Scientists now recognize that there is greater variation within racial groups than between them.[19] Geneticists attribute this to Africans descending from a large number of homo-sapiens, while the non-African races have very similar genetic constitutions because they descended from a very small number of homo-sapiens who broke out from sub-Saharan Africa around 100,000 BC.[20]

A haplogroup is a group of similar haplotypes that share a common ancestor having the same Single Nucleotide Polymorphism (SNP) mutation in both haplotypes. A haplotype is a set of alleles (an alternative form of a gene that can occupy a particular place on a chromosome) of a group of closely linked genes which are usually inherited as a unit. (Gale Encyclopaedia of Medicine) These haplotypes are how we find what genes and their mutations are responsible for. A haplogroup can be used to trace ancestry as it represents a major branch of the family tree of Homo sapiens. They are useful in tracking the early migrations of population groups so are usually associated with a specific region. A haplogroup can be tested by a Single Nucleotide Polymorphism (SNP) test, this looks for a rare mutation on the genes. Haplogroups are divided among maternal mtDNA or paternal Y-DNA. So for example, a mtDNA haplogroup is defined as all of the female descendants of the single person who first showed a particular polymorphism, or SNP mutation. A SNP mutation identifies a group who share a common ancestor far back in time, since SNPs rarely mutate. Haplogroups are assigned letters of the alphabet, and sub-clades consist of additional number and letter combinations, for example M1a4.[21] These are one of the most important factors in looking for biological affinities which we will see in Chapter 10.

Blood groups are another topic of interest. There are 30 blood group systems, the most important blood groups are ABO and RhD. Blood groups are determined by a protein (antigen) on the surface of the red blood cell, ABO has A and B antigens and RhD has D antigens. In the ABO system a person can either have A antigen on their red blood cells, B antigens or a combination of A and B (AB). An individual can also be blood group O, meaning they don't have either A or B antigens. The RhD system is a lot simpler, 85% of people have the D antigen on their red blood cells and are RhD positive, the remaining 15% lack the D antigen and are RhD negative. Your blood group is defined by your ABO group together with your RhD group. For instance, someone who is group A and RhD negative is known as A negative.[22] Blood types are inherited just like the colour of your eyes and hair and are important if you ever need a blood transfusion or else you could die! Your body's immune system works around your body to find antigens that aren't yours, any foreign body (bacteria or virus) will not have your antigen on its cell surface. Therefore if you are given B group blood when you are group A your body recognizes the B antigen as a foreign body and will kill the blood cell causing you to get destruction of your blood cells to a detrimental level. And vice versa. AB blood groups can receive blood from A or B. O can give blood to any blood group as it has no antigens but can only receive blood from O groups as the antigens on A, B and AB blood will be destroyed by the body. Luckily O is the largest blood group in existence, AB is rare, AB- is even rarer. Where it gets interesting is that certain blood types are only present or occur more frequently in specific races or ethnic minorities. 25% of Black and South Asian people are blood group B, compared to only 9% of Western European people. A rare blood type U negative is only found in African and Caribbean communities. 68% of the black population are Duffy negative whereas almost all white people are Duffy positive.[23] The reason so many blacks are duffy negative is because the antigen is also a receptor for malaria, therefore if black people had it in Africa they would all contract Malaria and die.

Picture 9.4 – Afro of an Egyptian man

The hair of African people is unique, in Nuwaupu it is called '9-ether hair', which manifests in the physical as tight curls, grown in the shape of a 9 symbolizing birth and growth. Hair is different between the races, and according to The Belgravia centre, (the UK's leading hair loss clinic and pharmacy) is split up into Asian hair, Afro-Caribbean hair and Caucasian hair. What differs between each group is the hair's density, speed of growth or the shape of the hair follicle in the scalp, each race has it slightly different. All hair regardless of race is essentially made up of the same thing. Each strand of hair consists of three layers, the cuticle, cortex and medulla, and a protein called keratin is the hair's main component. What determines the hair shape is the shape of the follicle. Afro-Caribbean hair sprouts from an oval hair follicle and grows in a spiral fashion, Asian hair grows from a round hair follicle and is usually bone straight and the follicles vary in Caucasian hair and can grow in between curly and straight but never as curly as that of a Negroids. The hair keeps its original shape during life. Caucasian hair has the greatest density of all three types, grows at 1.2 cm per month with an estimated 86-146,000 hairs. Afro-Caribbean's have the next most dense hair, growing at 0.9cm per month, with 50-100,000 average hairs. Asians have the least dense hair but the fastest growth rate at 1.3cm per month, and an average 80-140,000 hairs.[24]

Archaeogenetics

This section will incorporate archaeogenetics; the use of genetics, archaeology and linguistics to explain and discuss the origin and spread of Homo sapiens. This methodology can be used to gain valuable insight into human history and population movements in prehistoric times.[25] It is important this is evaluated and understood since part of the scope of real spiritual and universal knowledge includes the time and origin of races, cultures and what each race is supposed to represent, according to 'Our True Roots'.[26]

There are competing theories on the origins of anatomically modern humans relating first to the geographic location and secondly to the number of ancestors we descend from. With location; we have the *monogenesis* and *polygenesis* view. The first claims that humans originated from a single point in Africa and migrated across the world, the second that different populations independently evolved from homo erectus to home sapiens in different areas.[27] With ancestry; we have the mono-human or 'mtEve' (as I like to call it) view that we all come from a single ancestor, or the poly-human view that we come from more than one human. One could argue that by default the poly-human theory ties in with polygenesis since it is stated they evolved independently.

Cheikh Anta Diop discussed the Out of Africa theory in his video, 'The African Origin of humanity'. "A polygenetic; believes or contends that man was born in Africa and also in Asia in other words that there were several locations in the world where man finds his origin."[28] He later invalidates the polygenetic view by saying "but under closer scrutiny there are two things that made this theory fall apart more or less. The first is that nature never strikes twice in its evolution it doesn't ever hit the same place two times; nature doesn't create twice the same being. In the animal kingdom you can see that throughout the evolution of animals a being was created and it either disappeared or changed somewhat or a new being was completely, was created but never the same being twice and to remain strictly scientific it doesn't make common sense to say man was created twice." The psychic Edgar Cayce (though not very scientific) gave a reading stating that man *appeared* five times. "The period in the world's existence from the present time being ten and one-half million (10,500,000) years ago. When man came in the earth plane as the lord of that in that sphere, man appeared in five places then at once-the five senses, the five reasons, the fives spheres, the five developments, the five nations." (5748-1; May 28, 1925)[29]

American anthropologist Carleton S. Coon who I mentioned previously in Chapter 6 asserted that human evolution stemmed from Europe and Asia, a polygenetic view which omitted Africa. This idea was abandoned in the 1970's and 80's because of new findings and absolute datings,[30] an article published in the journal Nature proved that modern humans originated from "a single area in Sub-Saharan Africa,"[31] proving monogenesis. The tests mentioned previously by American Scientists in the 1980's confirm the mono-human or 'mtEve' view that man originated from a *single* common ancestor. So we have scientific confirmation of monogenesis and a mono-human. The Penguin Atlas of African History highlights the early history of 'homo sapien sapiens' the most modern form of man.[32]

1) purely sub Saharan phase involving the replacement of Rhodesian man with the modern form
2) a break out from sub Saharan Africa to Asia around 100,000 BC with spread across Asia to Australasia by 50,000 BC
3) an advance across Europe resulting in the extinction of the Neanderthals by about 30,000 BC. This 'out of Africa' hypothesis has now vanquished the rival candelabra theory. (In which modern races evolved in parallel from local varieties of homo sapiens i.e. Europeans from Neanderthals, Africans from Rhodesian man etc.

If science confirms the 'Out of Africa' theory and 'mtEve' then how and why are we all different? Part of the monogenesis belief is that because man evolved from one common ancestor, then when these descendants left Africa they mutated or adapted to different climates which resulted in the variety of skin tones and other differences we have today.

> Humans began to diversify as they migrated out of Africa and populated the rest of the world adapting to new climates, diets, and living conditions. Over tens of thousands of years, these ancient populations became isolated and their DNA changed until they became genetically distinct from one another. These deep ancestral groupings are referred to today as haplogroups.[33]

In Diop's video the presenter asked the question, "To what extent or in what way do blacks feature in the origin of man?" Diop answers, "the answer is the first man was black and it was he who gave birth to other races of the world."

There is a slide of 3 skulls, the first is a skull of a modern African man, the middle is one of a black man in prehistory called the 'Grimaldi' man and the right is that of 'Cro-Magnon' man, which you may remember from the Sliders TV show. "40,000 years ago the man in the middle left Africa and went to Europe... It was between 40 and 20,000 years ago that the man in the middle left Africa to go into Europe at a time during what is called the final or last glaciation. The climate in Europe was extremely cold it was much colder than it is now and during this period of some 20,000 years he underwent the adaptation to become what we know as white man." Dr York and Frances Cress Wellsing, author of the Isis papers say that white people were originally descended from blacks as melanin recessive beings who left Africa, and over a period of time and DNA mutations became the white race.[34] There is more to the story than this, see Canaanites and Flugelrods for a full overstanding.

Nina Jablonski, a distinguished professor of biological anthropology at Pennsylvania University also proposes that differing skin colours are simply our bodies' adaptation to varied climates and levels of UV exposure.[35] She mentions Charles Darwin recognized that dark skinned people are found close to equator, while light skin people are found close to the poles and quotes him in her talk.

> "Of all the differences between the races of man, the colour of the skin is the most conspicuous and one of the best marked..."
> "It was formerly thought that differences of this kind could be accounted for by long exposure to different climates... This view has been rejected chiefly because the distribution of the variously coloured races, most of whom must have long inhabited their present homes, does not coincide with corresponding differences of climate."
> [(Charles Darwin –The Descent of Man p.192-193]

Darwin's quote above disagrees with her idea that our bodies adapted to different climates but she explains, that's because he did not have access to NASA! She also goes on to say that as humans moved out of tropical regions, lightly pigmented skin evolved to maximize vitamin D protection in the skin. However the quote from the MacMillan website above says that skin changes colour to *deal* with the UV light, not to maximize vitamin D production.

Vitamin D production is determined by the amount of sunlight but it's not the *cause* of skin changing colour, so it can be argued that white people became better at absorbing vitamin D in less sunnier climates because they needed it more. This shows us that white people couldn't have been indigenous to Egypt or Africa because they would have darker skin as a result of the UV light which would be much less in Europe according to her map! Vitamin D is the only vitamin that cannot be gained by food intake, it has to be received by the sun. Sunlight converts two compounds 7-dehydrocholesterol, and ergosterol to vitamin D3 and D2.[36] I do however agree with her data that UV radiation levels on the Earth's surface would produce darker melanated people.

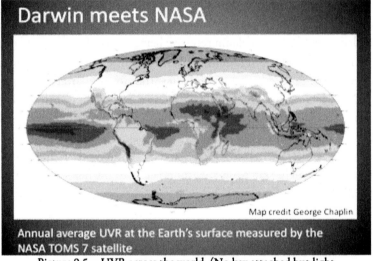

Annual average UVR at the Earth's surface measured by the NASA TOMS 7 satellite

Map credit George Chaplin

Picture 9.5 – UVR across the world. (No key attached but light colours probably represent sunnier/darker climates)

Science has confirmed both theories, and this theory of genetic mutation can be applied to blacks and whites in the sense that we are opposites or adverse to one another, but is it logical to do so for all the races and say we all descended from this one single being?' I am aware that life started out as a one celled organism and after billions of years evolved into multicellular life, which is why all organisms on Earth are genetically related, called the 'Tree of Life'.[37] So in *theory* the same thing could be said for human life. However with all the races and sub races in the world today "how could this one being be solely responsible for them." We know we are talking about one being because they refer to her as 'mitochondrial Eve' and a 'single' or 'common ancestor'. Nuwaupu speaks of parthenogenesis meaning 'virgin birth',[38] where females can procreate without a man by the secretion of seminal fluids from the bartholin gland located at either side of the vaginal orifice. Some species of reptile are able to do this today such as salamanders, newts and whiptail lizards. This would explain how she was able to reproduce without a man. Is there more to the story than human's adapting to different climates as a result of leaving Africa? I think the difference in race and genetics goes beyond the out of Africa theory and these differences were established at a very early part of our evolution. My work in chapter 7 suggested a multiregional origin theory so I am a polygenist by default. As much as I or anyone might have their own views or hypotheses, no one (not even me!) can argue with scientific fact, so the following is my attempt to find some truth within this rather than dismiss it altogether.

PERHAPS mtEVE WAS NINTI...?

Both Ninti and Eve can be traced to Hawwah. The Sumerian name Ninti means 'lady of the rib' or 'lady of life'. One of Ninti's names is Hawwah, which in Hebrew means 'mother of all living'. And she also goes by the name of Nekaybaw 'tribal leader'. The Black Book says Ninti mixed her blood with 14 females of the Homo-Erectus to fashion a new being Adam 49,000 years ago. One source says this superior Annunaki specimen used 20% of her genetic material and 80% of an inferior human specimen, (probably the homo-erectus).[39] Whoever the mtEve was, they go back to between 300-150,000 years ago determined by the rate of natural mutation of Mitochondria. (HT 1:9:259) The Annunaqi have been around long before this, so we cannot discount Ninti because of time. For if we all have a single ancestor there is no other explanation I can think of. Since we descended from primates, the final descendants in the evolution of a chimpanzee or orang-utan in any part of the world cannot account for racial differences, or can it? This is where it gets interesting. York suggests that people look different because we descended from different animals.[40] For example a branch of the gibbon evolved into the Indian race, a branch of the orang-utan evolved into the Mongolian race[41] and the earlier quote in the Holy Tablets 1:9:226 that the Chimpanzee and Gibbon evolved into Nubians. The Black Book says Ninti mixed the Homo erectus with lares/simians, chimpanzees, gibbons and orang-utans, which could explain these differences. The logic of this makes more sense than a sole 'Out of Africa theory' and it is a well known fact there is a missing link, whatever it may be. I cannot fathom the out of Africa theory *solely* as the truth and I think there is more likely to be a scenario that combined the two. The only way for this theory to work in my view is if other gods apart from the

Annunaqi came down to experiment with the humans on Earth. I found later in my 3rd draft that this was confirmed by Dr York who says:

> All races from this planet have had Extraterrestrial involvement
> from the Sumerians, to the Aztecs, the Hopis, to the
> Aborigines, to the Egyptians, to the original Nubian Hebrews
> in the form of prophets. The Aryans also had star visitations
> (The Ashtar Command from Pleiades and Aldebaran), the
> Procyonians, and the Venerians.[42]

The Indian race are said to come from the starship Nirvana so they could have also done their fair share of experimentation. The origin of these ET's is a million dollar question, but they could have manifested from their respective ethers (7, 8, and 9) just as the Etherians did. (HT 1:1:29). The problem here is that she only mixed with 14 test subjects, and the rest of the world would have missed her lovely DNA. The Earth would have to be very short in numbers for this to work, so this event could have been right at the very beginning or after a cataclysmic calamity. This single being or her descendants would have to mix with every other being and racial type if the scientists result's about a single ancestor is correct. Another possibility is that the beings without Ninti's DNA became extinct or were wiped out by Ninti's clan of Adamites similar to what is described by the fate of the Neanderthal man. Professor Goldstein a molecular biologist from UCL says because we all have remarkably similar genes, this suggests our ancestors survived a bottleneck in Africa just before 100,000 years ago. A bottleneck is an event that reduces the genetic difference, or diversity, in a population of animals.[43] If there were others separate from this entity who survived and mated to this day, then a single ancestor would not be possible. Perhaps this was even done in controlled breeding environments such as *Shimti* 'where the breath of life is breathed'.

An article published in the journal 'Science Express' to study African genetics "traced the genetic structure of Africans to 14 ancestral population clusters that correlated with ethnicity and shared cultural and/or linguistic properties."[44] I laughed when I read this article at the co-incidence that both parties confirm this number 14. Although this does not prove Ninti's existence it increase's tenfold the likelihood of the event in the Black Book. (Read Scroll #154 'Nibiru and the Annunaqi: Fact or Fiction') This proves the Black Book is divinely inspired and as Dr York classifies it 'Outformation'. Some place the exit point of modern humans out of Africa near the middle of the Red Sea in East Africa[45] some 100,000 years ago.[46] Point 3 above by Penguin does not mention the extinction of an Asian form of homo sapien e.g. 'Pithecanthropus erectus' more commonly known as Java Man, from Indonesia or sinanthropus so I dispute that an extinction in Europe justifies the monogenesis theory.

Science has made huge leaps since Charles Darwin's time, but the adaptation view posed by scientists including Diop and Jablonski bypasses an important principal of genetics, *inheritance*. If part of genetics is to study how genes are passed on to offspring, then their theory proposes that:

- we all started out as one race, for us to migrate and evolve into what we are today,
- environmental factors are more important than genes itself.

In genetics there is something called genotype and phenotype. A genotype is the genetic makeup of a cell or organism. A phenotype is the observable character, the expression of this genetic information. For example, some pea plants have either white or violet flowers. It is possible for two organisms to have the same phenotype but different genotypes. The flower colour for peas in this scenario has 2 possible genotypes that give rise to the violet flowered phenotype. If we duplicate this to the human level we know from Belgravia that hair in all races is made up of the same thing, genotype; but the phenotype in relation to the texture and curliness of the hair in Africans is distinct from other races. Was this texture lost by leaving Africa and adapting because there was a lack of sun heat to curl the hair, or was it passed down from the supreme beings with 9 ether hair? (HT 1:9:120/226). For example, given that Egyptian Gods in the Ogdoad and Sedjet are twins, and the Yoruba culture produces the highest rate of twins in the world this suggests an inheritance of DNA. It is believed but not proven that their high intake of yams and cassava make chemicals that release more than one egg. But I am sure there are other Africans with similar diets, so why don't they have a large occurrence of twins?

According to Oxlade 'Genotype is the major determinant of phenotype but environmental and developmental factors have a powerful modifying influence.'[47] Keita explains that phenotype is a complex issue and that an adult's morphological phenotype is the sum of that individuals genetic constitution and its reaction with the environment, which is affected by nutrition, disease and local climatic variables.[48] So I disagree with Jablonski's claim, in any case why should anyone believe NASA, they lied about the moon landing and the Martian sphinx. I mentioned the black couple who gave birth to a white baby earlier; this is likely to be the result of a genetic mutation not climate change. A good example is provided by Oxlade who demonstrates that

DNA in cell organelles can be used to prove that DNA is genetic material. He says, "sometimes plant cells contain chloroplasts with a mutation in their DNA that prevents the chloroplasts from making the green pigment chlorophyll. The chloroplasts are therefore colourless. The colourless character is inherited whenever a mutant chloroplast dies, and as the plant grows and more cells are produced, a proportion of colourless chloroplasts is maintained in the plant body."[49] This scientific introduction is important to overstanding race and what makes one 'black' at a genetic level. Having a better overstanding of this puts one in a better position to examine the physical and genetic evidence and solve the race problem of the Egyptians.

Summary

- Black Africans have the most amount of melanin and are the only race with nappy or 9-ether hair. These are the two distinct features of the black race.
- Human beings have been genetically manipulated by ET's. The Rizqiyians and Neteru claim to be our ancestors.
- All human beings are said to be descendants from a 'mitochondrial eve' who existed in Africa 300,000 to 150,000 years ago. I suspect this is Ninti.
- Ninti mixed her DNA with 14 test species. Science confirms there are 14 ancestral population clusters. The Holy tablets say there are 7 types of Negroid. So the 14 could include a man and woman from each type.
- Monogenesis (that humans originated from a single point in Africa and migrated across the world) is confirmed by scientists. Hence those that migrated evolved into other races and those that remained stayed black Africans.
- People in Africa can absorb more UVR which prevent it penetrating deeper skin tissue and as a result our skin turns darker. White people when exposed to the sun have a higher chance of developing skin cancer so therefore black people are more likely to withstand the hot temperature of Africa.
- There are different markers that can be used to identify race such as haplotype, DNA, blood type and skin colour.
- Blood group B, U -, and Duffy negative are popular blood groups amongst Negroids.

Notes and References

1. Bard K (1999) *Encyclopaedia of the Archaeology of Ancient Egypt.* Routledge, 3rd edition. p.328

2. Sarich V and Miele F (2003) *Race: The Reality of human differences.* Westview Press Inc.

3. Templeton A (1998). *Human races: a genetic and evolutionary perspective.* American Anthropologist. 100: 632–650.

4. Ibid (1) p.329

5. Oxlade E, (2007) *Genetics: The Science of genetics revealed.* Studymates Limited Second edition, Abergele UK. P.1&2.

6. Ibid p.13

7. York-El, Dr Malachi Z. Book #15 *666 Leviathan The Beast as The Anti-Christ. Part 1 of 4.* ISBN# 1-59517-143-6. Egipt Publishers, Athens, Georgia, 1996A.D. p.384

8. Ibid (5) p.27

9. Macmillan Website – *Risk factors and causes of skin cancer.* Available from: http://www.macmillan.org.uk/Cancerinformation/Cancertypes/Skin/About skincancer/Causes.aspx [Accessed 24/11/2011]

10. GCSE Bitesize Science: *The electromagnetic spectrum.* Available from: http://www.bbc.co.uk/schools/gcsebitesize/science/aqa/radiation/the_electr omagnetic_spectrumrev4.shtml [Accessed 24/11/2011]

11. Diop C (1974) *The African Origin of Civilisation: Myth or Reality.* A Capella Books. P.241

12. York-El, Dr Malachi Z. Book #133 *People of the sun.* ISBN# 1-59517-143-6. Egipt Publishers, Athens, Georgia. P.18

13. FOX News. *Whites genetically weaker than blacks Study Finds.* 2008. Available from: http://www.foxnews.com/story/0,2933,331949,00.html [Accessed 2/10/2011]

14. Sickle Cell Society. *What is Sickle cell anaemia?* Available from: http://www.sicklecellsociety.org/websites/123reg/LinuxPackage22/si/ck/le/s icklecellsociety.org/public_html/disorders/view/1 [Accessed 30/11/2011]

15. Genetics Home Reference: *What is DNA?* Available from: http://ghr.nlm.nih.gov/handbook/basics/dna [Accessed 1/12/2011]

16. Genetics Home Reference: *Mitochondrial DNA.* Available from: http://ghr.nlm.nih.gov/chromosome/MT [Accessed 30/11/2011]

17. Ancestry.com *Maternal Lineage Test* http://dna.ancestry.com/learnMoreMaternal.aspx [Accessed 24/12/2011]

18. Sutovsky, P., et al. (Nov. 25, 1999). "Ubiquitin tag for sperm mitochondria". *Nature* 402 (6760): 371–372.)

19. AAA (1998). "American Anthropological Association Statement on "Race". http://www.aaanet.org/stmts/racepp.htm. [Accessed 7/12/2011]

20. McEvedy, C (1995) *The Penguin Atlas of African history*. Penguin. 2nd Revised edition. p.20

21. *KKN Family association* http://www.kknfa.org/haplogroups.htm

22. *Give Blood, England and North Wales.* http://blood.co.uk/about-blood/blood-group-basics/ [Accessed 3/12/2012]

23. The Donor magazine 2008. http://www.blood.co.uk/pdf/publications/donor_sum2008.pdf [Accessed 30/11/2011]

24. The Belgravia Centre. *Hair types and racial differences.* Available from: http://www.belgraviacentre.com/blog/hair-types-and-race-differences/ [Accessed 25/1/2012]

25. Winters (2010) *Origin and Spread of haplogroup N*. Bioresearch Bulletin 3: 116-122.

26. York-El, Dr Malachi Z. Book # *Breaking the Spell*. ISBN# 1-59517-001-4. Egipt Publishers, Athens, Georgia, A.D. p.14

27. Science Daily. *New Research proves single origins of humans in Africa.* (2007) http://www.sciencedaily.com/releases/2007/07/070718140829.htm Accessed 13/12/2011

28. Video (Diop) *The African origins of Humanity*

29. Cayce E (2000) *Edgar Cayce On Atlantis.* Little, Brown and Company. P.49 Reading 5748-1.

30. "human evolution."Encyclopædia Britannica. 2011. Encyclopædia Britannica 2006 Ultimate Reference Suite DVD.

31. Ibid (27)

32. Ibid (20) p.18

33. Ibid (17)

34. Ibid (12)

35. Jablonski N (2009) Available from: http://www.ted.com/talks/lang/eng/nina_jablonski_breaks_the_illusion_of_skin_color.html Accessed 17/10/2011

36. "vitamin D." Encyclopædia Britannica. 2011. Encyclopædia Britannica 2006 Ultimate Reference Suite DVD.

37. BBC nature *Life.* Available from: http://www.bbc.co.uk/nature/life Accessed 16/12/2011

38. York-El, Dr Malachi Z. *The Black Book*. ISBN#? Egipt Publishers, Athens, Georgia, A.D. p.58

39. The Antiterrorist (2009) *The Antiterrorist Handbook.* p.14 Velluminous.

40. York-El, Dr Malachi Z. Book #80 *Man from Planet Rizq*, ISBN#1-59517-075-8, Egipt publishers, Athens, Georgia. P111

41. York-El, Dr Malachi Z. *Bible Interpretations and Explanations*. Egipt publishers, Athens, Georgia.

42. York-El, M. Book #190. *Mission Earth and Extraterrestrial Involvement*. ISBN# 1-59517-077-4. Egipt publishers, Athens, Georgia.

43. BBC Nature. *Wildlife* http://www.bbc.co.uk/nature/life/Human Accessed 12/1/2011

44. Science Daily. *African Genetics Study Revealing Origins, Migration And 'Startling Diversity' Of African Peoples*. Available from: http://www.sciencedaily.com/releases/2009/04/090430144524.htm Accessed 27/10/2011

45. Ibid

46. Ibid (20)

47. Ibid (5)

48. Keita S (1993) Studies and Comments on Ancient Egyptian Biological relationships. *History in Africa*. Vol. 20, African Studies Association. P.130

49. Ibid (5)

Chapter 10

Anthropometric and genetic analysis of African people

With the evidence of gods such as Ninti and Asaru (Osiris), there is a high probability of a 'God gene' being present in the Ancient Egyptians and their descendants. *Are There Black Devils* confirms this, "there are some people here today who have genes from these extra terrestrials" p.344 and The Holy Tablets 2:1:22 say they are coming back for their children. According to the laws of genetics, these children would inherit their biological characteristics. The existence of these 2 Gods substantially increases the probability of the Sumerian and Egyptian pantheon. A 'God gene' is out of the scope of this project so we will focus on ancient Egyptian genes. We will look at results on genetic studies in Egypt and the associated countries identified earlier particularly Sudan, West Africa and South America to see if genetic data can prove the cultural similarities. As well as genetics, several anthropometric indicators such as limb ratios, dental morphology, blood group analyses and cranio facial measurements will be taken into consideration. However these indicators aside from genetics and blood groups can be disputed or misrepresented as well as problematic.

The earliest metrical studies of Egyptian biological data were flawed, so now there are published standards for obtaining precise and accurate measurements whilst utilising relevant historical and geographic population comparisons. [1] Some of the anthropometric results are quite vague to leave a proper overstanding, i.e. 'this test series linked them to North Africans' so you rely on the anthropologist's judgement, which can lead to disputes. Modern studies of the origins of the ancient Egyptians are not concerned with identifying racial categories but with investigating the *affinities* of different chronological or geographical groups to whom they are most closely related to in terms of biogeography. Affinity means, 1) a liking or attraction 2) relationship especially by marriage 3) similarity of structure or character suggesting a relationship. [The Oxford Dictionary of Current English] These affinities are expressed as patterns of similarity or differences among local populations or skeletal samples that are believed to be representative of an ancient population. It is assumed that the degree of similarity in a set of biological characteristics is assumed to be related to the degree of genetic relatedness, while comparisons must be informed by other data. (Bard p.329) For example, in one study Van Sertima compares the affinities of the Egyptians to that of a Caribbean island.[2] Other disciplines such as geography, archaeology and history must also be employed to provide a context for assessing the meaning of biological similarity in a given case.[3]

Craniometric and skeletal studies

Franz Boaz argued in 1912 that cranial form was influenced by environmental factors from a study of European immigrants to the US. (Boaz, 1912 cited in Gravlee et al). By using modern analytical methods unavailable to Boas, Gravlee et al confirmed his conclusion.[4] Pictures 5.3/5.4 show an exact morphology of cranial type between Akhenaten's daughter and a Mangbetu woman from Congo, caused by a deliberate deformation of the skull in infancy. Though this can be used to infer contact and cultural diffusion between Egypt and Congo, it cannot be labelled exclusively as a Negroid trait, as other races could replicate it. (Mukhopadhyay and Moses 1997:523, cited in Gravlee et al) mention a divide between physical and cultural anthropologists, where the latter impede research on race and human diversity. I will present some of the studies here as they either overlap with skeletal studies or provide interesting conclusions about the population in Ancient Egypt.
One cultural anthropologist was an American anatomist Samuel Morton. In 1844 he examined numerous Egyptian crania and identified them as Caucasian and indigenous to the Nile valley. (Sertima, p.113) But he was bound by his own racist ideologies. However Sertima identified extensive skeletal surveys of pre-dynastic and dynastic Egyptians showing them to be roughly the same racial composition as the blacks of a modern Caribbean island, with a predominantly Negroid base and traces of Asiatic and Caucasoid admixtures. The Negro African element was the dominant racial element and they mixed in with Asians and Caucasians migrating into the North of Egypt. (Sertima, p113)

The general notion of the ancient Egyptian population is summed up by Giuffrida-Ruggeri who saw the indigenous southern Egyptians as authentic Africans and the Lower Egyptians as invading Mediterranean whites. (Keita, p145) Kemp also comments on the north south divide; "In the south of Egypt the population would have been close to and would have merged with that of northern Nubia. One trait was presumably a darkening of skin colour. As one moved north so local populations should in general have diverged more from those further south. This ought to mean if all factors worked equally (and they might not have done) that the population of the north eastern Nile delta merged with that of southern Palestine."[5] (Kemp, 2005, p.51)

Many studies including that of Thomson and MacIver suggested that the early Egyptians were a hybrid and/or composite group of non-Negroid and Negroid. (Keita, p.136) We can see from the Narmer Palette, that he defeated Asians and Caucasians who invaded Upper Egypt, so there *were* non black people in pre-dynastic Egypt, and by establishing the first dynasty meant he secured a victory over them and drove them out of the country. The level of intermarriage (if at all) to produce these hybrids needs to be backed up by historical data before this can be accepted, especially as intermarriage comes much later in Egyptian history. An article by Sonia Zakrzewski says "results suggest that the Egyptian state was **not** the product of mass movement of populations into the Egyptian Nile region, but rather that it was the result of primarily indigenous development..."[6] So since Africans are indigenous to Africa then the idea of a 'hybrid' or composite group can only be the result of migration and invasion.

Sertima also mentions a report by Arthur Thompson and David MacIver from 1905, who say that from the early pre-dynastic period to the Fifth dynasty, 24% of the males and 19.5% of the females were pure Negroid and between the 6th to 18th dynasties, the figures had changed to 20% males and 15% females. (Sertima p.114) Sertima accepts these statistics and labels them as an empty statistic saying we should focus on the contribution, participation and development of Black Africans toward the Egyptian civilisation. However these results do not coincide with the information from Dr York and Brewer. Dr York said in (Ancient Egypt and the Pharaohs, p.116) that Khufu lifted the ban on immigration and he ruled in the fourth dynasty.[7] If this is true we have good reason to assume that Egypt was predominantly inhabited by Negroids and foreigners only began arriving after this point. This means that from (2613 BC the start of the 4th dynasty to 2498 BC, the beginning of the 5th dynasty) a period of 115 years, Egypt went from a black country to having only a black population of 24% males and 19.5% females in the population. For this event to have any likelihood given the premise of Dr York would call for drastic measures. Egyptian priests told Herodotus that the Great Pyramid had taken 400,000 men 20 years to build, working in three-month shifts of 100,000 men at a time. This is not implausible, but archaeologists now tend to believe a more limited workforce of 20,000 workers were used, either way we see a very large number of people.[8]

The Ultimate Frontier said the pyramid builders were the Hyksos, under the supervision of the Brotherhoods. They are described as a Semitic white race that came out of Ethiopia who immigrated there from an area East of present day Turkey.[9] This *could be* the reason for a very low number of Negroid skeletons.

Risdon (1939) argued that the population of Upper Egypt underwent gradual change from the Badarian period through to the 18th Dynasty, and that by the New Kingdom, one group had almost entirely replaced the other in Upper Egypt. (Zakrzewski p.502) There is no mention of the *race* of these groups during these periods and it can be debated if he means Upper as in Northern or Upper as in Lower Egypt because of the Nile. If he refers to the Northern, which most scholars note was less African; this fits in with my original hypothesis that after wars and intermarriage Egypt lost its true identity. If he is referring to Southern this does not match historical evidence.

Diop examined Egyptian skulls and mummies from ancient to dynastic times and found that they differ in no respect to the anthropological characteristics of straight haired Dravidians and woolly haired Negroes. Upon scientifically cleansing the skin of the mummies the epidermis appears pigmented exactly like that of all other African tribes. Samples of these specimens were available in jars at the African Institute of basic research (IFAN) at the University of Dakar, Senegal.[10]

Most early craniometric studies concluded that there were two population groups inhabiting Egypt throughout the Predynastic period, and that the northern group (the Lower Egyptian type) replaced the more \Negroid" southern type during the Dynastic period. (Zakrzewski p.502)

Limb ratio studies

Allen's rule states that limb ratios are directly proportional to climate. Homo sapien sapiens tend to have shorter distal members of the extremities in colder climates. So the shin (tibia) and thigh (femur) of an equatorial African is expected to be longer than a Europeans. (Keita P.140) William Robertson Boggs stated these longer limbs and bodies help to easily dissipate heat, and I can link this to an indication of descendancy from the Watusi or Cuthite beings who were known to be 7 foot tall.

An early study by (Warren 1987, cited in Keita 1993, p.140) found that ratios for early Naqada Egyptians were similar to those of Negroes.

Trinkhaus (1981) performed a study on limb ratios for numerous populations including a predynastic Egyptian and Mediterranean European series. The results found the predynastic Egyptian values plotted near tropical Africans, not Mediterranean Europeans. A term 'supernegroid' was used by 'Robins and Shute' 1983/6 after evaluating predynastic and dynastic remains. "This suggests that the ancestors of the southern Egyptians were not cold-adapted immigrants to Africa. A sample of definite northern Egyptians may have given different results."

Zakrzewski conducted a study on limb ratios of 150 Egyptian skeletons from 6 time periods and her results suggest that Egyptians had the "super-Negroid" body plan described by Robins (1983).[11] (P.10 Zakrewski 2003)

Blood type

(Paoli 1972, cited in Keita 1993, p.140) found dynastic mummies to have ABO frequencies most like those of the Northern Haratin, a group believed to be largely descended form the ancient Saharans. The Haratin according to EB are 'black-skinned inhabitants of oases in the Sahara, especially in southern Morocco and Mauritania, who constitute a socially and ethnically distinct class of workers.'[12] Scholars speculate they are a result of ancient interbreeding between indigenous blacks and Indo-Europeans, possibly Berbers.

Hair

Strouhal (1971) microscopically examined hair preserved on a Badarian skull. His conclusion was that it belonged to a 'stereotypical' tropical African-European hybrid (mulatto) however Keita suggested it was no different to a Fulani's, and some Kanuri or Somali. (Keita p.140) Such a mixture could create many variations in hair texture. It is interesting that Keita compared it to a Fulani/Somali, as both groups show signs of visible and genetic differences to other Africans, explained later. Keita goes on to say that "Extremely woolly hair is not the only kind native to tropical Africa." (p.140) Because both people disagree on the affinity, other factors are needed in order to make a more informed decision and the hair made available for analysis by interested parties.

Dental

In dental studies it is believed by many that dimensions and crown variations of permanent teeth are largely if not solely determined by genetics, so are used in affinity studies. (Irish and Turner 1990, and Turner and Markowitz 1990) using dental morphology postulate an almost total replacement of the native/African epipaleolithic and Neolithic groups by populations or peoples from further north (Europe or the Near East). A similarity in dental traits is noted between epipaleolithic Nile Valley peoples and modern West Africans and also found for craniometric traits (Strouhal 1984) (Keita p.142)

In 2006 Professor Joel Irish conducted a bio archaeological study on the dental morphology of 996 mummies from Ancient Egypt. His results show dental traits more characteristic to North Africans than Southwest Asian and southern European populations. He included samples from the predynastic Badarian period, the Hawara tombs of Fayum and the dynastic period, all showing divergence (spreading out) from Lower Nubia.[13] The term 'North Africans' is broad, and does not refer to a specific race or ethnic group however this was the biological affinity he chose over SW Asian and S Europeans.

Some of the anthropometric results are open to discussion as they do not match historical information and are disputed amongst scholars. It is unlikely that unless you work or study in this field you would ever come across these fossils for your own personal study, however the work done by anthropologists is definitely worth reviewing. Other studies e.g. Zakrzewski's limb ratio study in 2003 with a clearly defined methodology and classification of results carry more weight to be trusted. It is necessary for the published standards mentioned by Bard to be employed, although some studies were completed earlier and were not subject to these guidelines.

A tidy conclusion on the physical anthropological evidence is written by Peck:

> "The physical anthropological evidence indicates that early Nile
> Valley populations can be identified as part of an African
> lineage, but exhibiting local variation. This variation represents
> the short and long term effects of evolutionary forces, such as
> gene flow, genetic drift and natural selection, influenced by
> culture and geography." [Bard written by Peck 1999 p.331]

He continues:

> "There is now a sufficient body of evidence from modern
> studies of skeletal remains to indicate that the ancient
> Egyptians, especially southern Egyptians, exhibited physical
> characteristics that are within the range of variation for ancient
> and modern indigenous peoples of the Sahara and tropical
> Africa. In general, the inhabitants of Upper Egypt and Nubia

had the greatest biological affinity to people of the Sahara and more southerly areas." [Bard written by Peck 1999 p.331]

Genetic

The analysis of ancient DNA is problematic due to contamination from human handling of material and fungi, bacteria, and agents that invade the bone when it is buried. Ancient embalming practices and the use of preservatives on skeletal and mummified tissues may also damage the DNA making it more difficult to analyse. It can also be costly and complex and so cannot be extracted from a large number of individuals.

The Ancient Egyptian fossils generally come from skeletons and mummies. Skeletal collections are preferred to mummies because they are more widely available and may more accurately represent local populations, whereas mummies are more likely to be individuals of royal or noble status and not entirely representative of Ancient Egyptian populations. (Bard p.330) Just think of Tutankhamun's tomb and his treasures, such wealth would only come from a royal family. Each dynasty as we know consisted of a direct line of descendants from a ruling family. It is said that Asar (Osiris) and Aset (Isis) were brother and sister twins who married but this is not entirely true, these stories are symbolic. Such close interbreeding produces birth defects because it increases the proportion of homozygous recessive alleles, two alleles of a recessive gene on both chromosomes. However the Egyptians, especially the royal family had a practice of marrying within their society group to keep the royal lineage pure and reduce the chances of recessive genes such as mental disorders. This is also commonly practiced among the Hindus of India and Native American tribes. The genetic differences between the royal family and the rest of the population, or differences of this kind are called 'genetic drift'. This is a term used to describe the apparently random genetic variation between a population. Another alternative is 'gene flow'; a movement of genes from one population to another normally by migration or invasion. If genes are carried to a population where those genes previously did not exist, gene flow can be a very important source of genetic variation.[14] Table 1 provides a description of some of the major haplogroups described in this chapter.[15/16]

Table 10.1: Major haplogroups

Haplogroup	Description
	mtDNA Haplogroup
L1	Haplogroup L1 was the earliest offshoot of Mitochondrial Eve, the ancestor of all humans dating back 150,000 – 170,000 years ago. This group is extinct and the earliest existing group associated to all humans is the second group L1. This group is found in West and Central sub-Saharan Africa. It is assumed that Eve lived in Africa as a result of this.
L2	Haplogroup L2 encompasses about a third of all sub-Saharan Africans arising about 59,000 – 78,000 years ago connecting with the evolutionary line of L1. L2 marks the group that stayed behind and did not migrate to other continents. There are fours subclades L2a, L2b, L2c,L2d. The most widespread of the four is L2a and it forms the most widespread cluster in Africa – the most common lineage of African Americans.
L3	L3 appeared around 80,000 years ago and is found only in Africa. M and N originated from L3 and these two groups bind all Eurasian lineages. So it assumes that although L3 was only found in Africa it is linked to many other populations.
U	Appearing around 55,000 years ago somewhere in the region of Europe and the North East, haplogroup U is found there at a frequency of almost 7%. Subgroups reflect their own geographical locations which tend to include the Indian and North African components. In North Africa the subgroup U6 is commonly found and may substantiate a theory of migration back into the region from the North East and Europe.
A	haplogroup A is found in eastern Eurasia and throughout the Americas. This haplogroup was present in the populations that initially colonized the pre-Columbian Americas, and dates to at least 30,000 years ago. Future work will resolve the issue of how many distinct colonization events there were in the original peopling of the Americas, and the origin and role of individuals bearing haplogroup A.
	Y Haplogroup
M1	M1 appears in Sub-Saharan Africa and is the only subgroup to do so. It is speculative as to whether M1 is a lineage of East African origin or a reverse migration from Asia or North Africa. This group is found in populations outside of Africa in the Near East, the Caucasus and in Europe (in lower frequencies)
M2	The Africans who chose not to leave their home continent developed the marker M2. They are a part of the larger African

	lineage group E3a. Predominantly in West Africa, most African American can trace their genetic history to this line.
M35	This group first appeared 20,000 years ago. It is the result of a genetic change in the Middle Eastern M96 populations who left Africa around 30,000 to 40,000 years ago. The Neolithic spread of these people out of the Middle East is associated with the marker M35 and now defines the haplogroup E3b. This group tends to appear in Italy, southeast Europe and North Africa. Migrating farmers where the likely cause of the spread, during the age of agricultural prosperity. This precipitated the geographical dispersal of M172 lineage.
N	This group resulted from the African haplogroup L3. It spread many sub lineages across Eurasia and the Americas. Although much research is needed, it is thought that there are many subclades which define more geographically distinct lineages within the Macro haplogroup N.
(R1) M173	This group first appeared 35,000 years ago and achieved the first large scale settlement in Europe by modern humans. This was a result migrant hunters on the Central Asian steppes moving to the west and east.
J1 (M267)	Haplogroup J1 emerged during the Neolithic Revolution in the Middle East. Members of the J1 clans shared the farming successes of the other J haplogroups. In particular, some J1 individuals moved back into North Africa and were quite successful there as well as evidenced by the highest frequencies for J1 appearing in this region. Other members of the J1 lineage remained in the Middle East, and some moved northward into Western Europe, where J1 is found at low frequencies.
EM81 E3b1b (Formerly E3b2)	E-M81 (E3b2; referred to as a "Berber marker"), which reaches frequencies of up to 80% in North Africa. It is thought of primarily as a Berber haplogroup, and is most common throughout the Maghreb region of North Africa and is absent in Europe, except for the Iberian peninsula and Sicily. It is considered to have entered the European continent as a result of Islamic domination over these regions of Southern Europe. But an earlier arrival may have happened through the late Mesolithic Cardium Pottery.[17]

We know from Chapter 8 that the present population in Egypt is not representative of Ancient times. There is evidence of mixing to have taken place between native black Egyptians and foreigners so it would be useful to test the present Egyptian population against:

1. ancient Egyptian DNA,
2. groups which have been identified with the Egyptians such as the Sudanese, Nigerians, Malians and Black Jews.
3. Populations from countries that invaded Egypt throughout its history for biological affinities.

I will present some of the best examples I have found to give a full picture and where possible, results will be displayed in quotes to keep the purity of the data.

The L haplogroup (LO to L6) corresponding to mtDNA is limited only to Africa. The LOd haplogroup is found at the base of human mtDNA and is said to be the most basal branch of the gene tree. It is a rare ancient mtDNA haplogroup that is limited to only West, East and South Africa.[18] The TMRCA (Time most recent common ancestry) for LOd is 106kya, this fits Penguin's time period minus 6ky of an out of Africa event. The L3 subclade is the parent haplogroup to M and N and is dated to 80-60kya. M and N were the progenitors of all non-African haplogroups (Gonder, 2007). Some say that M1 and N originated outside of Africa, I'm sure by now you are bored of the concentrated effort by scholars of whatever denomination, assigning African heritage to non-African people? However the science of genetics can't lie and Clyde Winters who we looked at in chapter 6 wrote several journals about the genetics of Africans, including 'The African Origin of mtDNA Haplogroup M1' and 'Origin and Spread of Haplogroup N.' The aim of the first paper was to determine the geographical location of the M1 haplogroup which some said originated in Asia, however the author was able to provide substantial evidence to disprove that claim. He also provided evidence that the haplogroups M1, M* and N are found in many countries in Africa including Tanzania, Uganda, Egypt and the Senegambian region; and is said to have originated from Ethiopia coinciding with the finds of Ardi and Lucy as the oldest fossils of our human ancestors to date. (See picture 10.1) This picture assigns the number 12 to Egypt, 11 (8+3) combined to Sudan and 75 to Ethiopia. Most carriers of M1 in Africa outside of Ethiopia are Niger Congo speakers. (See Picture 3.1 for a list of language families.) Of the people in Egypt that carry the M1 haplogroup, they speak Afro Asiatic languages which both Ancient Egyptian and Arabic are part of. The presence of M1 among Niger Congo and Afro-Asiatic speakers show an association with Nubia. The region of the Upper Nile Valley according to (Welmers, 1971) was the original home of the Niger Congo speakers, and in chapters 4/5 we saw how Egypt and Yoruba both stemmed from Nubia. Niger-Congo shares many linguistic similarities with Nilo-Saharan languages as well as the Y chromosome M3b*-M35 and R1*-M173 gene in both groups of speakers.[19] The second paper (Haplogroup N) reported that the majority of carriers of haplogroup N in Africa live in Sub-Saharan Africa. 85.5% of the total population of haplogroup N carriers live in East Africa whilst the remaining 14.5% percent live in West Africa. (See Picture 10.3)[20]

Figure 10.1 – Geographical distribution of M1 haplogroup in Africa. [Taken from Winters p.6]

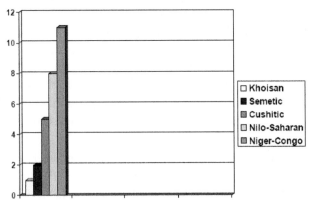

Figure 10.2 – Languages spoken by Haplogroup N populations in Africa. [Taken from winters p.118]

Paabo and Di Rienzo studied aDNA from the 12th dynasty pointing to multiple lines of descent including some from Sub Saharan Africa. The other lineages were not identified, but may be African in origin.[21]

A sedentary population was tested in Gurna near Luxor, Upper Egypt. The results showed the presence of the M1 haplogroup at (17.6%); nearly identical to the value of the Ethiopian population at (20%). Figure 10.2 by Winters gave Ethiopia 75 for M1 and Upper Egypt only 3, so this leaves inconclusive results in my view. Similarities were also present in the Ethiopian population for the L1 and L2 macrohaplogroup at a frequency of (20.6%). The Gurna population appeared statistically as close to Near Eastern as to sub-Saharan and Sudanese populations, even though these two groups were statistically different. This suggests Gurna could be the meeting point of two independent waves of migration from the Near East and from sub-Saharan Africa.[22]

Keita and Boyce wrote a paper on the genetic variation of the Y chromosome in Egypt. The three most common haplotypes were V, XI, and IV. V is associated with M35/215, and IV with the M2/PN1/M180 subclade (lineages). I am not sure of their association for XI, however they make reference to M145/M213. (*See note) In another system of classification, these lineages are in haplogroup E. The KKNFA website associate M35 with E3b and M2 with E3a.

M35 was labelled Arabian by some, however they say it is more accurate to call it "Horn-supra-Saharan African," because it is indigenous to Africa. The first speakers of Arabic, a Semitic language, came into Africa from the Near East. (Keita 2 - P.6) M35 has a high frequency in Moroccan Berbers (57.8), and Ethiopia (45.8), and a much lower frequency among core Semitic-speaking descendant communities in the Near East (i.e. Arabs and Jews). (P.14) Haplotype M2/PN1 is found in high frequency in west, central, and sub-equatorial Africa in speakers of Niger-Congo, which they say may have a special relationship with Nilosaharans (spoken by Nubians). Together they might form a super phylum called Kongo-Saharan or Niger-Saharan, but this is not fully supported. (Keita 2 - p.8)

Haplotype M2 has substantial frequencies in Upper Egypt and Nubia, greater than VII and VIII, and even V. Bantu languages were never spoken in these regions or Senegal, where M2 is greater than 90 percent in some studies. (Keita 2009, p9) Their results suggest that there is statistically no significant difference between Upper Egypt and Lower Nubia which has almost identical frequencies of XI and IV; Upper Egypt (XI-28.8%; IV-27.3%); Lower Nubia (XI-30.4%; IV-39.1%). Haplotype XI has its highest frequencies in the Horn and the Nile valley, the high frequency of XI in both Nilo-Saharan and Afro-

Asiatic speakers in NE Africa is striking. The Falasha, more properly Beta Israel (the "black Jews" of Ethiopia, traditionally Cushitic, not Semitic speakers), have such a high frequency of V and XI and none (yet found) of VII and VIII, that this shows them to be "clearly of African origin" and to have adopted Judaism.[23] This coincides with the results of Professor Goldstein the geneticist who linked the Lemba tribe from South Africa, Congo and Yemen to the tribe of Levi via the Kohen Modal Haplotype. 53% of men from the Bhuba clan (Judah priestly class) have these genetic markers called the Cohen modal haplotype while the lay Jewish populations have a frequency of 3-5%.[24]

Arredi et al studied the Y chromosomal variation in 275 men from Algeria, Tunisia, and Egypt. Here are some of the main results:

(1) Just two haplogroups predominate within North Africa, together making up almost two-thirds of the male lineages: E3b2 and J* (42% and 20%, respectively). E3b2 is rare outside North Africa, and is otherwise known only from Mali, Niger, and Sudan to the immediate south, and the Near East and Southern Europe at very low frequencies. (P2) E3b2 is known as a Berber marker and J is associated with the Middle East.

(2) E3a predominates in many sub-Saharan areas, being present at 64% in a pooled sample p.2.

(3) Haplogroup J reaches its highest frequencies in the Middle East, whereas the J-276 lineage (equivalent to J* here) is most frequent in Palestinian Arabs and Bedouins. P2/3

(4) The TMRCA of haplogroup E3b2 was estimated to be (~4.2 KY or 6.9 KY). The times for haplogroup J, the second most- common haplogroup observed in North Africa were (6.8 KY or 7.9 KY). This was done using the mutation rate measured in father-son pairs and assuming 30 years per generation, or using the deduced "effective" mutation rate calibrated by historical events. Both times are quite recent, supporting the idea of a recent demographic event.[25]

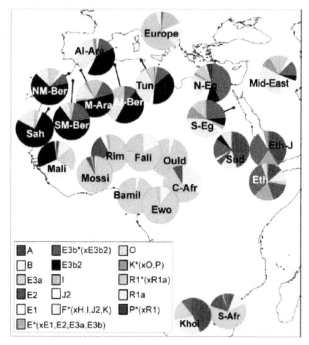

Figure 10.3 - Frequency distribution of Y haplogroup clusters in African, Middle Eastern, and European samples.

Luis et al's study involved testing the non-recombining region of the Y chromosome (NRY) in males from The Sultanate of Oman and northern Egypt. Here are some of their results:

(1) The NRY composition of the Egyptian and Omani collections exhibits a greater Middle Eastern versus sub-Saharan affinity. The cumulative frequency of typical sub-Saharan lineages (A, B, E1, E2, E3a, and E3b*) is 9% in Egypt and 10% in Oman, whereas the haplogroups of Eurasian origin (Groups C, D, and F–Q) account for 59% and 77%, respectively. (p.8)

(2) There are three E3b*-M35 sub lineages or mutations (E3b1-M78, E3b2-M123, and E3b3-M81) from the undifferentiated M35 lineage. The first two as well as R1*-M173 mark gene flow between Egypt and the Levant (Mediterranean) during the Upper Palaeolithic and Mesolithic.

(3) The complexity of the E3b-M35 fraction in Egypt may have been enhanced by several episodes of backflow, beginning with the introduction of agriculture into Africa, and, later, various historical events, such as the Greek, Roman, and Arab occupations. P10

(4) Egypt is the only African population that is known to harbour all three M173 subtypes (R1b-M269, R1*-M173, and R1a1-M17). This unique status is most likely due to Egypt's strategic location and its long history of interaction with Eurasia.[26] P11

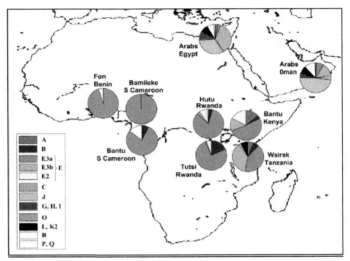

Figure 10.4 - Geographic frequency distribution of binary markers in eight African populations and one Omani population

Kivisild et al (2004) study tested mtDNA from Ethiopia and Yemeni populations to explore gene flow across the Red and Arabian Seas.

• The Ethiopian gene pool was found to contain a predominantly sub-Saharan substrate, as well as a considerable level of admixture with populations of Arabian and/or Near Eastern origin. Both Ethiopian and Yemeni populations can be considered to be hybrids of gene flow from sub-Saharan Africa and the Near East.

• An MDS plot (See Figure 10.6) of population differences grouped Ethiopian, Egyptian, and Yemeni populations together with Egypt in between the Near Eastern and the West and southern African clusters.

• The minor group M1b, defined by the motif 15884-16260-16320, is restricted to East Africans, having been observed, so far, only in Ethiopians and in Egypt (authors' unpublished results).

• Additionally J1-M267 chromosomes appear to be particularly frequent among southern Arabians (38% in Omanis) and well represented in Egypt (20%).

• A majority of mtDNA lineages of Ethiopian Jews (Falasha or Beta Israel) derive from African-specific clades L0–L5 (Shen et al. 2004), including exact matches with Ethiopians sampled in the present study. Consistent with Y-chromosomal findings, this fact points to extensive admixture of Jews with the local population.[27] This information would be useful to Rastafarians as their religion is centred around Ethiopia.

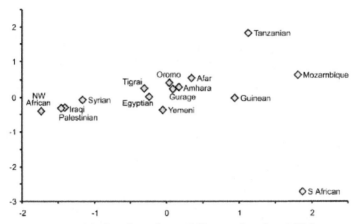

Figure 10.5 - MDS plot of population differences based on FST distances calculated from haplogroup frequencies. [Taken from Fig 3, Kivisild p.759]

Kring et al (1999) analysed mtDNA variation of 224 individuals from contemporary Nile River Valley populations in Egypt, Nubia, and the southern Sudan. Egyptian samples were taken from (Mansoura and Assiut), Nubians (Kerma, Assuan, and Dongola) and southern Sudanese from (Dinka, Nuba, Nuer, and Shilluk). Their results indicate that migrations had occurred bidirectionally along the Nile River Valley. This is supported by both the finding of 'northern' (Eurasian) mtDNA types at the southern end of the Nile River Valley and the finding of 'southern' (sub-Saharan) mtDNA types at the northern end of the Nile River Valley. Egyptians and Nubians appear to be more similar to each other than they are with the southern Sudanese, though this is expected as the historical evidence supports such interaction. They also suggest that Nile River Valley populations separated relatively recently (within the past few hundred to few thousand years) but that the population-separation times should be interpreted cautiously, because of assumptions involved in their analysis.[28]

Genetic study of West African populations

I mentioned earlier Keita's comment on a hair sample which he linked to the Fulani and some Somali. In a test by (Bryc et al 2009) the Fulani appeared to be genetically distinct from all other West African populations they sampled (average pair wise FST = 3.91%).[29] (Bryc p.3) They expressed a high similarity with many African groups but low levels of European and/or Middle Eastern ancestry was found among them. (Bryc P.4) This means Strouhal's comment that the sample belonged to a hybrid is correct to some degree but such labels need to be classified more accurately in the future to avoid the race problem. The table below shows genetic differences between West African populations. Of the 11 groups studied they found the Igbo, Brong, and Yoruba to exhibit little genetic differentiation from one another (average FST <0.4%) (Bryc p.3). The presence of genetic ancestry from West Africa was tested in African Americans and the estimated mean average was 77% consistent with prior studies. (p3) Tishkoff et al also came to the same conclusion. Most African Americans have high proportions of both Bantu (~0.45 mean) and non-Bantu (~0.22 mean) Niger-Kordofanian ancestry, concordant with diasporas originating as far west as Senegambia and as far south as Angola and South Africa. Thus, most African Americans are likely to have mixed ancestry from different regions of western Africa.[30] (Tishkoff, 2009, p.8)

These results show that although certain tribes like the Yoruba and Igbo might separate themselves culturally and socially, the fact is that they are genetically very similar (0.084%) Genetic knowledge of this sort will help true unity to occur.

	Igbo	Brong	Yoruba	Kongo	Bamoun	Xhosa	Fang	Hausa	Kaba	Mada	Bulala
Brong	0.350%	—									
Yoruba	0.084%	0.200%	—								
Kongo	0.282%	0.425%	0.291%	—							
Bamoun	0.293%	0.448%	0.318%	0.175%	—						
Xhosa	1.448%	1.636%	1.251%	1.106%	1.277%	—					
Fang	0.415%	0.594%	0.432%	0.150%	0.247%	1.165%	—				
Hausa	0.397%	0.560%	0.420%	0.588%	0.546%	1.796%	0.691%	—			
Kaba	0.516%	0.510%	0.471%	0.501%	0.484%	1.498%	0.567%	0.619%	—		
Mada	1.296%	1.336%	1.300%	1.282%	1.276%	2.319%	1.380%	1.299%	0.968%	—	
Bulala	1.862%	1.905%	1.879%	1.736%	1.806%	2.646%	1.929%	1.773%	1.280%	0.931%	—
Fulani	3.905%	3.684%	4.034%	3.770%	3.996%	4.133%	4.063%	3.761%	3.811%	3.967%	3.920%

Bold face font is used to emphasize the genetic similarity of the Igbo, Brong and Yoruba.

Figure 10.6 – FST distances between African populations

Additionally, the Nilo-Saharan speaking Luo of Kenya show predominantly Niger-Kordofanian ancestry in the STRUCTURE analyses and cluster together with eastern African Niger-Kordofanian–speaking populations in the phylogenetic trees. (Tishkoff et al p.7)

Manni et al found that "the Y-chromosome gene pool in the modern Egyptian population reflects a mixture of European, Middle Eastern, and African characteristics, highlighting the importance of ancient and recent migration waves, followed by gene flow, in the region."[31]

Genetic study of other African populations

Here are some interesting results from genetic studies that I have investigated:

- East Africa and its rich fossil content is the hypothesized origin of modern humans and has a remarkable degree of ethnic and linguistic diversity as reflected by the greatest level of regional substructure in Africa. (Tiskoff et al p.6)
- Africa contains more than 2000 distinct ethno linguistic groups representing nearly one-third of the world's languages. (Tishkoff et al, p.2)
- Tanzania is the only region of Africa where the population speak languages in all of the four major language families present in Africa: Afro-Asiatic, Nilo-Saharan, Niger-Kordofanian, and Khoisan. The Hadza and Sandawe speak a click language classified as Khoisan, are thought to be indigenous to Tanzania. However, populations speaking languages belonging to the other 3 language families are thought to have migrated into Tanzania from the Sudan (Nilotic Nilo- Saharan speakers), Ethiopia (Cushitic Afro-Asiatic speakers), and West Africa (Bantu Niger-Kordofanian speakers) within the past 5,000 years. (Gonder p.8)
- Another unique haplotype worthy of note is the Senegambian haplotype AF24 (DQ112852). According to Kivisild it is a branch of LOd; Chen says it stems from L3. The presence of AF-24 among the Senegalese and its absence in other parts of Africa, suggest a long-term population in the Senegambia preserved this rare haplotype from southern African Khoisan (SAK) populations who are linked exclusively with LOd. (Winters, 2010)
- The Dogon of Mali are the only African tribe/culture/people to show the highest levels of within–population genetic diversity. (Tishkoff p.3) This could be inextricably linked with the presence of the reptilians or Nommos who mixed with the Dogon tribe, meaning a large number of their genes are inherited from them.

Genetic study of Mexican populations

Clyde Winters wrote a paper entitled 'Genetic Evidence of Early African Migration into the Americas'. He introduces the paper by stating: the presence of Negroes in South America suggests a migration of Sub-Saharan Africans into the Americas 40-15 kya. The premise of the paper is that if Africans did colonize the Americas earlier then there should be genetic evidence in Amerindian populations pointing to Sub-Saharan haplogroups. The foundational mtDNA lineages for Mexican Indians are lineages A, B, C and D with varying frequencies among population groups. The mtDNA A haplogroup common to Mexicans is also found among the Mande speaking people and some East Africans. Haplogroup A is found among Mixe and Mixtecs. The Mande speakers carry mtDNA haplogroup A, which is common among Mexicans. In addition to the Mande speaking people of West Africa, Southeast Africa Africans also carry mtDNA haplogroup A. One Mayan male was found to have an African Y chromosome. This is very interesting because the Maya language illustrates a Mande substratum, in addition to African genetic markers. The Mixe Mixe carry African Y-chromosome DYS287 (YAP+) in Mixe individuals who harboured DYS199 C allele.

Dr. Gutherie also noted that A*28 common among Africans has high frequencies among Eastern Maya. It is interesting to note that the Otomi, a Mexican group identified as being of African origin and six Mayan groups show the B Allele of the ABO system that is considered to be of African origin. Green et al found Indians with African genes in North Central Mexico, including the L1 and L2 clusters. They observed that the discovery of a proportion of African haplotypes roughly equivalent to the proportion of European haplotypes [among North Central Mexican Indians] cannot be explained by recent admixture of African Americans for the United States. For example the Ojinaga area, is and has historically been largely isolated from U.S African Americans. He concludes that the genetic and molecular evidence support an early possible colonization of the Americas by Melanesians and Africans, and a two wave human expansion across America (by Africans from America and Africa). Some researchers claim that as many as 75% of the Mexicans have an African heritage. Although this may be the case Cuevas says these Africans have been erased from history! [32]

Professor Keita has contributed a great deal to the genetic and anthropometric studies of Egypt. Though I have quoted him a few times, his results were hard to follow. Keita is black, and I am not saying that all black people should adopt an Afro centric view just for the sake of it, however others seemed to share my view. One member of a forum called 'Caucasoid Affinities of Ancient Egyptians and Nubians' on the Anthroscape website asks, "*Why is it Keita's data seems to come out differently than so many other anthropologists? I mean I know he's black, but I doubt he's tampering with data or anything. It just always seems that his stuff goes against Brace or others?*"[33] I *will* mention a complete nobody here among 'qualified' anthropologists. Keita says on the National Geographic website that "There is no scientific reason to believe that the primary ancestors of the Egyptian population emerged and evolved outside of northeast Africa. Skeletal analyses have figured prominently in research..."

however he contradicts this by stating "The basic overall genetic profile of the modern population is consistent with the diversity of ancient populations that would have been indigenous to north-eastern Africa and subject to the range of evolutionary influences over time, although researchers vary in the details of their explanations of those influences."[34] Now, the evidence I have found in my studies, especially Luis and Arredi have shown that modern Egyptian populations show high signs of Eurasian and Middle Eastern affinities. We have also seen from Zakrewski that Ancient Egypt was the result of indigenous development. Modern populations might have been as diverse as ancient populations, only at the Greco-Roman period, but to say that these people were indigenous to North Africa is a fallacy. Keita also comments on the replacement theory by Turner et al of native/African's by people from further north. He replies "There is no evidence for sudden or gradual mass migration of Europeans or Near Easterners into the valley, as the term replacement would imply. There is limb ratio and craniofacial morphological and metric continuity in Upper Egypt-Nubia in a broad sense from the late Palaeolithic through dynastic periods, although change occurred." (Keita, 1993, p.142) Just to clarify the Valley refers to Upper Egypt, that area south of Cairo, and the key word here is 'replacement'. Well Kring's says in a paper dedicated to this area "Of course, additional migrations documented during the Ptolemaic, Roman, and Arabic times are also likely to have contributed to the current distribution of mtDNA types along the Nile River Valley." (Krings, 1999, p.9) And as I reported earlier he identified bidirectional migrations occurred between Eurasian and Sub-Saharan types along the valley. Krings also said "these migrations have not been extensive enough to genetically homogenize the mtDNA gene pools of Nile River Valley populations" so I can agree with Keita that the term replacement should not be used. Perhaps a numerical value to suggest at what level migrations occurred in the Nile Valley is the next question? Now here is my point! Since it is agreed that population replacement occurred in Lower Egypt by Northern groups, and some migrations by Eurasians/Near Eastern people occurred in the Nile Valley, what percentage of people in Egypt would have been indigenous? Results show the majority of black Africans in Ancient Egypt were replaced by foreign people, by saying all of them *were not* replaced is like taking ten pence from a child. Keita works for the Smithsonian institute who have been accused of dumping a large amount of artefacts into the ocean[35] so I take their results with a pinch of salt.

Genetic study of African populations is still relatively new and there are tons of published studies out there which carry useful information. I have selected those which were most relevant and available to me. I am not in a position to name an Ancient Egyptian haplotype, and there are likely to have been a combination of them. Haplotypes M1 and M2 show up in high frequencies amongst Egyptian, Sudanese and sub-Saharan populations so they are likely candidates.

Future large scale re-sequencing and genotyping of Africans will be informative for reconstructing human evolutionary history, for understanding human adaptations, and for identifying genetic risk factors (and potential treatments) for disease in Africa. (Tishkoff p.9) However this should only be done by black scientists, the last thing we need is genetically engineered weapons against us, nothing is out of the question these days, just watch District 9 and you will get the idea! Going forward the best course of action for Nubians wanting proof of their Egyptian origins would be to take ancestry tests and prove it to themselves. Don't believe me, or any one else, that's the benefit of living in this information age!

Summary

- It is important for Africans to have an overstanding of genetics and biological traits, especially those in relation to Africa, to know thyself and study our ancestral lineage.
- Scientists proved that life originated in Africa and studies have shown that the formation of the Egyptian state was an indigenous process and population continuity was carried across the Egyptian dynasties.
- The general conclusion from physical studies shows that Northern Egypt was occupied by white and Asian foreigners, who gradually mixed with the native black population. Southern Egyptians were typically Negroid but were gradually replaced by the Northern population of foreign or mixed Egyptians during the dynastic period.
- The Egyptian state was not the product of mass movement of populations into the Egyptian Nile region, but rather that it was the result of primarily indigenous development.
- The mtDNA LOd is found at the base of the human genome and haplogroups M and N are the progenitors of all other haplogroups since leaving Africa.
- Modern population studies of Egypt show them to be Mediterranean, or Middle Eastern.
- M35 or E3b is labelled 'Arabian' however it is indigenous to Africa and should be called "Horn-supra-Saharan African." This haplogroup shows affinities with Mali, Niger, and Sudan.

- The Sudanese/Nubians have high amounts of hg M1 and M2, but I cannot with certainty pinpoint an Ancient Egyptian gene common amongst black Africans. So I leave it to other Egyptologists and the related fields to expand on this study.

Notes and References

1. Bard K (1999) *Encyclopaedia of the Archaeology of Ancient Egypt*. Routledge, 3rd edition. Refer to: Peck W, "Egyptians, physical anthropology of,"

2. Sertima, I (2003) *They came before Columbus*. Random House USA. P

3. Keita S (1993) Studies and Comments on Ancient Egyptian Biological relationships. *History in Africa* Vol. 20, published by African Studies Association. P131

4. Gravlee C, Bernard H, Leonard (2003) Heredity, Environment, and Cranial Form: A Re-Analysis of Boas' Immigrant Data". *American Anthropological Association*. 105[1]:123–136.

5. Kemp, Barry (2005). *Who were the Ancient Egyptians? Egypt: Anatomy of a civilization*. p.51.

6. Zakrzewski S (2007) Population Continuity or Population Change: Formation of the Ancient Egyptian State. *American Journal of Physical Anthropology* 132:501–509. p.507

7. York-El, Dr Malachi Z. *Ancient Egypt and the Pharaohs* #190 ISBN 1-??. Egipt Publishers. P.116

8. Sacred Destinations. *Giza pyramids*. http://www.sacred-destinations.com/egypt/giza-pyramids [Accessed 1/2/2010]

9. Eklal Kueshana (2000) *The Ultimate Frontier*. The Adelphi Organisation. USA. 10th edition. p70/71

10. Diop C (1974) *The African Origin of Civilisation: Myth or Reality*. A Capella Books. P.237

11. Zakrzewski, Sonia R. (2003). "Variation in Ancient Egyptian Stature and Body Proportions". *American Journal of Physical Anthropology*. 121 (3): 219–29. p.229

12. "Haratin."Encyclopædia Britannica. 2012. Encyclopædia Britannica 2006 Ultimate Reference Suite DVD 29 Jan 2012.

13. Irish JD (2006). "Who were the ancient Egyptians? Dental affinities among Neolithic through post dynastic peoples". *American Journal of Physical Anthropology*. 129 (4): 529–43.

14. Berkeley Education: Gene flow:
http://evolution.berkeley.edu/evosite/evo101/IIIC4Geneflow.shtml
[Accessed 5/1/2012]

15. *Haplogroups*. Available from www.haplogroups.com [Accessed 12/12/2011]

16. *KKN Family association*. Available from:
http://www.kknfa.org/haplogroups.htm [Accessed 12/12/11]

17. Bionity.com. *Haplogroup E3b (Y-DNA)* Available from:
http://www.bionity.com/en/encyclopedia/Haplogroup_E3b_%28Y-DNA%29.html [Accessed 11/02/2012]

18. Gonder M et. Al (2007) Whole-mtDNA Genome Sequence Analysis of Ancient African Lineages. *The Society for Molecular Biology and Evolution.* 24(3):757–768.

19. Winters C (2010) *The African Origin of mtDNA Haplogroup M1. Current Research Journal of Biological Sciences.* P1-10. Maxwell Scientific Organisation.

20. Winters C (2010) Origin and Spread of Haplogroup N. *Bioresearch Bulletin* (2010) 3: 116-122. Bioindica press.

21. Available from: http://s1.zetaboards.com/anthroscape/topic/3973609/2/ [Accessed 19/1/2012] (Or cite Keita)

22. Stevanovitch et. al (2003) Mitochondrial DNA Sequence Diversity in a Sedentary Population from Egypt. *Annals of Human Genetics* (2003) 68,23–39

23. Keita S, Boyce A (2009) Genetics, Egypt, and History: Interpreting Geographical patterns of Y Chromosome Variation. *History in Africa* 32 (2005), 221–246.

24. York-El Dr M, (2003) Book #120, *Is Jesus God?* ISBN# 1-59517-073-1, Egipt Publishers, Athens, Georgia. P.196

25. Arredi B et al (2004) A Predominantly Neolithic Origin for Y-Chromosomal DNA Variation in North Africa. *The American Journal of human genetics.* 75:338–345, 2004.

26. Luis et al (2004) The Levant versus the Horn of Africa: Evidence for Bidirectional Corridors of Human Migrations. *The American Journal of human genetics.* 75:338–345, 2004. p.11

27. Kivisild et al (2004) Ethiopian Mitochondrial DNA Heritage: Tracking Gene Flow Across and Around the Gate of Tears. *The American Journal of human genetics.* 75:752–770, 2004.

28. Kring (1999) mtDNA Analysis of Nile River Valley Populations: A Genetic Corridor or a Barrier to Migration? *The American Journal of human genetics.* 64:1166–1176, 1999

29. Bryc et al (2009) Genome-wide patterns of population structure and admixture in West Africans and African Americans. *Proceedings of the National Academy of Sciences of the United States of America.* 107 (2) p.786-791

30. Tishkoff et. al (2009) The Genetic Structure and History of Africans and African Americans. *Science.* 2009 May 22; 324(5930): 1035–1044.

31. Manni et al (2002) Y-chromosome analysis in Egypt suggests a genetic regional continuity in Northeastern Africa. *Human Biology.* 74(5):645-58.

32. Winters C (2011) Genetic Evidence of Early African Migration into the Americas. Original Paper- Testing Evolutionary and Dispersion Scenarios for the Settlement of the New World.

33. National Geographic. Ancient Egyptian Origins. Available from: http://ngm.nationalgeographic.com/geopedia/Ancient_Egypt [Accessed 15/11/2011]

34. Anthroscape Human Biodiversity Forum. Caucasoid Affinities of Ancient Egyptians and Nubians Available from: http://s1.zetaboards.com/anthroscape/topic/3973609/2/ [Accessed 1/02/2012]

35. xpeditions magazine. *Egyptian Artefacts in the Grand Canyon.* The Phoenix Gazette - April 5, 1909. http://www.xpeditionsmagazine.com/magazine/canyon/canyon.html [Accessed 20/07/2011]

(*Note - Haplotype V is associated with the M35/215 subclade, as is XI (in Africa), and IV with the M2/PN1/M180 subclade, both of the YAP/M145/M213 cluster.)

Conclusion

This book should have has cleared up any misconceptions about the race of the Ancient Egyptians. By now you should know their origins, race, culture and who their descendants are. If you are a Nubian you can claim Egyptian ancestry by way of genetic inheritance from the Ancient Egyptians or as a descendant of the Neteru, Egyptian deities. You should be proud of your Ancient and royal heritage. The scroll 'Pa Ashutat' says, *"And we are the original Egiptians and we have our own flag, our own Egiptian Constitution, our language Nuwaupic, our own customs, culture, music, dance and dress."* (York, p.28) There is a scene from Dan Brown's 'The Da Vinci code' where the co star played by Audrey Tautou is in a state of euphoria after realizing she is a descendant of Jesus. Do you have the same feeling? Dr York calls it, 'genetic explosions'. Some people's DNA structures have been pre-encoded or designed to go off like an alarm clock at the sound of Dr York's voice or by reading his scrolls. It is like a catalyst which activates the DNA in order to accommodate more facts and right knowledge so you feel a surge of energy and genetic awakening like an explosion. It is time for the world to recognize and present Egyptians in their true light, and credit black Africans for their history and contribution to civilization. The authors of 'Black Genesis' say *"there is still much work to do in bringing to the world a new vision of the black origins of civilization."* We have done and will achieve even greater things. **Now it your job to spread this message.** This doctrine is not meant for everyone, the Bible says: Matthew 22:14 'For many are called few are chosen' and if you gravitate towards this information then fantastic, it is up to you to play your part. Here are some of the guidelines from a booklet, 'The Nuwaupian Universities: Amun-Re Institute Worldwide' also available on the UNW website. (unwonline.com)

1. We must teach ourselves our own customs, cultures and way of life, not alien education of religions.
2. A person, place or thing is alien to us **Nuwaupians** when it is not of and for us by our very nature.
3. We should not teach our own seeds alien ways, alien gods, alien religions, alien languages, histories before we teach and instil in them our four principles. Wu Nuwaupu (Anun-Re), Wu-Nupu (Atum Re) Asa-Nupu (Atun Re), Naba-Nupu (Amun-Re) which is rooted in Ma'at our way of life.

15. Our purpose in Wu-Nuwaupu and at our own schools as this The Nuwaupian Universities: Amun-Re Institute Worldwide is to set the stage and outline the facts and procedures necessary for restoration of our Nuwaupian culture and our true way of life.

16. The restoration of our own culture will make us masters of our own destiny...

What is a NUWAUPIAN? I have used the terms 'Nuwaupu' or 'Nuwaupian' many times, so here is some more information about Nuwaupu.

A Nuwaupian is a member of our organisation The United Nuwaupians Worldwide, who accepts and practices The Science of Right Knowledge, facts beyond any doubt. We aim to own, propagate, practice and extend our culture, customs, and way of life, while never losing focus on our future, the children. While we accept that no one wins the race in racism, we do not accept, support or propagate alien education, religion or influence. A person, place or thing is alien to us when it is not of, for and by us by nature. We endeavour to educate our family, utilising our own vast and original principles of divinity, language, and sciences, so great that all others have plagiarised and tried to emulate them.

Message to the Nuwaupians

There have been other Nuwaupian writers before me such as Haru Hotep and Brother Polite aka Nysut: Amun-Re Sen Atum-Re. They have both received comments, (positive and negative) by the Nuwaupian community. So in case I happen to be mentioned in a negative view I want to highlight any problems people may have, with an excerpt from the Master Teacher. It starts with this Bible quote: Matthew 8:32 "For you shall know the truth and the truth shall set you free." Dr York comments on this in a live audio class.

> "Make not set you free. There's a difference, let me stand there
> with you, the reason why it's not set you free is because you start
> thinking just because you got the truth your ass is free. It says
> it'll make you free, it'll motivate you to get free. So you still got
> some work to do once you get the truth you just can't sit on the
> truth and say I got the truth, and expect the food to come in the
> door. You gotta get your ass outside with the truth, and then
> you gotta plant and grow in order to get food cos the truth
> won't feed you. God won't food you, God would provide food
> for you. God would provide the health and the conditions in

nature that you can use to get food but God is not gona spoon food your ass. You will starve to death waiting for God... God gave you the ability to make things happen in his image cos he's a creating God. That you're in his image and likeness he's given you the power to create things and make them happen. If you sit on your lumpy ass, ain't nothing gona happen we gotta get up and get some stuff happening. We gotta become heard, we gotta become rough, people got to know we there, no more moving in the shadows, no more hiding behind the man, we gotta step out front and make ourselves heard." In a separate recording he says, "My disciples, brothers, all these young boys are being taught to act like me and go out and teach. If he's introverted I don't need him, I don't need quiet people sitting in the class absorbing knowledge. I want people that's gona take it in and go out and teach it. If they're not gona teach we're wasting our time..."

Well this is my work to the people, black people are in real need to know who and what they are and many are unaware of our true history.

I have referenced the psychic Edgar Cayce several times, and his students have written many books from his original readings, in the A.R.E: Association for Research and Enlightenment. Any one who is a true Nuwaupian knows that it is our job to propagate and get this information and outformation to our people. Nuwaupu contains a wealth of information from the physical and spiritual plane. Right knowledge, right wisdom and right overstanding is necessary to our development, so we have to take Nuwaupu to the next level and utilise it properly for our future development. Some of the updates have said: 'We Must Inform People because it's Our Job to Wake People. We Are Judged As A Species Not As Individuals'. (Jun 26th 2010 update) 'Once You Know, You Are Responsible For Everyone Who Asks A Question. We Are Judged As A Species. Not As individuals. We Are Responsible For Each Other. It's Our Responsibility to Get This Message Out. It's our job to break the spell of our brothers and sisters, they need The Actual Facts. If they fall behind I can't help them, but if they fall in front I can help. We need to be on every corner selling The Actual Facts'. (From update). One of the common sayings by Dr York is "No one wins the race in racism." The object of this book wasn't to prove the superiority of Nubians over other races, but to prove that Black Africans were the architects and inhabitants of Ancient Egypt, so we as a continent can turn to our original way of life and unite under one common goal. The majority of the black race have no knowledge of this, or their relationship to Egypt nor would ever admit to being Egyptian, and black people still follow alien religions and neglect their African culture. Nuwaupians recognize the diversity of the human race and wish to live in harmony with the Earth and other races. Another common saying is "Its not a black or a white thing, it's a grey thing." This means that *the greys*, one of the most common types of aliens are the ones really running the show. Whether you see things in black and white, the existence of alien life is real and it is amazing just what level of influence they have had in our history. It is naïve and egotistical for humans to think that we are the only ones in the entire universe and multiverse that exist, especially when scientists have confirmed there are billions of other galaxies in the universe and it is almost certain that in our lifetime we will again witness these beings. (HT 2:1:22) Nearly every culture speak of angels, Gods and star people in whatever language they belong to and to move forward it is our particular branch of Gods, ancestors that we must re-align ourselves with.

> I think you're find sir, that there will come a time when black
> people wake up and become independently intellectual enough
> to think for themselves as other humans are intellectually
> enough to think for themselves and the black man will think
> like a black man. [Malcolm X]

According to Genesis 11:5 "And the LORD came down to see the city and the tower, which the children of men builded. And the LORD said, Behold, the people is one, and they have all one language; and this they begin to do: and now nothing will be restrained from them, which they have imagined to do." This shows the power of unity and what happened when we were in unity with ourselves and nature. Nuwaupu is reaching Africa fast; the Malachi York Foundation in Ghana was set up to provide resources for underprivileged Ghanaian families. The Nuwaupian family across the world helped to send out goods to them. This is just the beginning. With time, a collective effort to rebuild the infrastructure and economy of our African continent and establish our true cultural identity Wu-Nuwaupu, we can get back to the plateau of being able to achieve anything! Look out for the sequel 'The cultural death of dynastic Egypt' coming soon.

'From Egipt you all come and unto Egipt you will return'
(Dr Malachi Z York)
THE END
www.blackegyptians.co.uk

Black Egyptians Workbook

I hope you have enjoyed reading Black Egyptians. Now try completing these questions to test your knowledge.

Questions

1. What is Nuwaupu?
2. Name two pictures which show the races of people living in Ancient Egypt and where they were found? How are the Egyptians painted?
3. Name 5 advocators of Black Egyptians and the books they have written?
4. Which countries or people invaded Egypt, from Ancient to modern times and when did they invade?
5. Which African countries have the strongest relations to Egypt?
6. How can a black person that is not from these countries claim Egypt?
7. Which haplogroups are the progenitors of all other non-African haplogroups and what is their parent haplogroup?
8. Was the Egyptian state a product of mass movement into the Egyptian Nile region or indigenous development? Who proved this?
9. The first signs of pharaonic Kingship come from where?
10. How can I find out more info about Ancient Egypt especially things which are hidden from the general public?
11. Which stories, people and books have been copied or plagiarized from Egypt?
12. Name the gods in the Sedjet and Ogdoad?
13. Why did Ancient Egypt have such an advanced civilisation?
14. Fill in the missing blanks:

Before settling in Ancient Egypt the Egyptians have been linked to have come from _____ on Earth. Before this they have been traced to outside of this planets atmosphere on _____. Two of the most important stars to the Egyptians were _____ and _____.The original planet of the Egyptian Gods also known as the _____ is on the planet _____ in the 19th Galaxy _____.

15. Why would someone of African descent choose to study Egyptology and Nuwaupu?
16. What are the repercussions of denying your Ancient Egyptian heritage and the knowledge explained within Nuwaupu?

Answers

1. Nuwaubu is the science of Sound Right Reasoning, and it's followers are the sons and daughters of Sound Right Reasoning. Belief is ignorance. Belief is to ignore to facts, intentionally or ignorantly. Also, Nuwaubu is Right knowledge, Right wisdom and Right overstanding. If one has to believe, it means he or she does not know, and if one does not know, that is ignorance. Hence, belief is ignorance, and religious beliefs, without the facts is ignorance. Knowledge can be checked out by one or more of 3 tests: 1. Experience 2. Evidence 3. Reason. Where the experience test is unavailable, evidence and reason should be used.

2. The Book of Gates in the tomb of Seti I and The Table of Nations Scene in the tomb of Rameses III. In the Book of Gates the Egyptian is painted with brown skin, lighter than the dark skinned Nubia. However in the Book of Gates both the Nubian and Egyptian have the same skin colour.

3. Supporters of a Black Egyptian race include:

• Dr Malachi York - What is Nuwaupu, Breaking the Spell, Right Knowledge etc .
• Cheikh Anta Diop - The African Origin of Civilization
• Robert Bauval and Thomas Brophy - Black Genesis: The Prehistoric Origins of Ancient Egypt.
• Ivan Van Sertima – Egypt Child of Africa, They Came before Columbus.
• Dr Ben Yosef Yochanon – Black Man of the Nile and his family
• Martin Bernal - Black Athena
• Robin Walker - Before the Slave Trade
• Anthony T Browder – Nile Valley contributions to civilization
• Ashra Kwesi
• Count Volney
• Herodotus

4. In order, starting from the earliest:

1) Protodynasty, (dynasty 0) 3100 BC – Narmer/Menes defeated Asians and Caucasians who invaded Upper Egypt; this is shown in the Narmer palette. The Egyptian dynasty as we know it may not have existed if he didn't win that war.

2) Hyksos, (15/16th dynasty) 1660 BC – This was the first time Egypt came under foreign rule. The Hyksos were from Western Asia.

3) Nubians (25th dynasty) 750 BC - The Nubian's led by King Piankhy ruled Egypt in 750. But this isn't considered foreign because they were the same people i.e. Black Africans.

4) Assyrian (25th dynasty) 667 BC – led by Ashurbanipal, the son of Esarhaddon. In 667 BC he defeated King Taharqa of Nubia who ruled Egypt at the time.

5) Persian (27th dynasty) 525 BC - Cambyses II of Persia defeated Psamtek III in 525 BC at the 1st Battle of Pelusium.

6) Greek (Macedonian period) 332BC – Alexander the Great

7) Roman (Roman period) 32BC – Augustus conquered Egypt in 30 BC

8) Arabs (642 AD) – General Amr Ibn al-as and an army of 4000 horsemen conquered Egypt in 642 AD.

9) Turkish Ottoman empire (1517 AD) – The Ottoman Empire defeated the Egyptian Mamluk Sultentate, an Egyptian state.

10) French – 1798 – led by Napoleon Bonaparte the French invaded in 1798 and occupied it for three years.

11) British (1882) – The British defeated an Egyptian army to further their own trade, political and military interests

5. Sudan, Nigeria, Chad, Ethiopia.

6. Nubians from the Caribbean and South America can claim ancestry from those countries as victims of the slave trade (in broad terms or with genetic testing). The Rizqiyians/Neteru claim to be the parents of Nubians on this planet, so all can claim Egypt through them.

7. M & N, L3.

8. Indigenous development. Sonia R Zakrewski, 2007.

9. Nubia now known as Sudan. Two incense burners were found at an A group cemetery in Qustul, with royal emblems at least 200 years before the Egyptian dynasty.

10. From the Black Egyptians official website:
http://www.blackegyptians.co.uk

There are many articles, links and information on the site. I recommend you read books written by Dr Malachi Z York and join the Ancient Egyptian Order. It is good to read standard Egyptology textbooks to get a wide scope.

11. Egypt's significance on religion.

• The Ten Commandments was taken from the Book of the Dead, from the declaration of innocence. 613 confessions of Ma'at.
• The story of Jesus and the virgin birth/immaculate conception comes from the story of Horus, the son of Isis and Osiris who was born after his father was killed. It is also linked with astronomy, and explains the sun's movement across the skies.
• The Enuma Elish. This is not Egyptian, but Sumerian; found in the Middle East, Mesopotamia occupying present day Iran/Iraq. The Enuma Elish consist of 7 clay tablets which the Genesis story of creation was copied from.
• Moses there are three pharaohs in Egyptian history with the name 'mose', Kamose, Ahmose, and the Thutmose's.

12. Sedjet (Atum Re, Shu, Tefnut, Geb, Nut, Aset, Asaru, Nebthet, Sutukh)
Ogdoad (Nun/Nunet, Heh/Hehet, Kek/Keket. Amun/Amunet)

13. Evidence shows the Ancient Egyptians came from Atlantis and they were visited Extra-Terrestrial beings called the Rizqiyians, while the Annunaqi visited the Sumerians.

14. Atlantis, Mars, Orion, Sirius, Neteru, Rizq, Illuwyn.

15. Because Nuwaupu is your true universal and spiritual science. By choosing an alien religion (not of African origin) you are giving up your physical and spiritual powers to 6-ether forces which don't have your best interests. 9 ether beings were the first to exist and can reach the highest plateau of spiritual transformation

16. It's all about spiritual advancement and the destruction of this planet. Believe it or not this planet has been destroyed many times and is on course for another Extinction Level Event. The Rizqiyians will return for their children and if you are not spiritually advanced enough to be able to transform your body into a different state you will not survive.

Join
This Mystic Order
A.E.O.
The Ancient Egyptian Order

1. Do you want to learn the secrets of Egipt?
2. Who or what built the pyramids?
3. Do you have guardian angels?
4. Were the Egiptians from beyond the stars?
5. How do prepare for death?
6. Egipt in the Bible and Koran.
7. Was Jesus found in Egipt
8. Is there an Egiptian face on Mars?
9. Did Mars have the first Egiptian Civilization
10. Is the Masonic Order from Egipt?
12. Were there U.F.O.' helping the Egiptians?
13. What is the true symbolism behind the obelisk needle?
14. How can spirits give you Health & Wealth?
15. What is Gods real name?

Has The Mystery Of Egipt Intrigued You?

You will have the answers to these most mystifying questions and much more. Abraham, Moses, and Muhammad were all taught by Egiptians. Enter the pylon and be a part of the most sought after and authentic order in the world ever... The Ancient Egiptian Order where truth & facts are waiting for you.

For More Info. Please E-mail Us At
aeo@unitednuwaubiannation.com
Or write to: The Ancient Egiptian
Order P.O. Box 5579 Athens , Ga. 30606

Index

P

Q

R

S

List of Illustrations, Tables and Figures

Picture 2.16 – Nibiru 'The Planet that crosses the skies'. (photo courtesy of Egipt Publishers)

Picture 3.1 – Language families of Africa.

Picture 3.2 – The Afar Rift Valley (photo courtesy of Penguin)

Picture 3.3 - Possible appearance of Ardi

Picture 3.4 - Different types of Negroid spread across Africa

Picture 3.5 - Arabia splits from Africa (photo courtesy of Penguin)

Picture 4.1 - Flag of Sudan

Picture 4.2 - Nubians bringing gifts in the tomb of Sebekhotep (photo courtesy of the British museum)

Picture 4.3 - Nubian prince Maiherpi

Picture 4.4 - Map of Sudan in ancient and medieval times

Picture 4.5 - Incense burner

Picture 4.6 - Nabta Playa 1

Picture 4.7 – The Nabta Playa Calendar circle megaliths (photo courtesy of Egipt Publishers)

Picture 4.8 - Pyramids at Gebel Barkal (photo courtesy of Louis Buckley: Black Nine films)

Picture 4.9 - Temple in Nubian desert (photo courtesy of MSN Encarta)

Picture 4.10 - King den smiting Asiatic enemy (photo courtesy of the British Museum)

Picture 4.11 - Great enclosure at Musawarat (photo courtesy of Derek Welsby)

Picture 4.12 - Temple of Isis at Philae

Picture 4.13 - Map of Nubia (photo courtesy of Oriental Institute, University of Chicago)

Picture 4.14 - Medjay 1

Picture 4.15 - Medjay 2

Picture 4.16 - Stone figures of Nubian pharaohs in the 25th dynasty. (Photo courtesy of Charles Bonnet)

Picture 4.17 - Tribal dispersion across Lower and Upper Nubia

Picture 5.1 - Map of the Yoruba Kingdom

Picture 5.2 - Head of an Oni (photo courtesy of the National Commission for museums and ornaments)

Picture 5.3 - Haggai's African Cruise (photo courtesy of Egipt Publishers)

Picture 5.4 - Yoruba African Orisha'sPicture (photo courtesy of Noire 3000: N3K Studios)

Picture 5.5 - Shabti box of Henutmehyt

Picture 5.6 - Seated dignitary

Picture 5.7 - Osiris carries crook and flail (photo courtesy of Anness publishing)

Picture 5.8 - Nigerian head with coiffure"From *The African Origin of Civilization* by Cheikh Anta Diop. English translation copyright (c) 1974 by Lawrence Hill & Co. Used with permission of Lawrence Hill Books."

Picture 5.9 - Statue of Amenhotep showing uraeus (photo courtesy of British museum – EA 30448)

Picture 5.10 - Queen of Punt

Picture 5.11 - Egyptian sculpture of Isis suckling Horus

Picture 5.12 - Nigerian statue of mother suckilng child in Whispering Palms, Nigeria.

Picture 5.13 - Numerous ram headed Ikenga wood carvings (photo courtesy of Catherine Acholonu-Olumba, CARC)

Picture 5.14 - Ichi head depicting winged disc (photo courtesy of Catherine Acholonu-Olumba, CARC)

Picture 5.15 - Maat with wings spread.

Picture 5.16 - Statues of Ibeji twins Nigeria

NUWAUPIAN GALLERY (photos 1-9 courtesy of Nuwbia Designs)
1. Our Pharaoh Dr Malachi Z York in Namuz
2. Our Pharaoh Nazdir A'aferti Atum Re
3. Re
4. Aset
5. Asaru
6. Anubu
7. Bast
8. Sakhmet
9. Ptah
10. Pyramids in Tama-Re, Eatonton Georgia 'Egipt of the West'.

Picture 6.1 - Egyptian kilt

Pictures '6.2- 6.7' "From *The African Origin of Civilization* by Cheikh Anta Diop. English translation copyright (c) 1974 by Lawrence Hill & Co. Used with permission of Lawrence Hill Books."

Picture 6.2 - Falcon and crocodile in Zimbabwe

Picture 6.3 - Elongated Skull – Akhenatens daughter

Picture 6.4 - Elongated skull of Congolese woman

Picture 6.5 - Ramses II/ Watusi Hairstyle

Picture 6.6 - Wooden doll

This book contains a variety of pictures and diagrams to enhance the points being made. I have tried without success to contact some of the copyright owner's and would be pleased to hear from him or her so that the matter could be cleared up.

Lightning Source UK Ltd.
Milton Keynes UK
UKOW06f0742171116

287836UK00001B/3/P